W9-CNN-754

DID MY
GENES MAKE
ME DO IT?

AND OTHER
PHILOSOPHICAL DILEMMAS

OTHER PHILOSOPHY TITLES FROM ONEWORLD

Descartes, Harry M. Bracken, ISBN 1–85168–294–5
God: A Guide for the Perplexed, Keith Ward, ISBN 1–85168–323–2
Kierkegaard, Michael Watts, ISBN 1–85168–317–8
Modern French Philosophy: From Existentialism to Postmodernism, Robert Wicks,
    ISBN 1–85168–318–6
Moral Relativism: A Short Introduction, Neil Levy, ISBN 1–85168–305–4
Nietzsche, Robert Wicks, ISBN 1–85168–291–0
Philosophy and Religion: From Plato to Postmodernism, Max Charlesworth,
    ISBN 1–85168–307–0
Political Philosophy: An Historical Introduction, Michael J. White,
    ISBN 1–85168–328–3
Postmodernism: A Beginner's Guide, Kevin Hart, ISBN 1–85168–338–0
Sartre, Neil Levy, ISBN 1–85168–290–2
Spinoza, Richard H. Popkin, ISBN 1–85168–339–9
What Makes us Moral?, Neil Levy, ISBN 1–85168–341–0
Wittgenstein, Avrum Stroll, ISBN 1–85168–293–7

DID MY GENES MAKE ME DO IT?

AND OTHER PHILOSOPHICAL DILEMMAS

AVRUM STROLL

ONEWORLD

OXFORD

For Mary

DID MY GENES MAKE ME DO IT?
AND OTHER PHILOSOPHICAL DILEMMAS

Oneworld Publications
(Sales and Editorial)
185 Banbury Road
Oxford OX2 7AR
England
www.oneworld-publications.com

ISBN 1–85168–340–2

Cover design by Design Deluxe
Typeset by Jayvee, Trivandrum, India
Printed in China by Sun Fung Offset Binding Co. Ltd

CONTENTS

ACKNOWLEDGEMENTS

Drafts of the first two chapters of this book were written while I was a visiting scholar at the American Academy in Rome in the Fall of 2002. I wish to express my gratitude to the Director, Professor Lester Little, for making this stay possible and to his wife, Lella Gandini, for her gracious hospitality. The Academy not only offers a unique opportunity for uninterrupted reflection and writing, but also a host of facilities, including its magnificent library and computer center, that are vital to the pursuit of research in the humanities. My appreciation for the support given to me by the many staff members of these various units is unbounded. I wish I had space here to thank them individually.

Given the wide scope of this study, I would have found it impossible to write it without abundant professional advice. I therefore wish to express my gratitude to Edward Frieman, Norman Kroll, and Marshall Rosenbluth for their help with string theory and the standard model, and to S. J. Singer and Russell Doolittle for their aid in matters biological. Since they are all members of the National Academy any scientific errors in this book are obviously my own. A special word of thanks to Burt Rodin for his assistance with transfinite arithmetic.

This is, of course, a book in philosophy, a discipline with an extensive history that encompasses an almost endless variety of different approaches to problems. Inasmuch as my area of expertise is mostly limited to twentieth-century analytic philosophy, I found the comments by colleagues about my interpretations of Aristotle, Aquinas, Leibniz, and Kant to be invaluable. Their sharp exegetical eyes, and detailed critical assessments of the text, produced new information and saved me from egregious blunders. I am thus enormously indebted to Zeno Vendler, A. P. Martinich, Danièle Moyal Sharrock, Alastair Hannay, Peter Sharrock, and Robert Rowan for the time they expended on the manuscript. I should emphasize that the interpretations offered throughout the work are my own and may not represent the views of any of the persons, scientific or otherwise, mentioned above. At various times I encountered computer glitches. A group of computer virtuosi at the University of California, San Diego, notably Erik Strahm and Steve Rusk, turned out to be life-savers without whose technical acuity this work would never have seen the light of day.

Finally, but most importantly, I wish to thank my wife, Mary. Her careful reading of the manuscript greatly improved its style, organization, level of argument, and content. That she took so much time away from her own research into twelfth-century papal politics is one, but not the only one, of the many reasons why I have dedicated this book to her.

La Jolla, California, February 2004

PREFACE

In one of the most beautiful passages in the philosophical literature, Aristotle explains why human beings philosophize:

> For it is owing to their wonder that men both now begin and at first began to philosophize; they wondered originally at the obvious difficulties, then advanced little by little and stated difficulties about the greater matters, for example, about the phenomena of the moon and those of the sun and of the stars, and about the genesis of the universe.
>
> *Metaphysics*, Bk. I: Ch. 2, 982b, 12–17

This passage is a prescient description of what this book, *Did My Genes Make Me Do It?* is all about. In its last chapter, arrived at "little by little," I do discuss the astral phenomena Aristotle mentions, including the genesis and future of the universe. I am not sure what he means when he contrasts "the obvious difficulties," with the "greater matters," but I am certain that he does not wish to confine the latter to astronomical considerations. Like most human beings I take these to include such deep questions as whether there is a God, whether post-mortem survival is possible, and whether one's thinking and behavior are determined by genetic factors. So although this book is in part about "the moon, the sun and the stars, and the genesis of the universe," it has wider scope. It deals with five pressing and difficult questions, including those I have just mentioned. But each of these splinters into a host of subordinate challenges, almost none of them "obvious." This book deals with those cases as well.

The matter of post-mortem survival is an example of such fragmentation. The greater issue can be stated in a sentence: "Is a person (i.e., a human being) a complex entity, consisting of a body and its various parts, *and* something else that is incorporeal and may survive the death of the body?" This query leads to a host of lower order perplexities: "If there is such an incorporeal component, what is it?" "Does it leave the body when a person dies, and is it immortal?" "Is it the same thing as that which some call 'the soul'?" "Is reincarnation possible?" "Do animals lack a soul?" "What is it that dies when a person dies?" An especially obdurate puzzle is the following: "How can one determine that a person has died?" For physicians who deal in organ transplants, and of course for their patients, it is a crucial question. An organ removed from a dead human being does not function well, or even at all, after it has been transplanted. Yet no doctor is willing to kill a dying patient in order to remove a functioning body part. But this is just one of a number of interconnected problems. Another is the fear of being buried alive. It has haunted human beings since time immemorial; and, as history teaches us, mistakes in this connection are not uncommon.

With respect to the question of whether post-mortem survival is possible my answer is that it is. I thus reject the claims made by many scientists and philosophers that medical and biological data establish that no person can survive the death of his or her body. I arrive at similar conclusions about some of the other issues mentioned above, such as whether God exists. It does not follow, of course, from the fact that post-mortem survival is *possible* that there is evidence to believe that such is the case, and similar remarks apply to the other major issues. My view is rather that none of these larger issues is a solvable problem.

This is unquestionably a controversial claim, since many intelligent persons are convinced that, given its distinguished record over the past four centuries, science can solve all problems. In 1918 a famous Austrian philosopher/physicist, Moritz Schlick, gave succinct expression to this point of view. He stated: "Since science in principle can say all that can be said there is no unanswerable question left." Schlick is, of course, referring to the sorts of problems that fall within the scope of scientific inquiry. These are generally called "empirical" or "factual." The phrase "in principle" that Schlick used is important. He did not mean that science has already solved all factual problems or even that solutions are in the offing. Rather his idea was that once certain technical hurdles are surmounted a solution to all empirical problems will be achieved. To speak about solving all such problems *in principle* is thus to distinguish between technical obstacles that impede progress and the success science will have should such obstructions be eliminated. This idea is sometimes recast as the notion that science will eventually arrive at a single, true theory of everything that exists. A major aim of this book is to challenge these claims. The "greater matters" I discuss are all factual (as distinct from normative), but I argue that none of them is solvable by science or indeed by any other discipline, including philosophy. But one will have to read the five chapters of this work to see how and why I arrive at this conclusion.

Let me emphasize that the thesis I am asserting is not a form of radical skepticism. That extreme outlook maintains that knowledge and/or certainty are unattainable. In a number of books and essays, including a work, *Skeptical Philosophy for Everyone*, that I co-authored with R. H. Popkin, in 2002, I disavowed such an incredible approach. Unlike radical skeptics, I have no doubt that knowledge and certainty are achievable – and indeed are everyday commonplaces. The position I am advancing here is more moderate. It is consistent with my rejection of skepticism. It is that some – a very few – deep and puzzling questions are not solvable by anyone; and this book explains why this is so. That there should be serious questions to which there are no answers is perhaps unsettling to many. But that is just the way the world happens to be. We shall therefore have to accept it as it is.

I should finally mention that this book has a hidden purpose; one you will not find expressed in the text. But it is what motivated me to write it.

I have attempted to recreate the kind of intellectual curiosity – Aristotle calls it "wonder" – that engenders philosophical speculation. I believe that virtually everyone is driven by the desire to know about these greater matters. In my opinion, they have a unique status: they are not scientific, historical, literary, moral or aesthetic. I call them "dilemmas," that is, intellectual predicaments in which one is attracted to incompatible alternatives and cannot decide between them. Like all philosophical problems they thus have their own autonomy. This book attempts to capture both the singular nature of these questions and the inquisitiveness and perplexity we feel in confronting them. If I have been successful in this endeavor, the outcome will neither put an end to wonderment nor will it quiet unease. It will not, for example, solve these problems, since they have no solutions. But it should at least be of some comfort to those of us who are perplexed that our deepest disquietudes have been given articulate structure.

1

IS SCIENCE THE ANSWER?

FROM MYTHOLOGY TO SCIENCE

The making of the modern mind begins in the West in the sixteenth and seventeenth centuries with the astronomical discoveries of Copernicus, Kepler, Galileo, and Newton. Their findings completely changed traditional beliefs about mankind's role in the broader scheme of things. For at least a thousand years before the Copernican revolution it was accepted without much dissent that the earth is the center of the universe, that humanity is a special creation of God, and that human beings are radically different from all other living things. Modern science and its close relative, technology, have shaken this outlook to its roots, and it is now widely rejected by many. What has given science and technology such compelling authority? In answering the question, we shall eventually want to distinguish science from technology, but for the moment let us treat them as being more or less the same. At least part of the answer must be the notable success that science, in this broad sense of the term, has attained in the past four hundred years. It has not only produced a clearer and truer picture of the animate and inanimate features of the natural world than any scheme that preceded it, but its achievements have extended the lifespan of humans, multiplied the food supply by orders of magnitude, and revolutionized communication. Many intelligent persons are convinced that, given its distinguished record, science can solve all problems. As mentioned in the Preface, the celebrated Austrian philosopher/physicist, Moritz Schlick, was a typical proponent of this view. In his magnum opus, *Die Allgemeine Erkenntnislehre* (*The General Theory of Knowledge*), he stated: "Since science in principle can say all that can be said there is no unanswerable question left." The idea it expresses is that science can eventually cope with all of mankind's problems.

The major aim of this book is to challenge such optimism. In the chapters that follow, I will present a series of problems that are palpably factual in nature, but that science cannot solve. In fact, my thesis is even stronger. It is that these problems, and others like them, are not capable of decision by anyone – philosophers, scientists, historians, or psychologists. I will also make the case that they are pressing problems, "deep disquietudes" as Wittgenstein characterizes them, that beset ordinary persons and professional philosophers alike. But in order to show that science cannot deal with them, I wish to make the strongest possible case for science, and the rest of the chapter will lay out that case.

Everyone will acknowledge, of course, that large numbers of scientific mysteries still exist. Whether there is extra-terrestrial life in the universe remains an open question. Chemists and biologists generally agree on the criteria of what counts as life – any form of life must be self-reproducing and capable of mutation. Accordingly, we *now* know what sorts of observations would have to be made to answer the question, even if we are not yet in a position to make them. That is what it means to say that the difficulty is solvable "in principle." The practical problem is different; it is how to get to some of those distant places and do the appropriate tests. But once there, the obstacles to discovery would not be much more formidable than they would be in order to find out whether there is life in the deepest trenches of the oceans. In both cases it is a matter of developing the appropriate technological means.

Of course, one should not underestimate the practical impediments. We don't have to leave the planet to encounter such difficulties. Even where the origin and nature of a medical ailment are completely understood, there may be no treatment for it. Sickle-cell anemia is a good example. In 1948 a team of biologists working at Caltech under the supervision of Linus Pauling was able to unravel the molecular basis of this serious blood disease. Nevertheless, more than half a century later, no cure is available. Again, the attempt to create energy by the process known as "fusion" is still years away from practical implementation. The difficulty is partly theoretical and partly technical and no solution is yet in sight. Despite the abundance of such practical barriers, many scientists conjecture that fusion will be in common use by the end of the century. Some investigators believe that cancer and many other major diseases will be conquered in the foreseeable future. The prospect of success over a whole range of problems seems ever brighter. A large number of literate persons in the West are optimists in this sense; they think that a scientific-technological Shangri-La lies just around the corner.

So given that there are many scientific questions still unanswered, why is there such general confidence? The answer turns on what counts as the best method for comprehending and managing nature. This is a complicated matter that we shall explore in the remainder of the chapter. But one can say at least this much: It is now widely accepted that science has no competition in this respect. To feel the full force of this attitude one should compare and contrast scientific and pre-scientific approaches to understanding and grappling with the environment. This we can do with a brief glance at the past. We know from historical, geological, and paleographical data that life for human beings has always been perilous. Nature produces violent rainstorms, floods, fires, earthquakes, volcanic eruptions, droughts, illnesses, and death. Just think about infective diseases for a moment. The average length of life for humans in England in the sixteenth century was about half of what it is today in advanced industrial societies. Why was the pre-modern world such a hostile place? How did humans attempt to cope with its threats? What explanation for this state of affairs was given by pre-scientific thinkers?

A distinguished contemporary biologist, S. J. Singer, has given plausible answers to these queries. In *The Splendid Feast of Reason*, he writes:

> In the absence of any scientific understanding, the universal response of primitive people to their predicament was to mythologize this alien and material world, to animate it with mythical living and immortal beings who were more powerful than humans and who could control the awesome forces of nature, beings with whom humans could identify and to whom they could turn in supplication in times of need. We rationalists must admiringly acknowledge that, for their time, these mythologies constituted a remarkably sophisticated achievement, ranking in brilliance with any ever created in history. The invention and elaboration of mythologies of a natural world inhabited by superhumans and eventually human-like deities generated a more pliant and friendlier kind of external world in which to live. What had previously been an utterly forbidding and unapproachable external world became humanized, a mythical outgrowth of human life, which rendered that external world no longer foreign and autonomous but instead anthropocentric, focussed on humans. All of this extraordinary achievement must have required a prolonged period of pre-recorded history to construct, and it eventually took on an immense variety of highly imaginative forms in primitive societies (p. 14).

As Singer suggests, until the development of modern science human imagination was the method used for explaining and coping with the happenings that beset mankind. Imagination created a set of stories in which the fragile powers of mankind were in constant battle with the overwhelming power of nature. Natural forces were eventually personified into "gods" and the human struggle for existence was seen as having some success only if the gods could be appeased by sacrifices and propitiative gifts. Explanation was thus given an anthropomorphic twist. In the *Iliad* and the *Odyssey* of Homer, who is thought to have lived around 750 B.C.E., gods like Zeus and Poseidon are depicted as having human forms, even as having sexual relations with humans. Unlike humans they are described as being immortal and enormously powerful. When angered they generate electrical storms and plagues of insects that wipe out crops; hence the need to conciliate them. The *Bible* begins with the picture of a local deity similar to those found in Homer. In its first book, *Genesis*, some of whose parts were written about the same time as the *Iliad* and the *Odyssey*, Yahweh – the Hebrew God – talks to Noah as he loads animals onto the ark, and closes its door after Noah embarks. With the passage of time, this anthropomorphic form of religion gave way to a more abstract conception. In *Deuteronomy*, thought to be composed during the Josiah Reform of 610 B.C.E., that same deity has become an immaterial force, no longer visualized in human shape or form. Nevertheless, as a later document, *Job*, tells us, Yahweh still continues to intervene in the world, punishing those who violate his commandments and rewarding those who follow them.

This mythological-theological explanatory system began to break down with the advent of science. It is now widely believed in the West that scientific method is not only the most successful way of understanding and controlling nature, but that it is the *only* way. This is believed because nothing having its explanatory and practical success has occurred in the millions of years that humans have been on earth. It is also believed that this is just the beginning, that "we haven't seen anything yet."

SCIENCE AND TECHNOLOGY

As I mentioned it is important to distinguish science from technology. Science is concerned with understanding how things work. It is essentially a form of curiosity, though of course disciplined by the requirement that its investigative activities lead to knowledge and truth. Technology is different. It is designed to control nature, to make it subservient to human needs, wants, and desires. In everyday life, and especially in sophisticated industrial societies, these two disparate activities frequently overlap and may be difficult to distinguish. But they can and should be differentiated.

It is generally true, for example, that science in its purest forms may have little impact on the everyday activities of human beings. The discovery by Kepler that the planetary orbits are not circular, but elliptical, has little, if any, significance for those shopping in supermarkets. It does have relevance to certain sorts of technological activities, such as sending instrument bearing satellites to explore the atmospheres of Mars and Jupiter. Without an accurate knowledge of planetary orbits such vehicles could well miss their targets. Of course, some scientific findings do have everyday implications. As mentioned earlier, the discovery that the earth is a minor planet revolving around a relatively small luminous celestial body, and that the solar system itself is located in a miniscule corner of a large galaxy, has had momentous significance for some persons who accept the biblical account of the cosmos as literally true. Similar remarks can be made about the impact of Darwin's theories about the origin of the human species.

It is also true that technology in highly sophisticated forms can exist in societies where there is no science – or to be more exact, no science in the contemporary Western sense of that term. China is perhaps the most celebrated case. Until fairly recently China never developed science as we now know it; yet its technology was extensive and much advanced over anything in the Western world. Such things as the wheelbarrow, the cross-bow, the kite, iron casting, iron-chain suspension bridges, the axial rudder, the magnetic compass, porcelain, block printing, the screw, gunpowder, the force-pump for liquids, the square-pallet chain-pump, the edge-runner mill with water power, the rotary fan and rotary winnowing machine, piston-bellows, the wagon-mill, silk-handling machinery (i.e., a form of flyer for laying thread evenly on reels), and water-powered textile mills, were in common use many centuries before their counterparts in the West.

How the Chinese could achieve such a complex technology without a concomitant development in science has been a puzzle to historians. One suggestion is that according to their Yin and Yang doctrine the universe consists of a totality whose parts are indissolubly welded to one another and therefore cannot be disjoined without conceptual distortion. It is thus impossible, even in principle, to isolate individual events, processes, or objects for examination. In contrast, the Western conception is that the universe is composed of discrete and autonomous events that can be separated from one another and investigated individually. This outlook is called "Reductionism." It is one of the essential features of Western science. What this term means is that single items, such as particular solids, gases, or liquids, can be removed from their natural environments, brought into a laboratory, and then manipulated experimentally in order to discover their basic properties. It is to a great extent the reductionist approach of modern science that has led to its deep understanding of nature.

Reductionism is not the only feature that distinguishes modern science from earlier approaches. Its quantitative approach is another. The ancient Greeks and their seventeenth-century counterparts, such as Galileo and Newton, were driven by the desire to understand the world. In both eras science and philosophy were not sharply discriminated from one another. The kinds of questions that each attempted to answer were remarkably similar – "What is the ultimate nature of reality?"; "Is there a fundamental, underlying principle that can ultimately explain the seemingly endless complexity of nature?"; "Is the earth the center of the cosmos?"; "What is the relationship between the sun, the earth, the planets and the stars?"; "Is there meaning in the universe or is it indifferent to human interests and desires?"; "Is there a God who is the cause of all that exists, and if so, what is his function?"

Aristotle (384–322 B.C.E.), who is often described as the last great philosopher of the ancient world, inherited these and other questions from his predecessors. Like modern scientists he thought that human reason and, where possible, careful observation, should be brought to bear on these queries. He also believed that the task of science is to discover general laws. But he was also strikingly modern in thinking that the basic ingredients of the natural world are individual. So unlike the holistic conception of the Chinese, his *Weltanschauung* assumed that science can isolate individual objects and by applying general laws can then explain their behavior. Invoking these principles, Aristotle became the first serious experimental biologist of whom we have any accurate historical record. (Darwin called him the greatest biologist who ever lived.) His philosophical view of the universe as consisting of discrete objects was thus conditioned by his biological outlook, and this affected his conception of scientific explanation. He thought that the basic question any theory should answer is: "Given that every object, whether man-made or natural, has a unique constitution (or essence) what is its special purpose or function?" Take knives, for example. They can be made of different materials and can be used for different purposes: as ornaments, paperweights, and so on. But that is not what knives are designed to do. Their main function – their purpose – is to cut things. Thus, as Aristotle saw it, a scientific investigation should uncover the essential purpose that any entity belonging to the natural world is designed to serve. As he wrote: "If, therefore, artificial products are for the sake of an end, so clearly also are natural products. The relation of the later to the earlier terms of the series is the same in both" (*Physics*, Bk. II).

In effect, the idea that all objects, whether artificial or not, are to be characterized in terms of their essential natures eventually gave rise, in Aristotle's system, to the notion that all activity is motion directed toward a particular end. Heaviness is the essential nature of solid objects and that is why such objects fall to the earth (their predetermined end); and lightness is the intrinsic nature of gases, such as smoke and steam, and that is why they rise toward the sky. And, he tells us, it is "by nature and for an end that the swallow makes its nest and the spider its web."

> This is most obvious in the animals other than man: they make things neither by art nor after inquiry or deliberation. Wherefore people discuss whether it is by intelligence or by some other faculty that these creatures work – spiders, ants, and the like. By gradual advance in this direction we come to see clearly that in plants too that is produced which is conducive to the end – leaves, e.g. grow to provide shade for the fruit. If then it is both by nature and for an end that the swallow makes its nest and the spider its web, and plants grow leaves for the sake of the fruit and send their roots down (not up) for the sake of nourishment, it is plain that this kind of cause is operative in things which come to be and are by nature ...
> If then, it is agreed that things are either the result of coincidence or for an end, and these cannot be the result of coincidence or

spontaneity, it follows that they must be for an end; and that such things are all due to nature even the champions of the theory which is before us would agree. Therefore action for an end is present in things which come to be and are by nature ... In natural products the sequence is invariable, if there is no impediment.

Physics, Bk. II, Ch. 8

Thus, according to Aristotle, every living entity goes through a process of development from "potentiality" to "actuality," if it is not interrupted. Kittens develop into cats, puppies into dogs, human infants into adults, seeds into vines, and so forth. Each of the later items is more complex than its earlier forms. Though the concept of genetic structure was, of course, unknown to him, he brilliantly drew the conclusion that each of these more simple entities has an internal composition, its essential nature, that gradually unfolds until it arrives at maturity. The resulting product often differs radically from its progenitor. A fully formed oak tree diverges in shape, size and appearance from an acorn. In describing the process of change, he was in effect giving a wholesale explanation of the motion of natural objects, whether organic or inorganic, in biological terms. This is a very natural and intuitive way of looking at things. If someone asks, "Where are you going this morning?" it is sensible to respond by describing your purpose, e.g., "I am going downtown to buy some stamps." Your response answers the question "*Why* you are doing something." In contrast, modern science replaces Aristotle's question by asking "*How*" not "*Why*" something happens.

Aristotle's science was thus *teleological*, not quantitative. When you explain that you are going downtown to buy stamps your response does not mention the rate of speed at which you are moving. The answer to this question is quantitative and disregards purpose. Modern science looks at nature as a machine, operating according to mechanical principles, and not as an organism that acts purposively. It thus replaces the biological analogy by a mechanical picture of nature. This change in outlook begins with Galileo's experiments of dropping iron balls down an inclined channel and measuring their rate of acceleration. (Since he had no exact chronometer he very cleverly used his pulse as a metronome.)

Galileo's approach proved that, setting the resistance of air aside, the velocity at which bodies fall does not depend on their weight, contrary to what Aristotle believed. It was known in antiquity that objects pick up speed as they approach the ground, but it was not known what the relationship is between their speed, the distance traveled, and the time required for the fall. Galileo's experiments demonstrated that a body that falls for two seconds, travels four times as far a body that falls for one second; and a body falling for three seconds travels nine times as far as a body falling for only one second. On the basis of this observation, it is thus possible to formulate, in mathematical terms, a law that will allow one to predict the distance that every freely falling object will traverse in a specific quantity of time. The law of falling bodies ($S = \frac{1}{2}gt^2$) or Newton's inverse square law of gravitation are examples of the modern approach to this mathematization of nature. Change for modern science is thus not identical with development or growth. It is basically transfer of position at a law-like velocity. In contrast, it was Aristotle's non-quantitative account that influenced his successors for nearly two thousand years and in part explains why the development of modern science was delayed until the seventeenth century.

SCIENCE AND THE REAL WORLD

We have seen that reductionism and a quantitative approach to nature are both essential features of modern science. But there is yet a third – one that is so obvious as to escape general notice. This is the notion that there exists a real world, a domain that is independent of human conception, speculation or fantasy. When Schlick asserts that science can solve all problems, he is talking about real problems: fires, floods, and earthquakes that kill people and damage property. Ordinary persons take it for granted that animals, the oceans, the cities in which they live, and the ground on which they walk, are all real. Most scientists are also realists in this sense. What they do not take for granted is what the real world is like and how it works. To answer these questions requires investigation, that is, the discovery of evidence that rules out certain conjectures and makes others probable. Yet to explain what is meant by "the real world" is not easy. Scientists do not normally discuss the issue – this is what it means to say that they take an external reality for granted. Therefore, in order to grasp what is meant by this concept we shall have to look elsewhere than science. Probably the most simple accounts are to be found in philosophy, where two forms of realism, "metaphysical" and "epistemological realism" are distinguished from one another. They correspond, roughly, to the presupposition that there is a real world and that a reductive, quantitative investigation is required to discover its nature.

Metaphysical and epistemological realism

In deepening the theme of whether science can solve all problems, let's begin with a look at metaphysical realism. This doctrine entails that the sole satellite of the earth – the moon – at which I am now staring does not depend for its existence on my mind, any state of my mind, on the state of any other mind, or collection of minds, past, present, or future. Even if all psychological awareness, whether human or non-human, were to be obliterated, the moon would continue to exist – assuming, of course, that no non-mental process had also obliterated it. States of mind include thoughts, guesses, intentions, beliefs, doubts, and desires. One's idea that guests will soon be arriving for dinner is a mental state. Whether pains, itches, and depressions are also mental states is a much debated question I shall bypass here. The important point is that according to this view there are objects, events, and phenomena whose existence does not depend on any form of sentience or awareness.

Metaphysical realism is also what philosophers call a dualistic theory. This term means that the world is composed of *at least* two different kinds 'stuff', neither of which is reducible to the other or to anything else. Traditionally, they have been taken to be mind and matter. In this characterization of "metaphysical realism," the term "at least" is important. Metaphysical realism does not mean that the world must contain exactly two kinds of irreducible ingredients. Some philosophers – among them, John Searle, the current writer, and the late J. L. Austin – have argued that the world contains many kinds of irreducibly different things: mental events, such as thoughts; physical processes, such as iron rusting; material objects, such as rocks; abstract entities, such as numbers; substances, such as gold and water; games, such as chess and baseball; institutions, such as governments; and the creations of governments, such as money. What every form of metaphysical realism maintains is that some of these are mind-independent.

As this description indicates, metaphysical realism affirms that there are minds and various states of minds. The very definition of "real world" requires this additional commitment. For "real" here means "mind-independent." But to assert that there are minds is not to assert that there *must* be minds. The realist holds that the existence of minds is a contingent fact. It is easy to imagine a segment of the universe that lacks any form of sentience. Indeed, this appears to be a true description of much of the past history of the earth and, as far as we know, of Jupiter and Saturn today. Long before living entities appeared on earth it consisted of inorganic substances: water, mud, and various gases. Even to assert that there are minds does not entail a commitment to dualism. So-called "philosophical idealists" argue that everything that exists is mental. Hence for the idealist nothing is mind-independent. Metaphysical realism, nevertheless, includes as one of its defining features the condition that there are minds. This is essential because its thesis is that some things exist independently of minds – so some reference to minds is necessary even to formulate the realist position at all.

However, it is not essential to metaphysical realism that it adopt any special view about the nature of mind. It has been asserted of the *human* mind, for instance, that it is a transcendental ego, a bundle of related perceptions, a complicated set of dispositions, a thinking substance, and so forth. Hence, one can be a metaphysical realist without coming to a decision about the nature of mentation. But every form of metaphysical realism presupposes the distinction between sentience, however it is ultimately analyzed, and events, objects, processes, and phenomena that do not depend for their existence on cognitive awareness in any of its various guises. Thus, the main distinction between metaphysical and epistemological realism is that the former generates conjectures about the nature of the real world whereas the latter attempts to determine whether those conjectures are true.

Metaphysical realism and monism

Epistemological realism is thus the investigative branch of realism; together they constitute explicit forms of the realism presupposed by modern science. There is, nonetheless, a difference between them. As we have seen, metaphysical realism is dualistic. But epistemological realism is not necessarily dualistic. Its investigative activities may eventually discover that all existents, including putative mental states, are really material. They may find the opposite to be true as well. The view is called "realist" in the sense that its inquiries begin with the assumption that mind and matter are fundamentally different. In practice, this assumption is the view that each human being participates in two irreducibly distinct realms, an inner, subjective, world of personal experience, and an external, publicly observable world. A contrast is thus drawn between a private, mental realm, to which only its proprietor has direct access, and an objective, material world that a reductive and quantitative approach can effectively explore.

In his *Biology & the Nature of Man*, the distinguished biologist W. H. Thorpe puts the contrast in this way:

> Let me say at the outset that, although I believe there to be an extremely close interrelation between mind and brain, I can only conclude that they are in some sense two things. All theories which imply that mind is merely a by-product of the activities of the brain, or that there is a complete parallelism over the whole range of man's mental experience between mental states and events and physico-chemical states and events in the brain I believe to be untenable. We know our own minds in a different way, at first hand, and better than we know anything else. I think the essential difference here is that between experience and observation ... There is no doubt that in the higher animals and in human beings, the brain is the main organ of correlation of the information flow received from all the various sense organs which are transmitting 'news' about the external world – including, of course, news from the body itself

and from the sense organs which tell us about tensions in the muscles and the positions of the limbs and joints ...

But even if we admit this much, this does not itself amount to saying that the brain is the sole organ of knowing since – returning to the kind of distinction I made just now – from the nature of the case, while it can cope with "knowing" it cannot cope with "experiencing." The kind of distinction between knowing and experiencing, coupled with the suggestion that the activity of the brain cannot provide a complete model of all mental states, events, and experiences, is likely to be highly repugnant to some people because of its dualistic implications. It implies two worlds, two systems, two events, where they would like, for plausible scientific reasons, to reduce everything to one only (pp. 21–24).

But as progress continues to be made in cognitive research, Thorpe's dualism may turn out to be an indefensible dichotomy. It may be that the mind is just an especially complex piece of matter, identical with the brain, and that thinking is simply a set of neurons firing at 40 Hertz. The question of whether the mental may ultimately turn out to be part of the objective material world is thus left open for future scientific exploration.

From a taxonomic point of view, the main alternative to metaphysical realism is thus not epistemological realism, but rather monism, that is, the idea that the world consists of only one kind of stuff. Monistic theories themselves divide into various categories: some maintain that the "stuff" is mental; others hold it to be "material." The philosophers, Bishop Berkeley, G. F. Hegel, and F. A. Bradley, were proponents of idealism; Thomas Hobbes and Karl Marx, of materialism. Russell once held that it was "neutral," that is, neither mental nor physical. He called this view "neutral monism." Most scientists are materialists. Some biologists, for instance, contend that human beings are nothing but complexes of matter; and that matter itself is simply a conglomerate of molecular, atomic and sub-atomic particles. But others – for example, the aforementioned W. H. Thorpe – defend a form of "vitalism," a dualistic view having a strong religious tint. The most common philosophical and psychological views today – behaviorism, eliminativism, and the identity theory – are all forms of materialism and thus are examples of monism according to this definition. All such theories are thus inconsistent with metaphysical realism, but not with epistemological realism, as described above.

Whether the private, human mental world will ultimately be found to be a form of materialism is still debated. But that there is at least an objective, non-mental realm is not a serious worry for modern science. For example, in collisions of electrons and positrons at the LEP accelerator at CERN (the European Organization for Nuclear Research), W and Z bosons were produced. These particles are too small to be seen even by electron microscopes, but their motions can be tracked by various types of instruments. That they are physical entities is thus beyond reasonable doubt, since predictions about their properties and behavior have been confirmed by such detectors. At the other end of the spectrum of size, astrophysical theory has identified a vast array of astral objects that existed long before there was any form of sentience in the universe. That the external world is wholly mental is thus rejected by modern science.

Metaphysical realism and the fundamental "stuff" of the world

Metaphysical realism has another facet, one with a long history that begins with the pre-Socratic Greek philosophers. This may be called the search for what is fundamental in nature. In a more sophisticated form than Greek thought could attain, modern science pursues a similar end. It wishes to discover the principles that govern nature from its tiniest ingredients to its most massive. Science begins with observations of and experiments on objects that one can see with the naked eye. The use of special instruments reveals these macroscopic objects to be composed of particles that cannot be seen with unaided vision. The aim of science is to explain how these miniscule objects become the building blocks of larger structures, including such massive objects as galaxies. The quest takes place at two intertwined levels of investigation. The first is highly theoretical; it concerns the discovery of principles or laws that tie diverse phenomena together. The other is descriptive; it attempts to account for the behavior of all the ingredients of nature, from the smallest to the largest.

Both levels of the quest are exemplified by the Law of Gravitation. It explains the behavior of smaller and larger entities and processes – for example, why an apple falls toward the ground, why the tides advance and recede in relation to a coastline, and why the moon does not drift away or plunge into the earth. It is an example of the kind of basic principle theorists seek. It explains in unexpected ways how diverse events, happenings, or structures in the real world are hooked together. It is the hope of modern science that if a single, synoptic principle, even more broadly encompassing than gravitation, could be found all the operations of nature could be explained. It could even answer the question whether the universe will eventually squeeze to a point or will go on expanding to infinity.

The earliest Greek philosophers, Thales, Anaximenes, and Heraclitus each attempted to discover such a fundamental principle. They found that what seemed to be a diverse and confusing set of events or happenings could be given a simple, single explanation. Thales, for example, noted that water, a liquid, hardens in severely cold weather, and becomes a vapor when heated. He also observed that if one digs deeply enough into the ground water bubbles up, and if one cuts persons or plants, the exposed surfaces are wet. His explanation of these diverse occurrences led him to the thesis that everything is composed of water. Using this explanatory principle, he thought he could account for the existence and behavior of all substances.

A later Greek philosopher, Democritus, argued that there were four elemental substances – earth, air, fire, and water – but even more importantly, that each of these was composed of even more fundamental entities that he called *atoms*. This view, arrived at without any observational backing, was given little credence for centuries until it was confirmed by two types of experimental evidence in the sixteenth century: first, by the detailed behavior of gases and, second, by the quantitative-weight relationships that accompanied a variety of chemical reactions. Two centuries later, John Dalton (1766–1824) explained the empirically derived laws of chemical combination by postulating the existence of atoms with unique sets of properties. His work generated numerous independent experimental verifications of the atomic hypothesis and today it is accepted by all scientists.

For about a century now it has been recognized that the atom also has a complex structure. What elementary particle physics has discovered in the past couple of decades is that the atom is composed of a bewildering array of smaller particles. Some congregate in small groups; others prefer to act singly. At present (2004), there are two main approaches dedicated to discovering a fundamental principle, comparable to the role played by DNA in biology, to explain the nature and behavior of these smaller particles. The earlier of these theories is called "The Standard Model." Its history can be traced to the work of Ernest Rutherford at the beginning of the twentieth century and even further back to the researches of John Dalton, the eighteenth-century English chemist. The other main contender for the grand master equation is String Theory. Both are too complicated to be described in any detail here but it is possible to depict some of their main features.

The Standard Model reduces to a handful the number of basic particles that compose matter and gives an account of how they are related. It tells us what these particles can do and what they cannot, how they come together and how they fall apart, all at dimensions a billionth of a billionth of the human scale. The model does not stop at the subatomic. Its theories attempt to explain the origin of the universe and the symmetries that frame its design. According to this view, matter consists of two kinds of particles – quarks and leptons. The matter particles interact by means of force particles or bosons. Bosons form another complex collection, including W and Z (the weak force); photons (electromagnetism) and gluons (the strong force). Experiments using the DELPHI detector at CERN indicate – for reasons physicists do not understand – that the elementary particles divide into three sub-groups. Our world is mainly built up from particles in the first group: electrons and up and down quarks. Although the elementary particles are all pointlike objects, their masses differ greatly – although why this is so is also not known. The top quark, for instance, is as heavy as an atom of gold, whereas the neutrino weighs almost nothing.

It is now generally agreed that the Standard Model should be extended since it is believed that hiding behind the quarks and gluons lie new particles and new forces. What these will turn out to be is a matter of speculation as yet; it is hoped that when more powerful accelerators, such as the Large Hadron Collider, come on line the question will be answered.

The Standard Model has one major liability to overcome and one major mystery to solve. The liability is that it does not explain the nature of gravitation – that is, that no "graviton" has ever been found. According to Einstein's theory of general relativity, gravity is linked to the curvatures of space and time, and is so weak a force it does not fit the pattern of the other forces. That it has not been accommodated by the Standard Model is considered a serious liability and is thought to limit its ultimate explanatory power. The mystery is complex. It is the question: "Why do particles have mass?" According to present theory, the answer lies in a particle that has never been identified. It is called the "Higgs boson," and is named after the British physicist, Peter Higgs, who first proposed its existence. It may explain the lopsided masses of the photon and the W and Z weak force particles. If such a boson is found it would not be just another particle, but would represent a field that exists everywhere, permeating space, and touching everything.

String theory attempts to provide a different fundamental explanatory principle. It holds that instead of particles, matter is ultimately composed of tiny loops of strings that vibrate at different frequencies in a universe made of 10 or 11 spacetime dimensions, not just four. Different vibrations become a quark or a lepton or the gravitational force or the strong force – indeed any particle or force. String theory has been enlarged into "membrane" or "brane" theory. This theory claims our universe is just one of many three-dimensional branes inside a mega-universe having another dimension. Most of the fundamental strings are confined to our three-dimensional space because they are attached to the surface of our brane. The strings of gravity crowd around a foreign brane and only a few gravitons escape and this may explain why gravity is so weak. It is also possible that gravity is spread out over other larger dimensions and this "thinning out" may explain why it is a weak force. Membrane theory also attempts to explain how large dimensions account for the differences in the masses of particles. It is a consequence of the theory that an electron is light because it straddles two dimensions, so part of its mass is located elsewhere. As metaphysical-sounding as these conceptions are, physicists are already designing experiments to test them. Even if 10^{-33} centimeters is beyond the reach of any proposed accelerator, experimentalists may still see the effects of these deep-lying phenomena at scales that are available even now.

THE SKEPTICAL CHALLENGE

Despite the evidence that biology and physics have supplied to support the view that there is a real world "out there," some thinkers of a skeptical persuasion have challenged this assertion. Curiously enough, in mounting this challenge, they find science itself to be a form of skepticism. Historically, skepticism comes in two versions, both of which rest on an assumption that science itself accepts, namely that most of the information we supposedly have about an external reality rests on sense experience. The first version is the more radical; it states that the only *direct* information we have consists of subjective sensations, what W. H. Thorpe calls "experiencing," and that it is conceivable that nothing outside of these sensations exists. It is thus possible that we are deluded into thinking that there is an external reality. The second, more moderate version, states that the senses are notoriously unreliable, so that we can never be sure that any account about external reality, even a scientific one, is accurate.

Let us examine these two forms of skepticism, beginning with the contention that most of our knowledge of external reality comes from seeing, hearing, smelling (etc.) things. I know there is a rosebush in my front yard because I see it there. I know that cars exist because I can hear them going by, and if I glance out the window, I can see them. It is the visual and auditory senses that provide us with information about these things. The ordinary person and the scientist tend to trust the senses, and to assume that the information they generate is reliable. But the skeptic finds such acceptance too facile. Consider some simple counter-cases.

We use mirrors for all sorts of purposes: to shave, to examine one's skin, and to observe the positions of cars behind us. When one shaves, for example, one assumes that the image of one's face that appears in the mirror is accurate, and therefore that the process of shaving will be successful. Yet, if one thinks about mirrors a little more carefully, one realizes that every mirror image distorts one's perception of the world's features. If one holds up an English language book to a mirror, one cannot read it, because the print runs backward. Yet the print on the book does not. One looking in a mirror never sees one's own face directly, that is, in the way other persons do. What one sees is reversed and subtly altered. We can shave because we adjust our habits to this situation, but it is a mistake to think that one is seeing one's own face as others do.

There are many ordinary, daily-life situations like this. A straight stick put in water looks bent; yet we do not believe it has become bent just because it was immersed in water, which is an easily penetrable liquid. Railroad tracks seem to converge in the distance, and yet when we walk to the spot where they apparently merged we find them to be parallel. The wheels of automobiles seen on television seem to be going backward when the automobile is seen to be moving forward. Yet this is impossible. Such examples of distorted perception could be multiplied endlessly. Each of these sense phenomena is thus misleading in some way. If human beings were to accept the world as being exactly how it looks they would be deceived as to how things really are. They would think the stick in water really to be bent, the writing on pages really to be reversed, and the wheels really to be going backward.

These are visual anomalies, and they represent the sorts of ordinary occurrences that provide ammunition for the skeptic. Starting from these cases, the skeptic can show that, when scrutinized, our common-sense beliefs become increasingly vulnerable to doubt.

Consider the case of the stick that looks bent when immersed in water. How can one be sure that it does not become bent when put in water?

How can one be sure that it is straight when it is out of the water? Of course it looks straight, but it also looks bent. What justifies giving priority to some sense impressions over others?

A person of common sense might respond by saying that seeing is not a sufficient condition for knowledge. One needs to correct vision by some of the other senses. Thus one might claim that the stick in water is not really bent because one can feel it with his hands to be straight when it is in the water. Thus, one corrects aberrant visual sensations by tactile impressions. But the skeptic can easily meet this move. What, he might say, justifies accepting one mode of perception as more accurate than another? After all, there are common occurrences that cast doubt upon the reliability of touch. Suppose one were to cool one hand and warm the other, and then insert both into a bucket of water having a uniform thermometric reading. The water will feel warm to the cold hand, and cold to the warm hand. But by stipulation, the water has the same uniform temperature, and therefore cannot be both hot and cold at the same time. Does this imply that one is not sensing the water at all? It is an interesting possibility and some skeptics have argued that such an inference is correct. But whether it is or not, the experiment surely suggests that the tactile sense cannot be fully trusted either, and that in particular, there is no justification for giving it priority over vision.

These remarks merely scratch the surface. In his famous Dream Hypothesis, René Descartes (1596–1650) propounded an even deeper skeptical objection to the commonsense view. He pointed out that the sensations we experience when asleep are intrinsically indistinguishable from those we experience when awake, and accordingly it is not possible by means of the senses to know *at any given moment* whether we are awake or asleep. But if this is so, we can *never* be sure on the basis of sense experience that we are apprehending the real world. This is radical skepticism in a full-blown form. It supports the first form of skepticism that we could have a panoply of sense information to which nothing external corresponds.

Suppose in the light of such difficulties, it is proposed that no mode of sense perception is sufficient to guarantee that one has knowledge, and hence that one needs to correct the senses by some other mode of awareness, say by reason. Reason tells us, that despite appearances, it is illogical to believe that parallel steel tracks, without any apparent reason, suddenly converge or that water bends rigid objects, like sticks. So independently of what our senses say, we can count on reason as a corrective that will give us an accurate picture of the world's features.

Yet reason has its own difficulties. It suffers from various liabilities: forgetting, jumping to unwarranted conclusions, miscalculations, misunderstandings, and misinterpretations. Almost everybody has forgotten or misremembered something important. One remembers having met a friend at the airport in Rome; yet that person has never been in Rome. One has added a column of figures incorrectly, getting the wrong sum. So why should one trust reason if its conclusions sometimes run counter to sense perception?

As these various examples show, the skeptical attitude cannot merely be dismissed. If it is ultimately mistaken, one will have to show why. That will require some hard thinking in order to arrive at a clear and defensible explanation of the apparently simple claim that the stick is really straight. In effect, a person who attempts to meet this challenge will need to develop a compelling theory that justifies the common sense and scientific beliefs that our senses are reliable. It would be viciously circular to appeal to science to decide this question since science assumes the reliability of sense experience, and that is just the point at issue. But that science does depend on data acquired through the senses is beyond question. And it is this fact that is the basis for the surprising claim made by some philosophers that science is a form of skepticism – moderate skepticism, to be sure, but skepticism nonetheless.

Apart from these considerations, there are other arguments in support of the notion that science is a form of skepticism. These call into account our mundane conception of the world, one that is based on sense experience. Our daily experience is of a *macroscopic* world, one whose components we can see, touch, hear, and feel. That world is composed of inanimate objects, like rocks and mountains, and of animate beings like insects, animals, and human beings. We can all see the sun, the moon, and feel ourselves standing on solid ground. As Ptolemy indicated, observation makes it plain that the earth does not move and that the sun revolves around it from East to West. Since time immemorial this has been the accepted picture of the cosmos. Yet science tells us that it is entirely wrong. The earth is in fact rotating and moving through space, and the sun does not revolve around it. It follows that if science is right the information generated by the senses is erroneous.

Consider a second case. The ordinary person tends to think of water as a liquid that is useful for various purposes: for drinking, washing, and mixing with other substances. Common sense also distinguishes between water, ice, and steam. Neither of the latter is a liquid, for example. What science tells us about water, ice, and steam differs from this conception. It claims that water, ice, and steam are basically identical because all are composed of H_2O. On this view, water is a collection of hydrogen and oxygen molecules – things we cannot see with the naked eye. Water is thus not to be identified with its observable properties, but with entities that are of microscopic size. In liquidity and transparency, we see the manifestations of these invisible ingredients, but the essential nature of water is hidden from the ordinary perceiver. Once again, our senses have misled us.

Now a third example. Common sense believes that many objects are perfectly solid. The table I am writing on is a case in point. But according to scientific theory, the table is mostly empty space and is not really solid. Its perceptible solidity is thus misleading as to its real nature. The truth of the matter is that the table is a cluster of invisible electrical particles occupying mostly empty space.

The conclusion to be drawn from these instances (and one could add an extensive list of others) is that we have good reasons for believing that everyday observation misrepresents the nature of reality. In undermining common sense, in favor of a highly complex, very counter-intuitive picture of an underlying reality, science supports skeptical doubts about the apparent knowledge the senses give us. It demonstrates that they do not provide an accurate account of how things are. But if science itself relies on observation, then are we justified in thinking its picture of the world is any more accurate than the ordinary man's? And if there is doubt about this, then are we justified in thinking that science can solve all problems?

THE SCIENTIFIC RESPONSE

Despite the seeming strength of the preceding skeptical arguments, they can be neutralized in various ways. If such counter-arguments are cogent – and the present writer thinks they are – one can support the scientific presupposition that there is an external world, and the concomitant belief that science can eventually come to discover what it is like and how it operates. Here are two arguments in support of science:

First, it is true that most, though not all, scientific knowledge of an external reality is based on observation. In the case of human beings it is the brain that processes such information. But observations depend for their existence on entities, such as the body and some of its organs, that are mind-independent. Even Thorpe, a dualist, agrees with this point. Here, we recall, is what he said in the passage I quoted earlier:

> There is no doubt that in the higher animals and in human beings, the brain is the main organ of correlation of the information flow received from all the various sense organs which are transmitting "news" about the external world – including, of course, news from the body itself and from the sense organs which tell us about tensions in the muscles and the positions of the limbs and joints.

In this citation, Thorpe is stressing that the human body, including its muscles, limbs and joints, is part of the external world and is not a mental entity. The essential point he is making is that subjective mental experience depends on bodily features and that these themselves are mind-independent. So here we have an argument that sentience depends for its existence on that which is non-sentient. Accordingly, science is justified in rejecting the skeptical contention that because mental experience is private we have no reason to believe in an external material reality.

There is a second source of support for science's view of reality that is strictly biological and is derived from the theory of evolution. It begins by contrasting unaided human vision with the extensions that telescopes and microscopes provide.

Prior to the development of such instruments most of the information about the world that human beings acquired was by means of a visual system that includes the eye, rods and cones, the retina, the optic nerve, and the brain. This system arose from and was refined by evolutionary development and natural selection. If we return to Aristotle for a moment and ask what is the purpose or point of this system, the answer, later given by Darwin, is that it makes survival possible. It enables humans to see and find sources of food and shelter, avoid predators and other hostile forces, and select mates for propagating the species. The fundamental thrust of evolutionary theory is thus to demonstrate that natural selection has allowed all species of animals, including human beings, to survive because they perceive a real world, not a supposititious, fanciful reality, but the real thing itself. Stalking and capturing a real rabbit will keep a hawk and its young fed rather than remaining hungry. What animals perceive of the world is limited by the range of their visual capacities. Accordingly, there are aspects of the real world that cannot be seen by the unaided animal eye, no matter how keen. As S. J. Singer writes:

> Things are seen with the unaided eye only if they emit or reflect radiation within a very narrow range of the electromagnetic spectrum (which we call light) and only if they are suitably contrasted with their background ... Humans do not see X-rays, ultraviolet or infrared radiation, microwaves or radio frequencies (that is, well over 99 percent of the electromagnetic spectrum) and were therefore entirely unaware of the existence of such phenomena as recently as 150 years ago. Likewise, our perception of distance is limited by the stereoscopic analysis provided by our two eyes and brain so that, for example, we cannot discriminate astral distances; to us, all the visible stars appear to be located on a single canopy in the night sky, much as we see them projected on the roof of a planetarium. We cannot distinguish with the unaided eye between a distant galaxy containing billions of stars and a nearby single star in our own galaxy, since both appear to us as single points of light.

These limits on our perception are further examples of the functional economy of evolution. Natural selection is parsimonious. It selects only for qualities that are important for survival. Our ancestors did not need to recognize objects at very long distances in order to capture prey or to avoid predators, and in view of the curvature of the Earth's surface, our ability to perceive long distances horizontally was in any event proscribed. In a similar vein, we did not need to, and therefore did not, see objects that are less than about 0.1 mm in size. The entire world of microorganisms was therefore invisible to us and remained unknown until microscopes were invented (pp. 144–145).

But what might be called the "middle sized furniture" of the world can be apprehended by the visual systems of most animals. Singer's point that natural selection is parsimonious and selects only for qualities that are conducive to survival is powerful. It means that evolutionary theory does more than take it for granted that there is a real world. It explains why there *must* be such a world given the millions of years that so many species have persevered. The existence of an external world is thus *proved* not by *observation* as the skeptical challenge assumes, but by the persistence of uncountable species of living beings.

SELF-CORRECTION, SCIENTIFIC TRUTH, AND SCIENTIFIC KNOWLEDGE

So far we have identified three essential characteristics of science: its reductive and quantitative investigative approaches to the world, its presupposition that there is an objective, mind-independent world whose operations are not obvious, and that the scientific task is to find out how they work. Let us now mention a fourth: science's quest for knowledge and truth.

Even though science is a form of curiosity, such wonderment is not idle; it is tempered by the requirement that its investigative activities lead to an accurate picture of things. This aim distinguishes it from many other disciplines, such as pure mathematics. A mathematician may construct a conceptual scheme of great elegance that has no application to reality. Yet that it does not may not affect its mathematical significance. But science is different. If a scientific idea does not fit the facts it will eventually be discarded despite its ingenuity. A famous case of this sort is the theory advanced by Claudius Ptolemaeus (fl. C.E. 127–145) to the effect that the earth is the center of the universe and does not move. Ptolemy argued that since all bodies fall to the center of the universe, the Earth must be fixed at its center, otherwise falling objects would not be seen to drop toward the center of the Earth. Furthermore, if the Earth rotated every twenty-four hours, a body thrown vertically upward should not fall back to the same place, as it was seen to do. Ptolemy also pointed out that no countervailing data had ever been observed. As a result of his arguments, the geocentric system became the accepted truth in Western Christendom until it was superseded in the sixteenth century by the heliocentric system of Copernicus. The Copernican view that the planets have circular orbits was in turn replaced by Kepler's discovery that the orbits are elliptical. A new explanation of why bodies fall to the ground was given still later by Newton's theory of universal gravitation. Yet as elegant and powerful as it is, the Newtonian system is now known to be a special case of a more general form of astrophysics that was developed by Einstein at the beginning of the last century, and it is this outlook, supplemented by quantum theory, that is currently accepted by most scientists.

There are many such developments in the history of science. The replacement of phlogiston theory by Lavoisier's discovery that oxygen is the causal factor in combustion is another example of scientific advance. Despite frequent misfires, science has a notable record for correcting its earlier errors. Most intelligent persons are impressed by this record, and it is widely believed today that science will continue to make steady progress toward a true view of things. The notion of self-correction is obvious and needs no further explanation here; but the concepts of truth and knowledge are less so. Even at first glance it is clear that they differ. The claim that there is life on Mars may well be true even if nobody knows that it is. But what, then, is the difference between these notions?

Scientific truth

Let us begin with the concept of truth. The most famous definition derives from Aristotle: "To say of what is that it is not, or of what is not that it is, is false, while to say of what is that it is, or of what is not that it is not, is true" (*Metaphysics*, Bk. 4, Ch. 7). It will be noticed that this formula distinguishes between two different categories of items, between *saying* and *what is*. According to this conception, truth is a relation that holds between a particular speech act and what that speech act is about. Philosophers call this a "semantic" relation. In modern philosophy there are many different accounts of the appropriate candidates for each category. For *saying* the main choices are *propositions, sentences, affirmations, beliefs, assertions, utterances, claims,* and *statements*. These are all different and each has its proponents. For *what is* the candidates include *the world, facts, reality, what is the case, situations, the way the world is, states of affairs,* and *state descriptions*. Again, each is different and each has its adherents. But despite such disagreements there is a consensus that truth is a relationship that holds between a specimen of language (or its analogues) and some feature or features of the world.

To illustrate: Suppose my wife and I have decided to go on a picnic and as we leave the house I say to her, "It is raining." I have made an assertion about the weather. If rain is then falling it is that fact that makes my utterance, "It is raining," true. If it is not raining that is also a fact; and it is that state of affairs that makes my assertion false. This is what Aristotle's formulation entails. It is called the "correspondence theory," because it holds that when there is a correspondence between an assertion, belief, or statement and the way the world is, we have truth. If that correspondence does not obtain we have falsity.

This concept of truth is relevant in the following way to our discussion of the main features of science. As emphasized earlier, metaphysical realism presupposes that the real world exhibits both sentience and non-sentience. The concept of truth satisfies this complex condition. It presupposes that the real world contains sentient beings capable of thought and speech, as well as non-sentient features about which such beings can and do make assertions or claims. Among such non-sentient features are facts. Truth, in contrast, depends on sentience. If there were no creatures capable of belief or statement-making, truth would not exist. Nor would science exist. But facts would. The fact that it is now raining has nothing to do with anyone's beliefs, doubts, thoughts, or any other psychological factors. As far as we know, the capacity for truth (or its antonym, falsity) is a distinctly human feature. To attempt to arrive at a true account of nature is a further distinctive feature of science. It is not, to be sure, the *only* aim of science. Knowledge is another. It is generally important and almost always relevant to ask: "But how can we *know* that any scientific claim *is* true?" The answer resides in epistemological realism, the investigative arm of metaphysical realism. It attempts to explain the nature and extent of the evidence that must be adduced in support of any truth claim if we are to know that the claim is true. Thus, together with truth, the quest for knowledge is a fourth distinctive feature of science. We have just discussed one of the two partners of this complex criterion; now let us look at the other. We shall find that what counts as evidence, and in particular that what counts as sufficient evidence for knowledge, is a complex matter.

Scientific knowledge

An investigation into the nature of knowledge ideally would begin with the study of the differing uses of the word "knowledge," found in everyday speech. These would include such expressions as "know him," "know that," "know how," "know why," "know whether," and so forth. But in general the philosophical and scientific traditions have focused on the kind of knowledge expressed when it is said that someone knows that such and such is the case. This sort of knowledge, called *propositional knowledge*, can be expressed in the formula, *A knows that p*, where A is a sentient being and p is a proposition, statement, assertion, etc. An example: "I know that our neighbor has a dog." It is this use of the term that we shall examine in what follows.

There is a direct connection between knowledge and truth, since it is universally agreed that A cannot know that p if p is false. If I assert that the moon is only 100 miles from the Earth that remark cannot be a piece of knowledge because it is false. Furthermore, A can be said to know that p only if A has evidence that supports the truth of p. Once again, there is a connection between knowledge and truth, via the evidential relationship. If the evidence is weak or if there is no evidence the claim to know lacks adequate support, and in such a case one cannot know that p. It is the requirement that there be evidence that rules out lucky guesses or superstition as cases of knowledge.

This brings us to two conceptions of propositional knowledge: "the Platonic" and "the Scientific." These overlap to some extent but they are basically opposed as we shall see. They coincide in agreeing that one cannot know that p if p is false. But they diverge over the issue of whether knowledge entails certainty. The Platonist says it does and the scientist says the opposite. Here is how the Platonist argues his case. He begins with an observation about the nature of possibility. His position is that if it is possible to be mistaken about p, then one cannot know that p. Thus, if it is possible that it will rain tomorrow or possible that it will not rain tomorrow, one cannot know today which it will do. Hence, if one knows that p, it is not possible to be mistaken about p. But if one can't be mistaken, then one is certain. And if this is so, then if one knows that p one knows that p with certainty. It is this conclusion that science rejects.

The notion of possibility also plays an important role in the scientific conception of knowledge. The scientist agrees that the existence of possibility is inconsistent with *certitude*. But he rejects the inference that it is incompatible with *knowledge*. Here is how he defends this position.

Let us agree, he will say, that all scientific explanations are generalizations based on past observation. Consider the discovery that water at sea level boils at 100 degrees Celsius. This finding was arrived at by means of observations conducted over a vast period of time. Would any scientist, therefore, be committed to the thesis that it is *absolutely certain* that water in the future will continue to boil at that temperature? The answer is "no." It is "no" because past experience is not an infallible guide to the future.

Nor can he say with certainty that water has always boiled at 100°C. It is thus *possible* that next week water will begin to boil at a different temperature. But in acknowledging this point, the scientist does not agree that knowledge – as distinct from certainty – is not attainable in such a circumstance. In fact he asserts the opposite. Knowledge, from a scientific perspective, is a matter of the strength of the evidence in support of a particular assertion. When the evidence is very strong, as it is in this case, one has knowledge about a particular feature of the world.

In distinguishing knowledge from certainty, science is in effect rejecting the Platonic conception of knowledge. This is not a verbal disagreement, but a substantive one. It is connected with the difference between a logico-mathematical and an empirical outlook. The Platonic outlook depicts knowledge as if it were identical with the kind of certitude found in logic and mathematics. But from a scientific standpoint this outlook is unrealistic and impracticable. It fails to understand that logic and mathematics have no factual content. Their theorems are tautologies and thus never get beyond the linguistic level to the world of fact. Knowledge about the world is not merely linguistic: it ultimately derives from observation, that is, from the kind of data that the senses provide. That is the only kind of knowledge that provides substantive information about matters of fact. But no observational data are sufficiently strong to entail certainty. The argument for this point is convoluted. It rests on yet another dichotomy: that between analytic and synthetic knowledge. Let us therefore take an additional, somewhat lengthy step and explore this contrast. We shall find in it justification for the scientific position that knowledge is to be distinguished from certainty.

The analytic/synthetic distinction

The analytic/synthetic distinction is the basis of what is perhaps the most widely accepted theory of knowledge today. It is a theory that has a long history and some version of it has been defended by most major philosophers since the time of Descartes.

According to this theory all knowledge claims are expressible as propositions that fall into two categories that are *exclusive* and *exhaustive.* To say that the categories are exclusive means that no proposition can be a member of both, and to say they are exhaustive means that they include all instances of knowledge claims. We thus have a synoptic theory covering all possible cases. One of the complications in describing the theory is exactly how these contrasting categories are to be defined or characterized.

Historically, there have been many different names and conceptions associated with each side of the distinction, but let us confine ourselves to three of the most important: Leibniz (1646–1714) distinguished between necessary and contingent propositions; Kant (1724–1804) discriminated between analytic and synthetic judgments; and both Kant and Hume (1711–1776) distinguished a priori from a posteriori propositions. In a longer essay, each of these pairs would have to be distinguished from one another. For instance, to say that a proposition is necessary is not identical with saying that it is analytic. To say the former is to say that the proposition holds (is true) in all possible worlds; to say the latter is to say that the predicate term is part of the meaning of the subject term and in that sense gives us a (partial) analysis of the meaning of the subject term. Some philosophers have maintained that "Every event has a cause," is necessary because it holds in all possible worlds, but that it is not analytic because "being caused" is not part of the meaning of "event." Some propositions, however, are both analytic and necessary. "All husbands are married" is necessary because it is true in all possible worlds, and it is analytic because "being married" is part of the meaning of "being a husband." Similar differences hold between the other notions.

For our purposes here, the important idea is that historically all of the propositions belonging to the analytic (necessary, a priori) side of the distinction have been thought to possess an important epistemological characteristic that marks them off from those belonging to the synthetic (contingent, a posteriori) side of the distinction. The characteristic is that they can be determined to be true without any reference to experience. The operative point can be brought out by considering how we come to establish the truth of the following propositions:

(a) All husbands are married.

(b) All present-day laptop computers weigh less than 20 pounds.

It is clear at some relevant time in the past we could only have determined whether (b) is true by an appeal to experience, that is, by investigating the weights of laptop computers, or by checking the production records of manufacturers, say. The idea is that in order to determine the truth of (b) some research would be requisite. It is not enough merely to have understood the proposition. This is what it means to say that (b) is *a posteriori*; namely, that its truth can be ascertained only *after* some resort to experience. This proposition also has the feature that it might have been false: one can imagine that a certain firm made some heavy, experimental laptops it did not sell to the public. So to say that (b) might have been false is equivalent to saying that it is not a necessary truth, since there are imaginable circumstances in which it might not have been true. But now let us contrast (b) with (a). We can tell without any research that (a) is true. We know this *prior* to any sort of investigation of the facts of the matter. The kind of knowledge we have in this case is thus said to be *a priori*. All we have to do is to understand the proposition and we can *see* that it is true. Moreover, it is not merely true; it is necessarily true. For it is impossible to imagine or describe any circumstances in which, as those terms are customarily used, someone could be a husband without being married. So (a) is both a priori and necessary.

Now Hume and many subsequent philosophers saw this exclusive–exhaustive division, however it was expressed, as having important implications for the theory of knowledge. They contended that propositions belonging to the category of the synthetic, contingent, a posteriori side of this opposition are never certain, and they bolstered this inference with the argument that all such propositions can be determined to be true only on the basis of past experience; and since past experience, being only a sample of all experience, might turn out in the light of future happenings to be unreliable, such propositions could never be certain. At most they could be known to be true only with some degree of probability. In contrast, a priori, analytic, or necessary propositions can be certain. To say that they are certain entails that they hold in all possible circumstances, so that no future experience can run counter to them; and this in turn entails that one asserting them cannot be mistaken. But such certitude produces no information about the world; it is a product of the special, usually definitional, relationships holding between the terms in a proposition. From the truth of the sentence, "All giants are tall," it does not follow that there are giants. Or as Wittgenstein wittily remarked: "I know, for example, nothing about the weather, when I know that it rains or does not rain" (*TLP*, 4.461). Such propositions thus provide information about conceptual relationships, not about matters of fact. Accordingly, this analysis issued in the following conclusion about knowledge, namely that insofar as propositions are descriptive of the world they can never be certain; and insofar as they are certain they are devoid of information about the world. The contention that science can have knowledge that is less than certain is supported by such an analysis. Science is content to rest its case on probability. The highest degrees of probability obtainable about the world are cases of knowledge for science. As Bertrand Russell once wrote:

> What shall we regard as having the greatest likelihood of being true, and what as proper to be rejected if it conflicts with other evidence? It seems to me that science has a much greater likelihood of being true in the main than any philosophy hitherto advanced ... Therefore, we shall be wise to build our philosophy upon science, because the risk of error in philosophy is pretty sure to be greater than in science.

In using such terms as "likelihood," and "the risk of error," to characterize the scientific endeavor, Russell is implying that certainty is not to be expected as the outcome of its investigative pursuits. Instead, it is knowledge and truth. That this is so is bolstered by the line of reasoning we have just advanced. We thus have arrived at a fourth criterion – the quest for knowledge and truth – that defines modern science.

There are doubtless other criteria that distinguish modern science from other intellectual activities but the four we have cited are sufficient to explain why many people accept Schlick's dictum that in principle science can answer all questions. Moreover, when we add the success of technology to the preceding account one can even more fully appreciate why such optimism is widespread. Let us, therefore, complete our case for the overweening confidence in science by a glance at how technology has altered nature for the benefit of the human race. Before beginning such an account, we concede, of course, that technology has had, still has, and always will have a dark side. But we shall ignore that fuliginous aspect here. Our aim, instead, is to present the strongest case for the proposition that science in principle can solve all problems. So let us reinforce this endeavor by appealing to the aid that the troops of technology can supply. The case can be made in two sentences: "Would you rather have lived four hundred years ago before science and technology altered the world or today?" The answer for most persons, as we shall now indicate by a brief, fictional narrative, is obvious.

THE POWER OF TECHNOLOGY

It is almost impossible to overestimate the effect of technology on daily living. Its use today is widespread and deeply ingrained. Technological devices are so familiar as to be virtually invisible – that is, until something goes wrong. A washing machine or a television set that stops working is tantamount to a crisis. Then we take notice. Of course, when a new technology is introduced it tends to make a splash. Consider the impact that the first movies made on Western culture. But as time passes the new is taken for granted and is absorbed into the routine of everyday practice. The effect of technology is thus subtle; it is quickly internalized and its profound effects pass undetected. Most of us wear wristwatches. In the middle ages there were no watches. Human behavior was mostly regulated by the ringing of church bells. The intervals at which these were sounded depended on gross observations – the season, the position of the sun or moon, and so on. Today, in contrast, most of us maintain rigid schedules, frequently checking our watches or clocks in order to keep appointments. We rush from one thing to another as if we were automata governed by control towers. Meetings, lectures, classes, and games are fixed to take place within minutes. Yet most of us are unaware of how the precise measurement of time has affected our lives. The pace of the contemporary world is hectic when compared with how persons have conducted themselves through most of recorded history.

Examples, making the same point, can be multiplied indefinitely. But there is also another way of illustrating the profound influence of technology. Consider the following fable, for example. It begins in fifth-century b.c.e. Athens. Its protagonist is a young Greek named Georgios. As the narrative opens he is listening to one of the most famous political speeches ever given: the Funeral Oration of Pericles. Georgios never hears the whole speech. He suddenly falls into a trance, and is transported, unconscious, via a magic carpet to sixteenth-century England. En route he somehow learns English, while not forgetting his life in Greece. When he awakens he is again listening to a speech. The orator is Henry VIII, King of England. The year is 1533. Henry is announcing to a crowd assembled at his court in Windsor that Pope Clement VII has refused his request to divorce his wife, Catherine of Aragon. Henry is also explaining why he wishes to divorce Catherine and to marry a twenty-year-old beauty, Anne Boleyn. He points out that after many years of marriage Catherine has been unable to provide a male heir to the throne. Their only child, Mary (born in 1516) is female. The crowd murmurs its approval, since they wish a male to carry on the royal line.

After the speech, Georgios (now called George) goes to London and finds lodgings there. He is struck by the similarities between the Greece he knew and sixteenth-century England. Though Athens was a democracy and England is a monarchy, there is otherwise very little difference between the two cultures. Travel in Periclean Athens was by ship, horse, horse-drawn carriage, or on foot, and two thousand years later he finds that this is still how the English get from one place to another. Athens, at night, was gloomy, and London is not much better. (Frying-pan shaped lamps, using fat derived from animal intestines, were not be used in London for another century, and then they were a failure.)

He remembers only too well the plague that decimated Athens, and now here in London he notes that smallpox, typhus, typhoid, and dysentery are commonplace. In the more than two thousand years that have passed, the system for disposing of human waste has not really improved. An open cesspool is used by the richer Londoners; the poor urinate and defecate wherever there is a sheltered spot. No streets are paved. Homes are hovels, made of clapboard, and are the sites of filth, squalor, and disease. Most people live with their animals – swine, chickens, dogs, cats, horses and donkeys. The dwelling places of the poor are overcrowded – ten to a room is common. Rooms are generally without furniture, even without beds. Refuse is thrown into the street, where it festers. George is told by neighbors that only about one child in four born in London survives infancy. In the midst of death people seek every possible means of assuaging the futility of existence. The consumption of alcohol is prodigious and much of the population is in a state of irremediable inebriation. Crime is rampant; burning, looting, rape, prostitution, and civil unrest are endemic. London is in most respects like the Athens he knew. He feels quite at home here.

But suddenly George falls into a coma. Deeply asleep, he is transferred, again by magic carpet, to New York City. Now the year is 2004. When he awakens he is in a place called an airport. As he looks around, he sees a group of people who are standing in front of what seems to him to be a painting of a man. As he moves forward to join them, he realizes that they are listening to a speech. He sees the lips of the figure move and he can hear his voice clearly. The man in the painting thus seems alive. He has never seen a painting in which a figure moves and makes sounds that one can hear. He is told that the orator is the leader of the American people, and that he is called The President of the United States. Someone adds that the President is speaking to a group called "The Congress." He is puzzled because he is also informed that though he and the other auditors listening to the man in the picture are in New York, that same man is at that very moment speaking in Washington. Yet George is somehow hearing and seeing the President. It is just as if he were in Washington. Yet he is not. He could not have heard or seen Pericles or Henry if he were not in their immediate presence. Someone tells him this is possible because he is watching television. He has no idea what this is.

Things quickly become more confusing. As he glances around the room, he sees large glass windows and through them objects that are totally unfamiliar. They gleam in bright lights. He asks what they are and is informed they are airplanes. Asking about these he is told that they carry people from one place to another while flying through the sky. He wonders if they are a special species of bird and is told "no;" that they are machines, made by man. He has no conception of what a machine is. And how can things that fly through the air be made by human beings? It is incredible and unbelievable. Perplexed, he decides to leave the airport. As he walks through doors that open magically as he approaches, he becomes increasingly bewildered by what seems to him a fantasy world. He sees people rapidly conveyed away by horseless carriages that someone calls "taxis." He cannot understand how these strange objects move without being pulled by an animal. As he stands amazed, he hears someone holding an object and talking into it. The person is clearly carrying on a conversation with someone who is not present. George wonders how this is possible. He is witnessing a conversation by means of a cellphone.

As he walks around the city, he becomes aware that it does not look like either Athens or London. There are innumerable high buildings – so high he has to crane his neck to see their tops. The streets are paved and smooth. There are sidewalks for pedestrians. The people look clean and well-fed. He sees human beings of all races, black, brown, and white. There is a babble of languages, one of which is a dialect of English. People say "erl," but don't mean a nobleman as they did in England. Here they mean "oil." But he can still understand most of what they say.

For George, New York is wholly different from Tudor London or Periclean Athens. He has entered a domain of which he cannot make sense. Without knowing what has produced this world, he is witnessing the effects of modern technology. In less than five centuries, it has revolutionized human existence. It has altered the quality of human life in ways that are entirely unprecedented. George will eventually discover that technology has not allowed human beings completely to defeat their ancient adversary, nature. He will learn that there are still hurricanes, floods, droughts, and a variety of diseases and illnesses. But he will also learn that technology has done much to level the playing field. When he discovers that he will live much longer now, that his life will be easier, that he will be healthier and have options for travel and enjoyment he could never have imagined in his earlier incarnations, he will be glad to be living in the twenty-first century. It is like the difference between being rich or poor. It is not a difficult choice at all.

THE PRICE OF SUCCESS

Much of the success of modern science can be accounted for in terms of its technological applications and its reductive and quantitative approaches to nature. But there is almost always a price to be paid for success. For modern science it is that the qualitative aspects of human experience cannot be accommodated by a quantitative approach. Yet these are some of the most important features for living creatures: the taste of an apple, the appreciation of a sunset, the beauty of a great painting or a musical composition, the pleasures of friendship, of love, of accomplishment, and so forth. None of these is quantifiable in the way that the motion of inanimate bodies is. There is thus a domain of (especially) human existence that is non-factual and hence seemingly not accessible to scientific analysis. Its natural turf is generally called "the humanities," that group of disciplines that include the arts, literature, music, history, cultural anthropology, and philosophy. When Schlick asserts that "Since science in principle can say all that can be said there is no unanswerable question left," he is possibly mistaken. Perhaps in the humanities there are unanswerable questions. Schlick's is a controversial statement, and some thinkers have rejected it. One of the greatest philosophers of the past century, Ludwig Wittgenstein, said: "We feel that if all possible scientific questions be answered, the problems of life have not been touched at all." But Wittgenstein then added: "Of course, there is then no question left, and just this is the answer." Perhaps Schlick meant that the humanities do not "say" anything. If their functions are not those of describing or discovering facts, but in dealing with "the problems of life," or with values, then he may be right after all in claiming that it is only science that can access the natural world. And if this is what he meant then it would seem that he and Wittgenstein are in agreement.

But I do not think they are. I think that Schlick's remark has to be understood in a different way from Wittgenstein's. Wittgenstein is saying that what he is calling "the problems of life," and which he associates with ethics, aesthetics and more generally with values, are not solvable by scientific means. My view is that Schlick would agree with Wittgenstein on this point. He would agree, that is, that there are human problems which are not open to scientific resolution; but then he would add that this is not what he was referring to with his aphorism. What he meant is that if a problem is factual in nature then in principle it is capable of scientific solution. In my opinion this is a much more interesting challenge than Wittgenstein's. It is generally agreed that science does not and even in principle cannot deal with moral and aesthetic dilemmas. Science is a fact-finding activity and most moral and aesthetic problems cannot be resolved by an appeal to the facts.

Hume was among the first of the post-Cartesian philosophers to make the distinction. He said from an "is" one cannot derive an "ought." What he meant is simple and compelling. From the fact that humans drink alcohol in various forms nothing follows about what they ought or ought not do, that is, whether it is right or wrong to drink alcohol. Whether people actually drink alcohol or in what quantities they drink it is a scientific, factual question. Whether they should or should not drink alcohol and in what quantities is a question of a different order. The two should not be conflated. Most, though not all, philosophers agree with Hume. I think that Schlick was well aware of the distinction and, accordingly, that his aphorism was limited to questions of fact. So that is the challenge: Are there any questions of fact that science – even in principle – cannot solve? I assert that there are, and the rest of the book will be devoted to proving that this is so. Let us turn to the first of these problems now – "Is There Life After Death?" With respect to this issue science will draw a blank – and so will everybody else.

2

IS THERE LIFE AFTER DEATH?

"Is There Life After Death?" The query seems simple enough when posed in this stark form, but as one tries to answer it a host of complexities arise. There is, however, one central problem on which all the subordinate issues turn: *Is a human being (i.e., a person) a complex entity consisting of a body and its various parts, and an element that is incorporeal and is generally called "the soul"?* The puzzles that this question generates form a virtually endless list. Here are a few of them: Is there such a thing as the soul and if so, what is it? If there is such a thing as the soul does it leave the body when a person dies and is it immortal? Is reincarnation possible? Is the soul a distinctively human thing, that is, do animals lack a soul? Is the soul identical with conscious awareness? If not, how do they differ? If they are identical, is the brain the source of such awareness, so that if the brain dies, consciousness also dies? Is there a difference between the death of a body and the death of the person whose body it is? Historically, there have been many answers to these questions, and we shall explore them as the chapter develops.

Unfortunately for the impatient reader – and also for the impatient author – there are a number of preparatory conceptual and biological matters to address before we can deal with these substantive questions.

The last half of the chapter will focus on two of them: first, whether there is such a thing as the soul, and second, whether it is the soul (if anything) that persists after the death of the body. But some of the questions raised in the preceding paragraph will arise almost immediately – for example, whether a person is identical with his or her body, so that when the body dies the person necessarily dies; and if the body and the person are not identical, does anything survive the death of a person and if so what is it? So let us turn to these preliminary considerations now.

WHY THE QUESTION IS NOT TRIVIAL

One matter we should dispose of at the outset is whether the answer to the question "Is there life after death?" is trivially "no." One might argue that this is so on the ground that "death" simply means "the termination of life." The problem is thus solved by definition. This way of looking at the matter provides a neat solution, but it is wrong for at least two reasons. First, by defining "death" in this way one converts the response into an analytic truth. But as our discussion of the analytic/synthetic distinction in the previous chapter indicated, such definitional truths are tautologies that do not provide factual information about the world. Even many of those who have denied that any form of life persists after death have offered physiological or medical evidence to support their position. That they have done so indicates they do not suppose the issue to be resolvable by conceptual means alone. In this respect, they join the vast majority of human beings who have answered the question in the affirmative. Both groups believe that what is at stake is whether a certain "something" *in fact* survives death. I concur that this is the issue. In the discussion that follows I will try to explain why so many persons believe that the question is a substantive one.

Second, to answer in this way is to presuppose that we know with indisputable clarity what life and death really are. We shall find that this is an unwarranted assumption. History teaches us that there have always been discordant views about these notions. Consider death, for example. The fear of being buried alive has long haunted human beings. Such a concern suggests that it is not always easy to determine whether someone has died. Even today, using the latest technology, physicians may disagree about particular cases. Here are a couple of "amusing" examples from the past to illustrate the point. The sixteenth-century Flemish medical doctor, Andreas Vesalius, one of the greatest anatomists of all time, professor of surgery in Padua for three years, and later physician to the Holy Roman emperor, Charles V (1500–1558), had to leave Spain in a hurry in 1564. He was performing an autopsy when the "cadaver" began to move and showed other signs of life. His mistake caused a furor. The incident occurred at the height of the Spanish Inquisition and Vesalius was pardoned only on the condition that he make a pilgrimage to the Holy Sepulchre in Jerusalem. As far as we know, he was not sued by the victim. A cynic later remarked that the only sure sign that a man is dead is that he is no longer capable of litigation. In the nineteenth century, a Russian count, Karnice-Karnicke, patented a coffin that allowed a "corpse" that had been buried to summon help from the surface by activating a system of flags and bells. Advertisements described the price of this construction as "exceedingly reasonable, only about twelve shillings."

CLINICAL DEFINITIONS OF DEATH

The triviality issue may also arise in science. In this form it appears as a seemingly empirical thesis, namely that when a living human organism has been deprived of oxygen for a short time, its biological systems deteriorate to such an extent that post-mortem survival is impossible. As one physiologist put it, oxygen deprivation "not only stops the machine but wrecks the machinery." Those who believe in life after death accept the medical data, but reject the conclusion that post-mortem survival is impossible. In particular, they challenge an assumption on which such an approach depends: namely that a human being – a person – is to be identified with his or her body. Their view is that a human being is a complex totality, some of whose elements are somatic and some of which are not, and it is one or perhaps more than one of these that survives the death of the body. In order fully to understand their objections we must see what it is that biology and clinical medicine actually claim and what, according to "post death" survivalists, its supposed limitations are. The issue to be explored is thus whether the total package we call a human being or person is simply identical with his or her body. We turn to this topic now.

Biologists and physicians normally distinguish the death of parts of an organism, such as its red blood cells, from the death of the whole entity. It is clear, of course, that a complex organism, such as a human being, may continue to survive even though many of its components have died. Cells that determine the color of human hair, for instance, may become inert without affecting the vitality of the person whose hair it is. In such a case, the person will exhibit a classic sign of longevity: "uncolored" white hair. Let us look first at the mechanisms involved in the death of cells and then at those concerning the death of the total organism. The former situation is relatively straightforward whereas the second is more complicated. We turn again to the eminent biologist, S. J. Singer, for a description of cell death. In *The Splendid Feast of Reason*, he writes:

> In 1945, Rudolf Schönheimer, using the newly available stable nitrogen isotope N^{15} as a tracer, showed that most protein molecules in the body were "turned over" – that is, destroyed, and new ones generated – in a matter of hours or days. Outside the body, though, in a sterile solution in a test tube, a protein molecule can remain unchanged for months at a time. Why the rapid protein turnover in the body? The answer in part is that in the body and inside most cells, many kinds of protein molecules are subject to unavoidable chemical attacks that render them dysfunctional, attacks from poisons like hydrogen peroxide that arise during normal metabolism, from free radicals, from radiation, and so forth. In other words, the operations of chemistry and physics inside the body inescapably wreck protein molecules in time. These chemical defects in protein molecules cannot be reversed. Rather than allowing these defective molecules to clog up the cell's operations, other proteins recognize these defectives and rapidly break them down to reusable pieces (amino acids). New protein molecules are then made in cells to replace the ones destroyed, so as to maintain the amount of a functional protein fairly constant.

Most cells in the body also turn over. The average red blood cell, for example, has a half life of about 100 days in the human body, until it is inevitably destroyed by, among other traumas, the continual physical wear it receives from being squeezed through the capillaries numerous times. Mechanisms that program cell death exist in the simplest single cell as well as in the most complex organisms. Presumably these mechanisms detect a cell that has undergone some initial chemical events that would ultimately and inevitably result in cell death and then proceed to accelerate the cell-killing process. The cells that die are replaced by new ones. (Nerve cells of the brain by contrast, however, have long lives; and when they finally die, new ones are not normally regenerated in humans.) (pp. 72–73)

Controversies about the demise of a human being, that is, a whole organism, typically arise as a result of modern technological developments in medicine. These have made it possible to maintain breathing in comatose individuals by respirators and to eliminate metabolic waste products by dialysis. The problem of determining when the organism is defunct is especially acute in cases of prospective organ transplants. Traditional signs of mortality, such as cardiac arrest and the cessation of circulation, are often absent in patients who are in an irreversible vegetative state. Because such individuals never recover and yet, when assisted by technical devices, exhibit signs of life, doctors tread a fine line in deciding when to remove a vital body part. If the patient dies before such a procedure is initiated, the organ normally does not function well or sometimes not at all when inserted into another person. Yet no physician wishes to expedite death in such a circumstance. As a result of such problematic situations, a medical definition was developed in the late 1970s that identified the death of a human being with the death of a special part of the brain: the brain stem.

The distinction recognized that some vegetative organisms had approached, though they had not yet reached, a point of "no return." With the death of the brain-stem the point of no return had indeed arrived, and from a clinical standpoint the restoration of life was no longer possible. In 1981, a presidential commission issued a report, which was subsequently endorsed by the American Medical Association, the American Bar Association, and the National Conference on Uniform State Laws, that defined the death of a human being as being identical with the irremedial loss of brain-stem function. This definition became the law in many states in America.

In July of 2001 the California Medical Association issued a new protocol that distinguished irreversible coma from what they called "brain death" or "cerebral death." This they described as the irremediable loss of the clinical function of the *entire* brain and is characterized by (a) coma or unresponsiveness, (b) absence of brain-stem reflexes, and (c) apnea (suspension of respiration). The new definition differs from that adopted in 1981 in that it distinguishes between the death of the entire brain and that of the brain stem. The death of the entire brain includes the death of the brain stem according to this characterization. The new view also states that the older term "irreversible vegetative state" is to be discarded as a definition of death since patients in a prolonged coma may nevertheless exhibit vital signs.

The clinical problem in such cases is how to ascertain whether an irremediable loss of brain function has occurred. According to the medical literature, the death of the brain is confirmed only after three criteria have been satisfied. First, the cause of the coma must be determined, and it must be demonstrated that all attempts to remedy the condition have failed. Second, all possible reversible causes must be excluded, such as drug intoxication or hypothermia. Third, the absence of all brain-stem reflexes must be established, including apnea, no matter how strong the stimulus. An article in the 1990 edition of *The Encyclopedia Britannica* describes the testing of brain-stem reflexes as follows:

> It may take up to 48 hours to establish that the pre-conditions and exclusions have been met; the testing of the brain-stem function takes less than half an hour. When testing the brain-stem reflexes, doctors check for the following normal responses: (1) constriction of the pupils in response to light, (2) blinking in response to stimulation of the cornea, (3) grimacing in response to firm pressure applied just above the eye

socket, (4) movements of the eyes in response to the ears being flushed with ice water, and (5) coughing or gagging in response to a suction catheter being passed down the airway. All responses have to be absent on at least two occasions ...

The developments in the idea and diagnosis of brain-stem death came as a response to a conceptual challenge. Intensive-care technology had saved many lives, but it had also created many brain-dead patients. To grasp the implications of this situation, society in general – and the medical profession in particular – was forced to rethink accepted notions about death itself. The emphasis had to shift from the most common mechanism of death (i.e., irreversible cessation of the circulation) to the results that ensued when that mechanism came into operation: irreversible loss of consciousness, combined with irreversible apnea. These results, which can also be produced by primary intracranial catastrophes, provide philosophically sound, ethically acceptable, and clinically applicable secular equivalents to the concepts of "departure of the soul," and "loss of the 'breath of life,'" which were so important to some earlier cultures (vol. 16, p. 986).

The article describes such tests as "the secular equivalents" of certain non-secular concepts. It thus leaves it open whether such notions as "the departure of the soul," and the "loss of the breath of life," might have non-secular applications. This is a matter we shall explore below. But first a terminological point. The term "secular" is usually contrasted with such expressions as "religious" or "spiritual." In the preceding context, it is clear that "secular" means roughly the same as "medical" or "scientific." Let us therefore (but with some trepidation) assume that in this context "non-secular" will mean the same as "non-medical" or "non-scientific." On this assumption, it will not follow that "departure of the soul," has a religious connotation. What does follow are two things: first, that "departure of the soul," cannot be explained medically or scientifically; and second, that the definition of "brain death" does not entail that nothing survives the death of the whole organism. These inferences are, in effect, alternative ways of saying that the question of whether there is life after death is a substantive one. The following quotation, taken from the 1990 Encyclopedia article, supports this construal. It distinguishes between cell death and the death of a human being. In so doing it implies that a human being is the same as the total organism, and then expressly affirms that the problem of defining human death is not resolvable in purely biological terms. I take this last comment to mean that "departure of the soul," cannot be explained scientifically and accordingly that it is possible that something, such as the soul, *may* persist after the death of the whole organism. Here is the quotation that supports these inferences:

> At the opposite end of the spectrum from cell death lies the death of a human being. It is obvious that the problems of defining human death cannot be resolved in purely biological terms, divorced from all ethical or cultural considerations. This is because there will be repercussions (burial, mourning, inheritance, etc.) from any decisions made, and because the decisions themselves will have to be socially acceptable in a way that does not apply to the fate of cells in tissue culture (p. 985).

WHAT DIES AND WHAT (SUPPOSEDLY) LIVES?

In both the scientific and non-scientific literatures one commonly finds the claim that the death of a human being is identical with the death of the body. In the non-scientific, especially religious, literature, it is also often asserted that if something survives death of the body, it is the soul. We have two different assertions here that may give rise to diverse answers. It is possible, for example, that when the whole organism dies it is not *just* the body that dies, but a larger entity, and that it is the soul that lives. It is also possible that when a person dies the body also dies and that something other than the soul survives. Hence the scientific and non-scientific assertions may both be mistaken. A post-mortem survivalist point of view may thus take a more general form that does not depend on these claims. In our inquiry into the nature of the survivalist outlook, we should avoid committing ourselves to the position that when a whole organism dies it is only the body that dies and that it is the soul that survives. So how, if we wish to avoid what may turn out to be misleading assumptions, shall we begin to explore the question "What dies and what survives?" We shall start by separating the questions:

IS IT JUST THE BODY THAT DIES?

It is illuminating, if depressing, in trying to decide what dies, to read newspaper memorials and obituaries, especially of individuals who are not famous. There is an important difference between memorials and obituaries. The former are usually addressed to a decedent as if that individual were still alive and can see and read the memorial. They often contain references to a place which the deceased now inhabits, indicating that the authors of the memorial (usually relatives or parents) feel comforted in knowing that he/she is safe "and at home" with others who have died, such as Grandma Joan, Grandpa Tom, and Grandpa John. They sometimes expressly affirm that "your name and spirit live on." There is no doubt that such writings presuppose the continued post-mortem existence of the individual being to which they refer. Obituaries generally do not make this assumption. They are notices indicating that a death has recently occurred. I will reproduce one such notice, changing all the names and omitting dates to avoid possible identification. It is taken from a group of twelve that appeared in *The San Diego Union-Tribune* in the summer of 2002. The twelve obituaries follow an identical format. The item I will cite is thus typical. It will be helpful in our attempt to answer the first part of the question: "What dies and what survives?" Here is my revised version of the notice:

Wilma L. Johnson.
Wilma L. Johnson, 87, of San Diego died Wednesday. She was born in Mason City, Iowa. Mrs. Johnson was a homemaker. Survivors include her husband, Thomas A. Johnson; daughter, Megan R. Williams of La Mesa; son, Donald R. Johnson of Valley Center; and four grandchildren. Viewing: 4 to 9 P.M. Thursday at the Happy Ground Mortuary, 3355 Laurel Rd., El Cajon. Services: 10 A.M. Friday at the mortuary. Arrangements: Happy Ground Mortuary.

As this notice tells us it was Wilma L. Johnson that died. The other eleven obituaries also name recent decedents. The notice says nothing about the body of Wilma L. Johnson, though if it had been absent at her demise it surely would have been mentioned. It is thus a plausible assumption that she had one at the time of death. None of the other eleven notices refers to the death of a body. Such repeated omissions suggest that a complete and accurate death notice need not contain any reference to a body. In the particular case of Wilma Johnson the notice is informative in two ways: it gives one a reason for doubting that when Wilma Johnson died it was *only* her body that died and a strong reason for believing that it was Wilma Johnson that died.

Of course, most persons who wish to know whether there is life after death would not be satisfied to be told that it was Wilma L. Johnson that died. They would like a "deeper" answer. They might put their point this way. "Of course, we know that Wilma L. Johnson died; that is not the issue. The real question is: 'Who or what was Wilma L. Johnson?" This is a complex question. We know the answer to the first part – "Who was Wilma Johnson?'" Her obituary supplies the answer. It describes her age, place of birth, marital status, and so forth. But to say this will probably not satisfy those who want a deeper answer. They wish to know "*What* was Wilma Johnson?" They mean by this question: "Was she a complex entity, composed not only of her body, but of something else, that some survivalists would call 'the soul?'"

Once again those who jump from the simple answer that it was Wilma L. Johnson who died, to ask such a "deep" question are moving too quickly. Let us slow them down a bit to see if we can accommodate their worry. Of course, people have all sorts of reasons – religious, psychological, etc. – for supposing that a human being is not simply identical with his or her body, and for assuming that the total bundle includes a feature that survives the death of the body. I shall now formulate an argument that provides a different ground than any traditional set of reasons in support of the survivalist position. It will thus constitute a kind of logical reconstruction of the intuitions that religious and non-religious folks have who insist that something persists after the death of the whole organism. I am not saying that this argument is decisive or that I accept its conclusion. It is primarily designed to explain why the belief in a life after death is not to be dismissed out of hand. It thus supports the thesis that such a belief is non-trivial. Its main thrust is directed to showing that a human being is not identical with his or her body and hence that something may survive the death of the body. Here is how it goes.

The obituary does not indicate the cause of Wilma Johnson's death. Let's construct a scenario that might help us with the question of *what* died when she died. According to her obituary, Mrs. Johnson was eighty-seven when she expired. As part of the scenario let us also assume that she had been ill and in pain before the terminal event took place. If so, Mrs. Johnson may have complained about the distress she was suffering. She may have said: "My leg hurts," or "My head aches," or "My whole body aches," or "I have a terrible pain in my back." So agreeing that it was Wilma Johnson who died, we can rephrase the question under consideration in this way: "What did such words as 'my' and 'I' pick out in the complaints she made about the discomfort she was feeling?" It is obvious from these linguistic clues that she did not identify *herself* with her leg or her head or her body. She was clearly distinguishing herself from those things that ached. Those who pose the deeper question about what died would not only concur with this statement, but would say something even stronger, namely that Wilma Johnson *was not identical with* any of her body parts taken singly or collectively or even with her whole body. They would say this because they believe that even if her body dies, something survives. The philosopher, Wittgenstein, ends *The Blue Book* with a remark that supports this stronger point of view. He writes:

> The kernel of our proposition that that which has pains or sees or thinks is of a mental nature is only, that the word "I" in "I have pains," does not denote a particular body, for we can't substitute for "I" a description of a body (p. 74).

It is striking that Wittgenstein describes that which has pains or sees or thinks as mental. His outlook is thus to be distinguished from clinical views that identify the whole organism with the body or from those that contend that the brain – a physical organ – is the item denoted by "I." I also find his statement curiously suggestive of the survivalist outlook, since many of its proponents believe the soul to be mental – to be a form of disembodied consciousness, for example. But whether this is the only or even the best way of describing what persists after the death of the body is a complex issue that I shall address later. Therefore, without committing ourselves to the mental nature of the "I," while following the rest of Wittgenstein's linguistic clues, we can then ask: "What was Wilma Johnson when she died if she wasn't the same thing as her body or any collection of its parts?"

A possible, even a plausible, answer to this question is that Wilma Johnson was a person and it was that person that died. The idea that when a human being dies it is a person, and not some bodily part, that dies has some impressive corroboration; it was the conclusion of a lengthy report of the Twenty-Second World Medical Assembly held in Sydney, Australia in 1968. As its authors put it "clinical interest lies not in the state of preservation of isolated cells but in the fate of a person." Unfortunately, their report did not go on to define personhood. If we add their conclusion to that arrived at, on linguistic grounds, in the case of Wilma Johnson we find medical support for the survivalist view that a person is not identical with any set of somatic features. But in order to gain a full understanding of that view – and especially whether anything can survive the death of a person – we shall have to determine what it is to be a person. And how does one determine that?

It is often useful to consult a dictionary to find out what something is. As J. L. Austin pointed out:

> When we examine what we should say when, what words we should use in what situations, we are looking again not *merely* at words (or "meanings," whatever they may be) but also at the realities we use the words to talk about: we are using a sharpened awareness of words to sharpen our perception of, though not as the final arbiter of, the phenomena.
>
> "A Plea for Excuses," p. 130

Thus, a dictionary not only describes the uses and meanings of words but in doing so it can give the reader a sharpened perception of the phenomena themselves – in this case persons. And that is what we are really after. But there is still another benefit. Here is what Austin said in this connection:

> our common stock of words embodies all the distinctions men have found worth drawing, in the lifetimes of many generations; these surely are likely to be more numerous, more sound, since they have stood up to the long test of survival of the fittest, and more subtle, at least in all ordinary and reasonably practical matters, than any that you or I are likely to think up in our arm-chairs of an afternoon – the most favoured alternative method (ibid.).

So in trying to figure out what a person is, one is wise to follow Austin's advice. Instead of an armchair, we shall start with a dictionary. In this case, the entry under "person" is indeed helpful. It provides a welter of significations, only two of which are relevant to our problem. Some that are not germane state that a person is one of the three modes of being in the Godhead as understood by Trinitarians; or that it is an inferior human being, as used in the sentence: "People in our position could scarcely know a person in trade socially." Those that bear on our inquiry say that a person is:

1. "A human being as distinguished from an animal or thing."
2. "A being characterized by conscious apprehension, rationality and a moral sense."

These descriptions apply to the death of Mrs. Johnson. The first mentions that in being a person Mrs. Johnson was a human being and not an animal or a thing. That she was not an animal or a thing is something we suspected all along. The second is even more informative. It tells us that a person is a being characterized by *conscious apprehension (awareness), rationality,* and *a moral sense.*

Each of these features is thus worth further investigation. But before doing so let us pause for a moment to summarize the survivalist position as it appears on the basis of our investigation so far. With respect to the question: "What died when Wilma Johnson died," survivalists maintain that though various parts of her body, such as certain cells, died, and even that her whole body died, it was not *simply* her body or any of its parts that died, and finally that it was not an animal that died. Their view is that it was a human being that died. In effect, they are drawing a distinction between a corpse and a human being. They find support for this view in the dictionary. It states that a corpse is "a dead body," and it adds, "usually of a human being." Since it also says that a person is a human being we can assume that survivalists regard these terms as interchangeable. The survivalist position is thus that what died when Wilma Johnson died was a person and what was later buried was her corpse.

But they do not state what it is to be a person; so we do not know how they would answer the question, "What dies when a person dies?" As we have seen, in their view a person is a complex entity, in part consisting of a body and its parts. But apart from these components what other elements comprise personhood? If there are such other elements which, if any, of them dies or survives, when a person dies? Let us now see if we can make some headway with that question by investigating what is meant by conscious apprehension, rationality, and a moral sense. Is it possible that one or perhaps all of these features ceased to exist when Wilma died? It may be that Wilma's capacity for rationality and her moral sense vanished when she died, but that her capacity for conscious apprehension did not. Other variations are also possible. Those who believe that "something" survives when a person dies may think that it is perhaps one, or more than one, of these features that persists after death. Or it may be that what survives the death of a person will be different from any or all of them. Is the soul, for example, different from any of these features?

It will be noticed that all three characteristics are, in a certain sense, non-physical. Whether any is, or whether all are, *mental* is a difficult question. For example, is a moral sense mental? The query would cause a divagation in the line of reasoning we are pursuing, so I shall skirt it here. Instead, we can explore how a survivalist might conceive the nature of personhood without using the term "mental." We can do this by contrasting the ways in which large dictionaries present their definitions of "person" with the ways in which they give the definitions of animals. In the latter cases, they tell us what those animals *are* by telling us what they *look like*. They do this by enumerating their physical attributes and providing drawings or pictures of them. Consider the turtle, for instance. The dictionary states that it is a reptile enclosed in a two-part shell (consisting of a carapace and a plastron) from which its head, tail, and four legs protrude. It also provides a sketch. Writers of prose or poetry can use the description and the depiction for various literary purposes. Here, for instance, is a four-line poem that makes the turtle's appearance a source of humor:

> The turtle lives twixt plated decks
> Which practically conceal its sex.
> I think it clever of the turtle
> In such a fix to be so fertile.

Ogden Nash, in The New Yorker, Nov. 15, 1930

But in the entry for "person" dictionaries do not mention any physical attributes and do not provide accompanying visual representations or portraits. On the basis of a lexical entry one cannot determine what a person looks like.

The contrast between the treatment of animals and persons emerges clearly if we consider the entries for "tiger" and "dodo" that follow. (In *Webster's Third New International Dictionary* there are sketches of both animals.)

Tiger. 1a: a large Asiatic carnivorous mammal (*Felis tigris*) having a tawny coat transversely striped with black, a long untufted tail that is ringed with black, underparts that are mostly white and no mane, being typically slightly larger than the lion with a total length usu. of 9 to 10 feet but sometimes of more than 12 feet, living usu. on the ground, feeding mostly on larger mammals (as cattle), in some cases including man, and ranging from Persia across Asia to the Malay peninsula, Sumatra, and Java, and northward to southern Siberia and Manchuria – compare BENGAL TIGER, SABER-TOOTHED TIGER.

Dodo. 1a: a large, heavy, flightless, extinct bird (*Raphus cucullatus*, syn. *Didus ineptus*) related to the pigeons but larger than a turkey, that had dark ash-colored plumage with the breast and tail whitish, the rudimentary wings being yellowish white with black-tipped coverts, the bill blackish, and the legs yellow; that inhabited forests and laid a single large white egg in a nest of grass; and that was present in great numbers on the island of Mauritius prior to the arrival of European settlers but became extinct by 1681.

Note that the definition of "tiger" describes the creature as having a tawny coat transversely striped with black, and a long untufted tail, and also gives its size. The accompanying sketch tells us more about its appearance. The definition of the extinct dodo contains a large quantity of descriptive language about its semblance (it looks like a pigeon but is larger than a turkey), the colors of its bill, legs, and plumage. The sketch confirms the accuracy of the account. Neither entry says anything about rationality, conscious apprehension, or a moral sense. In the case of "person," by way of contrast, there is no mention of size, color of skin, weight, or habitat.

Now why the difference between these types of definitions? A survivalist might offer the following conjecture as an answer:

The conceptual model of the world that most human beings have is such that persons are not identified with any physical feature or set of such features and the opposite is true of animals.

If this surmise is correct, it explains why many persons subscribe to the Cartesian outlook that beasts do not have souls. From this perspective animals are simply identical with their physical properties. The conjecture also explains why survivalists insist that something survives the demise of the body. For if rationality, conscious apprehension, and a moral sense are not physical features, some or all of them may survive the death of the body. The conjecture also bears on the profoundly different question of whether anything can survive the death of a person. For it may be that some of these features persist when a person dies and that some do not. Our candidates are three. Which, if any, can we exclude? Let us begin with rationality.

RATIONALITY

There are two questions to be addressed in this connection: "What is rationality?" and "Can rationality exist by itself, independently of a person?" The second is deep, and will require careful analysis. It also turns on what is meant by "rationality." In responding to the first query, we seek (again, as a first step) assistance from the dictionary. This time it is not very helpful. It says: "The quality or state of being rational." It also says "more at RATIONAL." Therefore, following its advice, we go to "rational." Here we find an abundance of entries. Most of these we can discard as irrelevant. But one is important. It states:

> RATIONAL usu. implies a latent or active power to make logical inferences and draw conclusions that enable one to understand the world about him and relate such knowledge to the attainment of ends, often in this use, opposed to *emotional* or *animal*; in application to policies, projects, or acts, RATIONAL implies satisfactory to the reason or chiefly actuated by reason (the triumph of the *rational* over the emotional side of man).

As this definition indicates, a rational being has the power to make logical inferences and to draw conclusions that enable one to understand the world. The definition states that in this use *rational* is opposed to *animal*. What is the intended opposition? It is not, I submit, that animals cannot, at least to some extent, understand the world about them. Instead, I take the point to be that there is at least one use in English in which "rational" and its antonym "irrational" primarily apply to human beings. In this respect, we might compare these terms with "even" and "odd." Though one can say of a person that he or she is odd, one cannot sensibly say that a person is even – in the sense of being divisible by two. "Even" and "odd" thus have their primary turf in mathematics. The lexical characterization of "rational" has similar boundaries. Whether and when one can also apply this epithet or its antonym to animals are difficult and controversial issues. A person who eats to the point of obesity might be said to be irrational but this would probably not be said of a dog who is radically overweight. Though one might say of a pet that it can think and even that it is intelligent, it is dubious that one would be willing to affirm that it can deduce from its hearty appetite that its prospects for early death are increased. But in knowing that Wilma Johnson was a person, we know that she was in principle capable of perceiving a logical relationship between obesity and the possibility of impaired health. Unlike one's favored pet, she was clearly capable of making reasonably sophisticated logical inferences and of drawing conclusions from them that enabled her to understand the world about her.

So the next step in our investigation is to determine whether rationality, as so defined, can survive the death of a person that has this capacity. This is a question we can ask of Wilma Johnson but probably not of the dog beside the chair on which I am now sitting, and certainly not of the chair itself.

That we cannot say this of a chair is significant. It presupposes that rationality is an attribute that only a living being can possess. Even more narrowly, the term is generally applied to creatures occupying comparatively high places on the scale of evolutionary complexity, and thus only rarely, if at all, to bacteria or nematodes. Still more narrowly, it is normally used only of beings exhibiting a considerable degree of intelligence – as the definition indicates, of those capable of making logical inferences and drawing conclusions about the world. Conscious awareness of one's environment is a clear precondition for rationality. The word "conscious" is important here. Probably all animate entities have some sort of awareness of their surroundings. But to say of an entity that it has "conscious awareness" is to say something more. The concept includes self-awareness and the ability to organize the world under rubrics that transcend those that the lower order animals are capable of, such as familial relationships. To be aware that A is J's uncle is to allow the inference that either J's father or mother is a sibling of A. Such logical inferences are probably beyond the capacities of animals. Conscious apprehension or awareness of familial relationships is thus a special feature possessed only by human beings. This leads us to the conclusion that rationality depends on conscious apprehension and cannot exist independently of it. Therefore, if when a person dies he or she were to lose the capacity for conscious awareness that individual's capacity for rationality would also cease to exist.

HAVING A MORAL SENSE

A similar conclusion follows about the concept of a moral sense. This notion refers to the conscious awareness by human beings that certain kinds of obligations and degrees of respect are owed to other living beings sharing a common ambience. Thus, the notion primarily applies to those creatures, including pets, that are recognized members of a community. As far as we know, the possession of a moral sense is uniquely a human feature. We do not think that animals are guided by moral principles, such as the maxim that equal crimes deserve equal punishment or that one should treat each individual as an end and not as a means. Wittgenstein expressed this difference in a famous apothegm, saying: "If a lion could talk we could not understand him" (*Philosophical Investigations*, p. 223). What Wittgenstein was getting at is that the contexts in which a lion operates are so different from those in which human intercourse takes place that even though a lion might use the same words as we humans do they would not be comprehensible to us. A lion belongs to a community whose other members are not human beings but lions. Their relationships, customs, and practices are radically different from ours. Could a lion who sheds a mate be said to have "divorced" that mate? Could a lion understand that a potential prey, say a deer, has a right to life and that taking its life is murder? Would it make sense for us – or to the lion – to try it for murder? Lions do not have lawyers, judges, courts, or a constitution. Wittgenstein's point is that we humans could not communicate with one another without having more or less the same backgrounds. It is a radical disparity in communal practices, institutions, and customs that separates us from animals; and it is this disparity that justifies the belief that animals do not have a moral sense. A corollary of this point is that the possession of a moral outlook is uniquely a property of human beings.

Like rationality, a moral sense can exist only where there is conscious apprehension of, and sensitivity to, the attitudes, feelings, desires, and needs of the other members of a community. We thus conclude that when a person dies and if the conscious awareness of others were to cease to exist, then one's moral sense would also cease to exist. In other words, the latter depends for its existence on the existence of the former. We have thus reached the conclusion that conscious apprehension is more basic than either rationality or a moral outlook. It is more basic in the sense that it is the only feature of personhood that *might* persist when a person dies. But to say it might persist does not mean that it can persist. So now a key question: Can it?

CAN CONSCIOUS APPREHENSION SURVIVE THE DEATH OF A PERSON?

The main argument that it cannot is based on scientific, especially on bio-medical, evidence. The aim of the argument is to show that humans in deep comas lack conscious apprehension, and the evidence supporting this conclusion is that such persons fail to exhibit responses to external stimuli. When death finally occurs the lack of response is even more obvious; and hence physicians conclude that conscious apprehension in dead persons is impossible. In arriving at this judgment proponents of the argument distinguish consciousness from awareness. Persons in a deep sleep, for example, are conscious, but may be unaware of such external happenings as rain, thunder, or lightning. The example illustrates that apprehension is a more fragile state than consciousness. It lends credence to the notion that apprehension cannot exist apart from consciousness. The evidence that patients in comas are not conscious in turn supports the conclusion that neither consciousness nor apprehension can survive a person's death.

Survivalists do not find the argument convincing. They contend that what the medical data show is simply that persons in comas can neither speak nor act. Conceding the point, they contend that it does not follow from such observations that comatose persons are aware of nothing at all. They point out that, for all we observers know, comatose individuals may be aware of external and internal phenomena, such as dreams, itches, and pains, though they cannot communicate about or react to them. This riposte is not without evidential support. There are substantiated reports that some persons who have emerged from prolonged comas have stated that while in that condition they were aware of the voices and caresses of family members, that they had dreams, felt pains, and were even wondering whether they would ever recover. This response creates a challenge for science. In effect, it shifts the onus onto physicians, demanding that they prove that a comatose person lacks *any* awareness at all. The real issue, according to survivalists, is thus:

> *Can a physician ever know with certainty that a comatose person is not consciously aware of various kinds of happenings, whether internal or external?*

They believe the answer is "no." They believe this on the ground that conscious apprehension is not a physical feature and thus is not detectable by an external observer. Hence, it is possible for a comatose patient to have experiences of which only he or she is aware. That the patient cannot react to or speak about such experiences does not mean that they do not exist. So survivalists arrive at a first step in a complex argument whose conclusion is that conscious apprehension may exist even after a person has died. Just because a dead person cannot speak it does not follow that such a person cannot continue to be aware of phenomena that no one else can detect.

The survivalist response does not depend solely on this line of reasoning. A second objection to the medico-biological argument is that it is question begging. It assumes that when the body dies the entire physiological system, including conscious apprehension, also dies. The medical view (mentioned earlier) is that oxygen deprivation not only stops the machine but wrecks the machinery. But survivalists stress that to speak of a human being as a machine is essentially to speak of the body or its parts. So even if it is granted that the machinery is "wrecked," it does not follow that a non-somatic constituent of a human being is also "wrecked." Biologists are assuming exactly what is in question: that if the body dies it follows that conscious apprehension also dies. The survivalist challenge to this line of reasoning is: "How does a physician or biologist prove that?"

Both the bio-medical argument and the survivalist responses to it are capable of further elaboration. Physicians state that as long as a comatose person is not brain dead it is possible for an external observer, using modern instruments, to determine whether the individual is having certain sorts of sensations. In particular, it is possible to ascertain with a high degree of probability whether a person is dreaming. Even if the person cannot speak, areas of the brain "light up" when the person is dreaming, and it is possible by sophisticated probes to detect such brain activity. Scientists admit, of course, that they cannot determine the content of dreams but they can determine *that* dreaming is taking place as long as the brain continues to function. In those cases where the patient has a flat brain scan, no neural activity is taking place at all, and accordingly it is plausible to infer that the patient is not aware of anything. In the case of a dead person, such an inference is even more compelling, since brain activity has ceased entirely.

Once again, survivalists do not find this line of argumentation convincing. They do not contest the claim that instruments can detect neural activity in comatose patients who are not brain dead, and they agree that it is probable that such patients are having dreams, and perhaps other experiences. But they argue that such medical findings do not demonstrate that when no brain activity is detectable it therefore follows that conscious awareness has ceased. They say the situation is analogous to the following. From the fact that some fish in a large body of water make waves so that their movements can be tracked it does not follow that where there are no waves there are no fish. Their position is thus that from the lack of observational data no inference about the possibility of sensation follows. Their counter-argument thus depends on the thesis that conscious apprehension is not a physical feature, and therefore that it cannot be detected by instruments capable of measuring only neuronal or other sorts of physiological happenings.

As a non-participant in the debate, I judge that these various arguments counter-balance one another, and that the contest has resulted in a dead heat. Neither side can demonstrate that conscious apprehension vanishes when a person dies nor, on the contrary, that it does not. In my opinion, we have reached an impass that is irresolvable. If this were the end of the story we could conclude that the question of whether there is life after death has no decisive answer. However, it is not the end of the story, but only a phase in a broader controversy. There still exists a substantive issue that does not depend on medical findings. This is the question of whether the soul is identical with conscious apprehension. Some survivalists think it is and others think it is not. In either case, the question raises new complexities. In its simplest form it can be formulated as follows: "Is it possible that an entity, traditionally called 'the soul,' can exist after the death of a person?" Obviously the answer to a great extent depends on what is meant by "the soul." As we shall now see, this is a controversial matter, made more complicated because of its lengthy history.

THE SOUL

That history reveals some curious views about the nature of the soul. Since time immemorial survivalists have affirmed that the soul is immaterial, but there have been exceptions. Here are two.

1. Some years ago, a team of French scientists decided to use the experimental method to determine whether the soul exists and if so what it is. They weighed a dying person's body and then weighed the corpse. They found that the corpse was lighter. They concluded that the difference was due to the evanescence of the soul. On this view, the soul is a physical entity since it has mass. Interestingly enough, this experiment exactly paralleled the argument, widely accepted in the seventeenth and eighteenth centuries, proving the existence of phlogiston. A log was weighed before it was burned and the ash was weighed after combustion was complete. It was found that the ash was lighter than the original piece of wood. The difference was attributed to the evaporation of an invisible substance called *phlogiston*. As Lavoisier later demonstrated, it was the loss of oxygen during combustion that accounted for the difference in weight.

Curiously enough, the eminent British chemist, Joseph Priestley, who was the discoverer of oxygen, never abandoned his belief in the existence of phlogiston. Just as the non-existence of phlogiston was proved by experimental evidence, so the difference in weight between a dying person and a corpse was found to depend on physical factors, especially the loss of fluids accompanying death. The argument that the soul accounted for the difference was thus rejected.

2. An earlier, equally unusual demonstration that the soul was material took place in the third century C.E. In a book that was to become famous, the *Glossa magna in Pentateuchum*, published in 210 C.E., Rabbi Oshaia stated that there was a bone in the human body, located below the eighteenth vertebra, that never died. It could not be dematerialized by fire or water and it could not be broken by any force. He argued that God would use this bone in resurrecting the body. This would happen because other bones would unite with it to form a new body. The name he gave to this "immortal" bone was "lus," an Aramaic word meaning "almond." Some Roman intellectuals were skeptical of these various claims, and demanded observational evidence that such a bone existed. A colleague of Oshaia's, Rabbi Joshua, son of Chanin, agreed to bring the bone to a workshop so that it could be tested. When struck with a hammer the bone remained intact while the hammer and the anvil on which it lay were shattered. The demonstration seems to have overcome Roman, and much subsequent, doubt. For more than a thousand years the "bone of Luz," or *Judenknöchlein*, as it was called by early German physiologists, was taken to be identical with the immortal soul. However, in 1543, the famous anatomist, Vesalius, showed that no such bone exists in the human body. As a result of his findings, immaterialism has been the dominant survivalist position ever since.

But even within this consensus there has been and continues to be dispute. It would be impossible to survey all the variations that have been held historically or conceptually. Let us instead focus on a main distinction around which most of these notions center. This is the difference between conceiving of the soul as the essence of a human being and conceiving it as the human mind. The difference is between thinking of the soul as an entity that confers identity on a person, and thinking of the soul as a mental entity, something that deliberates, believes, doubts, and has opinions. On this latter conception conscious awareness is an aspect of the soul serving a particular function.

Though different, these views are not inconsistent; and historically have often been presented as a single complex theory. The converse is also true. Each has been defended as capturing the soul's true nature. In effect then we have three closely related notions that I will call the "E" view for Essence, the "M" view for Mind, and the "C" view which is a Composite of the E and M views. C is thus not a distinct conception. It becomes important only at the end of *The Republic* where the doctrine of the immortality of the soul is connected with Plato's defense of reincarnation. In the theory of reincarnation, both M and E play their usual roles, M as the mind that transmigrates, and E as giving personal identity to the resulting fusion of mind and body. In this connection, E takes on a relativistic tinge it does not have in the *Phaedo*, since the same soul is depicted as occupying different bodies at different times. In each case, the new combination defines a particular person or animal. When the body dies, the soul will choose and then inhabit a new body, giving the resulting combination its identity as a particular entity or thing. In the *Phaedo*, by way of contrast, the soul is always identified with a particular individual only, such as Socrates or Cebes, and there is no suggestion of reincarnation.

In the history of Western thought, the greatest "theorist" of the soul is unquestionably Plato. With the possible exception of the theory of forms, the nature of the soul is the central theme in his most important writings. The E version is found in the *Phaedo*, and the M and C accounts both appear in *The Republic*, though in different places. Let us begin with the E account. The *Phaedo* consists of a long conversation between Socrates and some of his disciples. It takes place in a cell in which Socrates has been imprisoned after being sentenced to death by an Athenian court for impiety and other offenses. On this particular day, the sentence will be carried out. Socrates will be given poison to drink and will die. The main question that he and his acolytes address is whether death is final. This query is taken to be merely a terminological variation on the question of whether the soul is immortal. It is assumed by his followers that every person has a soul and that if the soul is immortal death is not final. Agreeing with these assumptions, Socrates accepts the burden of proving that the soul is immortal. He arrives at this conclusion by means of a lengthy and complex line of reasoning that when simplified contains three main steps: that death consists in the separation of the parts of a whole organism; that the soul is a totality that lacks parts; and therefore that it is exempt from death. Since the soul is an essence that defines each person it follows that because Socrates's soul is immortal his "death" will not be a terminal event.

We find the first step of the argument early in the dialogue in an interchange between Socrates and Simmias. Socrates asks: "Do we believe that there is such a thing as death?" Simmias agrees that there is such a thing. Socrates now inquires:

> And is this anything but the separation of soul and body? And being dead is the attainment of this separation when the soul exists in herself, and is parted from the body and the body is parted from the soul – that is death?
> Exactly: that and nothing else, he replied.
>
> *Phaedo*, 64–65

In *The Republic*, Book X (608–609), Socrates asserts that the body is a composite entity containing parts. When certain parts die, the body will also die. It follows from the Socratic definition of death that because the body is susceptible to dissolution it cannot be immortal. A similar thesis is implied in the *Phaedo*. Contemporary biologists would agree, though giving different reasons for this claim. The next step of the argument is an assertion to the effect that the soul is a simple entity that has no parts or sub-units. Since death is a consequence of the separation of the parts of a totality, resulting in the dissolution of the whole organism, it follows that the soul is exempt from death.

The argument presupposes that each person's soul is unique and is the source of that person's identity. The particular soul each has is thus the real Socrates or the real Cebes or the real Simmias and so forth. Socrates makes this point plain in the following interchange. Crito, believing that Socrates will soon die, asks: "But in what way would you have us bury you?" Socrates answers: "In any way that you like; only you must get hold of me, and take care that I do not walk away from you." The text continues as follows:

> Then he turned to us, and added with a smile: I cannot make Crito believe that I am the same Socrates who has been talking and conducting the argument; he fancies that I am the other Socrates whom he will soon see, a dead body – and he asks, How shall he bury me? And though I have spoken many words in the endeavor to show that when I have drunk the poison *I* shall leave you and go to the joys of the blessed, these words of mine, with which I comforted you and myself, have had, as I perceive, no effect upon Crito. And therefore I want you to be surety for me now, as he was surety for me at the trial: but let the promise be of another sort; for he was my surety to the judges that I would remain, but you must be my surety to him that *I* shall not remain but go away and depart; and then he will suffer less at my death, and not be grieved when he sees *my* body being burned or buried. I would not have him sorrow at my hard lot, or say at the burial, Thus we lay out Socrates, or, Thus we follow him to the grave and bury him; for false words are not only evil in themselves but they infect the soul with evil. Be of good cheer then, my dear Crito, and say that you are burying my body only, and do with that as is usual, and as you think best.
>
> *Phaedo,* 115

I have italicized the words "I" and "my" in the sentences, "I shall not remain but go away and depart," and "when he sees my body being burned or buried," because his use of "I" and "my" in these instances indicates that Socrates is identifying himself with his soul, and distinguishing *himself* from his body. It will be recalled that this is essentially the thesis we attributed to Wilma Johnson who, using these same locutions, was discriminating herself from her body and from the pains she was suffering before her death. In the *Phaedo* we thus have a paradigmatic expression of the E view, namely that each soul constitutes the identifying essence of the particular individual who has it. It is also a classic expression of the post-mortem survivalist position. The body that will be buried after Socrates drinks the hemlock is not identical with Socrates. *He* will have departed and gone to the joys of the blessed.

The E view as expressed in this dialogue and more generally as providing one formulation of the survivalist thesis contains an apparent contradiction. Consider the following statements:

1. Socrates dies at time T as a result of drinking hemlock.
2. Socrates' soul does not die at time T.
3. Socrates is identical with his soul.
4. Therefore, Socrates does not die at time T.

It will be noted that propositions (1) and (4) are incompatible, since (1) states that Socrates dies at time T and (4) states that Socrates does not die at time T. The difficulty arises in Plato and more generally in widely espoused versions of the survivalist position because both identify the person who dies with the soul that does not die. The dilemma does not simply depend on the soul's being immortal. As long as the soul is identical with Socrates then if Socrates dies at a specific time and the soul persists beyond that time the paradox arises. Of course, if the soul is immortal, as Plato, speaking through the voice of Socrates, claims, then the contradiction is even sharper; for then Socrates dies on a particular occasion and never dies on any occasion.

There are several ways out of the paradox, none of them very appealing to survivalists. The first and simplest is to identify what dies at time T with the body. Thus what Crito will bury is not Socrates but a body. As Socrates puts it in the previous passage: "say that you are burying my body only." This is surely the most traditional solution. But it has a liability. It does not neutralize the paradox as it stands, for there is no mention of the body in its formulation. No doubt Socrates' reference to the burial only of his body is a way of attempting to deny (1) that he dies at time T. But to speak about the death of the body does not contravene the statement that it is Socrates who dies at time T. What is thus needed is a rewriting of (1) to read something like: "What most persons regard as Socrates is really *only* his body, and it is his body that dies at time T." But this move creates another paradox, which can be expressed as follows:

a) The total organism that is Socrates consists of his body and his soul.
b) Socrates is identical with his soul.
c) Therefore the total organism that is Socrates does not consist of his body and his soul.

The attempted revision has thus created a dilemma at least as perplexing as the previous one. Now it is a) and c) that are inconsistent. A possible way of neutralizing this second paradox is to reject b), the premise that Socrates is identical with his soul. This option also allows inferences that will help with the first paradox. According to that argument, it is Socrates who dies at time T, though his soul does not. Thus premises (1) and (2) of the original paradox go through. But the problem with this construal is that it entails the rejection of a commitment that, at least in the *Phaedo*, Socrates (and Plato) cannot abandon. To discard (3) would be inconsistent with what is essential to the E doctrine, namely that Socrates is identical with his soul. If one were to abandon (3) it would also raise the problem of what the function of the soul is if it is not to confer identity on an individual.

All sorts of additional difficulties arise for E if one claims that the soul is immortal. If it is held that every individual has a soul and is identical with it, it follows that nobody ever dies. Clearly this is counterintuitive and violates common sense. Still, that a metaphysical doctrine is far removed from common sense is probably not a concern for most survivalists. But even granted such an exemption from the pressures of common sense, they still face a condundrum: *What dies?* This is the difficulty we encountered earlier in the chapter. As we saw at that time, there are good reasons for thinking it is not *merely* a body that dies. A suggested, compelling alternative was that it is a person or a human being that dies. However, if one insists that the soul is immortal, that Socrates is a person, that Socrates the person is identical with his soul, and that it is not merely a body that dies, then one comes dangerously close to running out of candidates for the entity that dies at time T.

Nevertheless, even in this contingency there is a solution, but it is one that most survivalists would not find palatable. It is to reject a), the proposition that Socrates is a composite of body and soul. Unfortunately, such a move would not only be inconsistent with the text of the *Phaedo*, but it would also entail finding some other entity, which, when added to the body, would amount to the total organism that dies. It is not clear what that additional factor could be, though conscious awareness is a possibility. But since conscious awareness is a functional feature of the mind, fixing on it would mean abandoning E for M. As far as I can see, there is no resolution of these paradoxes that a survivalist committed to E can accept.

M, OR THE SOUL AS MIND

Given this situation, let us turn to M to see if it eases some of these troubles. We shall deal with C and the theory of transmigration later. But before worrying about whether M is a viable alternative to the above puzzles, let us be clear about what M is and how it differs from E. M is mainly found in *The Republic*. It holds, as originally formulated by Socrates, that the soul is divided into three parts and is a mental entity, roughly equivalent to what ordinary persons would call the human mind. The description of these parts first appears in a lengthy passage in Book IV (434–440). Socrates designates them as the appetitive, the spirited, and the rational. As these names indicate, the appetitive concerns desires, such as the urge to drink when thirsty or to eat when hungry, the spirited with anger and other attitudes, and the rational with thought, broadly construed. Toward the end of *The Republic*, Socrates comes to realize that the appetitive and the spirited elements are somatic functions and therefore cannot be constituents of the soul, which would be "marred by association with the body and other evils." A supportive reason he gives for this conclusion is that if the soul were complex it could not be immortal. M and E thus both affirm that the soul is simple. The basic difference between them is that M construes the soul as a mental entity, whereas E regards it as the essence that defines personal identity. Here is a late passage in which Socrates rejects his earlier view that the soul is composed of parts:

> We were thinking just now of the soul as composed of a number of parts not put together in the most satisfactory way; and such a composite thing could hardly be everlasting ... Well, then, that the soul is immortal is established beyond doubt by our recent argument and the other proofs; but to understand her real nature, we must look at her, not as we see her now, marred by association with the body and other evils, but when she has regained that pure condition which the eye of reason can discern.
>
> *Republic*, Bk. X, 611

His disavowal of such partitioning leads Socrates to identify the soul with what he earlier called its rational element. This thesis is to be distinguished from that found in E, that Socrates is *identical* with his soul. M is not committed to that view. What M characterizes as the soul is an immaterial entity, something akin to Descartes' *res cogitans* and to what in *The Concept of Mind* (1949) Gilbert Ryle was to call "The Ghost in the Machine." According to M, it is the soul that inhabits the machine that is the body. It – not the body – thinks, believes, deliberates, judges, solves problems, and makes decisions. Though multifunctional, it is an indissoluble unity and is thus exempt from the ravages of time. In holding the soul to be immortal, M resembles E; but the resemblance ends there. E simply confers identity; it does not entail that the soul possesses deliberative or cognitive functions. M gives it those mental powers, without committing itself to the identification of Socrates with his soul.

Can the M view avoid the paradoxes that beset the E conception? I believe that it can. Let us present M in the following argumentative form to see why this is so.

(i) Socrates is a person.

(ii) All persons have bodies and souls.

(iii) Socrates dies at time T.

(iv) Socrates's soul persists after time T.

(v) Therefore, Socrates's soul survives the death of Socrates.

Both paradoxes are avoided because M does not claim, as E does, that Socrates is identical with his soul. M asserts something weaker: that Socrates *has* a soul. The relationship between personhood and soulhood (to coin a phrase) is, in this view, a contingent one. According to M, it is possible for a given soul to leave a particular person and enter another body, thus forming a new person. This is indeed what the theory of transmigration maintains. The fact that the relationship between a person and his or her soul is contingent permits both premises (iii) and (iv) to be true, namely that Socrates dies at time T and that his soul survives his death. (v) follows from (iii) and (iv). Hence, M captures, without any inconsistencies, the position that many survivalists wish to defend – that the soul survives the death of a *person*. It also accommodates the common sense idea that when Socrates dies it is a person that dies. The result achieved is thus stronger than the traditional thesis that it is only the body that dies.

Despite these advantages, it does have a serious flaw. It does not explain how body and soul are related. What is it for a soul to invest a body and how does immaterial thought move physical body parts? Since these issues come up in connection with the doctrines of reincarnation, resurrection, and metempsychosis (also known as transmigration of the soul), I shall turn to these topics now. Again there is no better place to start than with *The Republic*.

REINCARNATION, RESURRECTION, AND METEMPSYCHOSIS

It is important to distinguish between these three views. They are often conflated because they all presuppose that body and soul form a cohesive unit. There are also religious traditions that presuppose that they all entail the immortality of the soul. But logically speaking, immortality is not an essential feature of any of them. It is theoretically possible, for example, to have transmigration provided that the soul endures for a sufficiently long time – a period that is not necessarily endless. It is logically possible that shortly after the death of a person the soul might "vanish like a puff of smoke" (a worry expressed by Simmias in the *Phaedo*). Resurrection differs in several important respects from reincarnation and metempyschosis. Its focus is on the body rather than on the soul. Moreover, with metempsychosis the soul is a wanderer. In most versions (in particular in Plato, as we shall see) the soul is depicted as *always* investing a different body from the one it last left. But resurrectionists generally hold that a particular soul inhabits a particular body before and after it has been revived.

In the Bible, the emphasis is on resurrection – whereas in Hinduism reincarnation and transmigration play dominant roles. Isaiah, for example, states: "the dead shall live, their bodies shall rise" (Isa. 26:19). As just mentioned, the assumption in the Hebrew bible is that the same soul has always inhabited the same body and will continue to do so after its resurrection. In Hinduism, on the contrary, each being is predestined to undergo innumerable different incarnations (*samsara*) and one's aggregate moral balance sheet (*karman*) will determine the length of each life and the specific form of each rebirth. Indeed, the prospect of innumerable lives is generally regarded with horror. To escape the cycle of constant rebirths is to achieve final emancipation (*moksa*). As one historian remarks: "Life everlasting is the last thing a Hindu would aspire to."

Though the concept of metempsychosis has been extensively studied in the books of Hindu sacred law, such as the *Dharma-sastra* of Manu, it is in Plato's *Republic* that we find the most explicit and best developed Western account of this doctrine. Generally known as *The Myth of Er*, it occurs at very end of *The Republic* (Bk. X, 613–620). Socrates is speaking. He says:

> My story will not be like Odysseus' tale to Alcinous; but its hero was a valiant man, Er, the son of Armenius, a native of Pamphylia, who was killed in battle. When the dead were taken up for burial ten days later, his body alone was found undecayed. They carried him home, and two days afterwards were going to bury him, when he came to life again as he lay on the funeral pyre. He then told what he had seen in the other world.

According to Er when his soul had departed from his body, it journeyed to a "marvelous place," where many other souls had gathered. At that place a being described as "an interpreter" scattered lots before each of the souls, asking them to choose one. The lots were human bodies. The bodies varied enormously: among them were despots, or men renowed for beauty, or for strength and prowess, or for distinguished birth and ancestry; there were also bodies of unknown men and woman. Each soul was asked to choose one of these lots. As Er points out, the choice determined one's subsequent fate. One might choose the body of a ruler, not knowing that he was "fated to devour his own children." Others might be more fortunate. After all choices were made each soul was forced to drink of the water of Lethe and thus would no longer remember its past life.

I have labeled this transmigrative story the C doctrine. It is a mixture of M and E. From M it accepts the concept that the soul is the mind, a thinking thing that can choose and deliberate. Once the body dies, the soul will return to that "marvelous place" and, after reflection, will select another body. From E it takes the notion that the soul gives that body its (new) identity. This version of E differs from the canonical formulation described above only in its relativism. The soul will move from person to person with the passage of time. Both the M and E narratives tie transmigration to reincarnation. The soul does not merely hover endlessly in immaterial space but invariably becomes incarnate. For many religions incarnation is an essential element of the salvation story. We find a version of incarnation (without transmigration) in the New Testament where it is concisely expressed in a single sentence: "And the Word became flesh, and dwelt among us" (John 1:14).

A MAJOR DIFFICULTY: THE MIND-BODY PROBLEM

The Myth of Er initiates a problem that has traumatized Western philosophy ever since. This is a difficulty that concerns the relationship between the mind (or soul) and the body. Historically, the problem takes two different forms, both arising from the fact that the mind/soul and the body are considered to be entities of an entirely different order: one immaterial, the other material. One version of the problem involves investing or incarnation. How can something immaterial become an indissoluble part of something that is material? The problem is particularly acute for many traditional religions, but it transcends parochial concerns and is more general. In my judgment, it turns on the difference between the concepts of "inhabiting" and "inhering." I shall speak to this distinction in a moment. The other version of the problem arises from the recognition that mind and body frequently interact. Interaction is not conjectural or hypothetical. It is an obvious fact. We constantly experience such interaction. I decide to read a book. In order to do so, I must pick it up and open it. How does my decision cause my muscles to move? The mind is immaterial: it has no bulk or weight, is invisible, and does not occupy space. It cannot be apprehended through any of the senses but only, as Plato tells us, through "the eye of reason" (*Republic*, Bk. X, 611). The body, in contradistinction, is a physical object. It has mass, displaces space, and is apprehensible through the five modalities of perception: vision, touch, smell, taste, and hearing. It is composed of ingredients – bones, skin, and flesh – that also have mass. So how can an invisible, massless mental act, my decision to read a book, move something heavy and fixed, my body, that by its very nature is resistant to motion? It is as if one were to ask: "How can nothing, nothing at all, move something solid?"

A FIRST DIFFICULTY: INVESTING THE BODY

In this essay we have frequently spoken of the soul as *investing* the body. However, the notion of "investing," is ambiguous between two different concepts: *inhabiting* and *inhering*. To say, for example, that Smith inhabits a particular domicile does not entail that Smith is identical with his house, or even that his presence affects its independent existence. Yet, those who believe in reincarnation think that the soul becomes an ineradicable part of the body, that the two meld together like whisky and water in a glass. When the body is resurrected the admixture of body and soul produces a single autonomous individual. The idea that the soul

75

"inhabits" the body when so-called investment occurs does not accurately represent the viewpoint of most believers in reincarnation. The relationship is too weak. Their conception of what happens is probably better expressed by the idea of "inherence." In one of its main uses "inherence" means "existing in someone or something as an inseparable quality." It is the notion of inseparability that reincarnationists wish to capture. From their perspective, body and soul join to form an autonomous unit, each of whose parts contributes essentially to the total organism.

The puzzle that is generated by this conception is how do these diverse ingredients lose their independence and become one? How does an invisible, immaterial entity become an indissoluble component of a material object like a human body? The problem is a little like dividing an integer by a large number of zeros. The zeros contribute nothing to the dividend. How can an entity having no mass contribute *substantially* to an entity that has mass? That is the question. Neither M nor E can provide a solution to this dilemma. M contends that body and soul form a unit but that its elements are not inexpugnably tied to one another. As we have seen, M allows for the departure of the soul in cases of transmigration, and accordingly fails to meet the inseparability challenge. E does not fare any better. It holds that each person is identical with his soul. When the soul leaves the body and transmigrates, what dies is not a person but a body. It is thus not clear what the total organism is supposed to be either before or after the soul leaves the body. On the story E tells it cannot be identical either with the body or with the soul. We are left with a mystery. In my judgment, neither the inhabitation nor the inherence conceptions can resolve the dilemma.

A SECOND DIFFICULTY: THE CAUSAL CONNECTION

The difficulty about the causal connection between thought and physical movement is equally troublesome. The canonical answer to the question derives from Descartes. In his *Meditations* mind/soul (l'âme) and body are said to be two separate, independently existing *substances*. The problem the distinguished French thinker faced was how to get two such diverse substances together to merge into the union traditionally called a person or human being. Descartes' solution was that such a mixture occurs in a gland in the brain – the pineal gland. But even in his own time this "solution" was found to beg the question. It simply shifted the problem to a different physical site, the brain. But the question still remained: How does something immaterial, such as a mental event, cause movements in the fluids, tissues, and integuments, that the pineal gland contains? Neither Descartes nor his followers could provide an acceptable answer. The conundrum is still with us. It is called "The Mind–Body Problem," and there is a vast cognitive/scientific and philosophical literature devoted to it. It is clearly impossible to survey the multiplicity of analyses and attempted solutions to it. Let me just say, in conclusion, that these range from denials by scientists that the soul exists, or even more radically that the mind exists, to more sophisticated versions of Cartesianism, such as the thesis that each of us has private access to his or her pains and thoughts in a way that no external observer does. On this modified form of Cartesianism it is denied that mind and matter are two distinct *substances*. But, whatever mind is supposed to be, it is also agreed that it cannot be something physical.

Both approaches have a large number of variations. But each founders on shoals that by now should be familiar. To deny that the soul (taken to be mind) exists is to embrace paradox and to deny the existence of personal experience – the experience of pain, for instance. To hold that the mind or soul is not physical is to leave the obvious fact of causal interaction unexplained. My conclusion is that, given these obstacles, the problem about post-mortem survival is irresolvable. It is a question of fact whether something survives the death of a person. But it cannot be answered decisively. As David Hume said in a different context, the arguments pro and con do not admit of refutation and do not produce conviction.

SUMMARY OF THE ARGUMENT

The basic question the chapter addresses is whether it is possible that there can be life after death. My ultimate answer is that this is an undecidable question. I begin by considering some trivial negative answers to the question. I also mention that there are positive answers that derive from religious conviction, psychological factors (such as the fear of death), or pragmatic considerations, such as Pascal's Wager. I have shunted aside all such arguments, whether negative or positive. My intention instead has been to discover whether there are any logical arguments supporting such a possibility. I have found a number of these and they are scattered through the text.

These arguments support the thesis that the total organism that is a human being or person is more than a body, and therefore that what dies when a person dies is not simply his or her body. The assumption that a person is a complex entity, consisting of the body plus some component or components that are not physical is the key notion in the discussion. It captures the outlook of those that I label "post-mortem survivalists," or "survivalists" for short. I do not contend that their view is correct; my concern is only whether it raises a significant factual question. In my view, the supporting arguments demonstrate that it does.

If a person is more than a body, what is the non-somatic factor that in addition to the body forms the composite entity that is a human being? Or if there are two or more such components, what are they? Two different answers are considered: first, that the candidates are rationality, a moral sense, and conscious awareness. Second, that the added element is what has traditionally been called "the soul." I advance a series of arguments to demonstrate that neither rationality nor a moral sense can be this factor, but that conscious awareness may be. This result leads to the question: Is conscious awareness the same thing as the soul? Toward the end of the essay I show that it is not. I also show that conscious awareness is a component of what I call the M view (see below) and therefore cannot be the additional feature. By a process of elimination, we are thus left with the option that the only non-physical component when added to the body is possibly the soul.

The question thus arises: What is the soul? Historically there have been many different conceptions, most of which, I argue, are variations on two competing views: the soul conceived as an essence, that is, as something that determines the identity of a person, or the soul conceived as the mind, something that thinks, judges, decides, and chooses. I call these the E (for essence) and M (for mind) conceptions, respectively.

Both notions are discussed at length. The investigation results in the conclusion that neither fulfills the requirement of being the added factor that forms a human being. The E conception is too strong. When a human being, say Socrates, dies, E holds that only the body dies but that (the real person) Socrates continues to live. It follows that a person, in this case, Socrates, has not really died. M in contrast is too weak, since it considers the relationship between the body and soul as contingent. This is why transmigration is possible. The soul may leave the body and invest itself in a new body. The original requirement that something be a total human being was much tighter. It mandated that the composite entity, called a person, be composed of elements that meld into one another indissolubly, like water and whisky in a glass. The elements in such a case are inseparable. But according to M they are separable so M does not capture the notion that a human being or person is a composite entity whose ingredients each contribute substantively to the total package.

The preceding line of reasoning thus leads to the conclusion that the scientific arguments, based on biological data, are question begging, and that the arguments based on the two divergent views of the soul are flawed. I end the chapter with the judgment that the issue, about post-mortem survival, is both factual and significant but that it is not resolvable.

3

DOES GOD EXIST?

"Does God Exist?" They are just three little words. Yet the question they raise is one of the most complicated in the history of Western thought. In various forms and under various interpretations it has been debated for more than two thousand years. There have been and still are ingenious and compelling arguments pro and con. We shall examine the most important of these in what follows. Our investigation will lead to the conclusion that the arguments nullify one another and that none of them is decisive. Like the issue about whether there is life after death, this is an exemplary case of a factual question that is irresolvable.

Two of its three words – "God" and "exist" – are responsible for the complexities that the question raises. It would require an entire book – indeed several books – to follow the main rivers, let alone the tributaries, that course through the history of the subject. Therefore in order to identify and then focus on a small set of central issues we shall narrow the contours of the question. Such a shaping will perforce bypass some interesting bayous, especially those traditionally designated as "primitive religions," but in the end it will produce a query that is reasonably clear and factual in character. The first part of the chapter will thus be concerned with making the question precise enough for conceptual analysis. With those preliminaries out of the way I shall then formulate and evaluate the most important arguments on both sides of the dispute.

SHAPING THE QUESTION

It is frequently pointed out by anthropologists that every society about which we have a reasonably accurate historical record has had some form of religion. Two further points are made in this connection: that most of these cultures draw a distinction between the sacred and the secular (or profane); and that many of them depict the sacred as a domain inhabited by incorporeal beings that dwell in such things as rivers and trees. In order to avoid misleading assumptions, that is, to identify such beings as gods, let us use a more neutral term and call them "spirits." Of course, it is also true that in many of these communities the distinction between spirits and gods is fuzzy or a matter of degree. Since our focus will be on the question, "Does God Exist?," we shall avoid the belief systems of such animistic or polytheistic cultures for at least three reasons: First, the question: "Does God Exist?" may be interpreted to mean, "Is there a *multiplicity* of spirits or gods?" whereas the question we wish to address is rather, "Is There Exactly One God?" Second, it is only in comparatively advanced religions that we encounter sophisticated and incisive arguments about the possible existence and nature of a single God. Most primitive religions lack this feature. Third, in many primitive cultures spirits are expressly differentiated from gods. To avoid confusing conflations, we shall therefore eliminate these belief systems from consideration in what follows.

But this is just the beginning. The question needs further tightening. I will also exclude those religions that conceive their central figures, such as Buddha or Confucius, to be *human* beings of supreme excellence. Accordingly, I shall confine the inquiry to religions in which God is a transcendent being and not *merely* an impeccable person conveying an important moral message. I will turn the screw a notch further, by limiting the investigation to those religions that have a well-developed argumentative tradition about the nature of God. There is virtually no theology in the canonical twenty-four books of the Old Testament or in the Koran. The progressive narrowing of our question, "Does God Exist?" will thus leave us with only one familiar option, Christianity. This is a religion that has an extensive theology, the cumulative work of such persons as Origen, Augustine, Pelagius, Anselm, Aquinas, Descartes, Leibniz, Paley, Kant, Gilson and Copleston, *inter alios*. Each of these authors takes such questions as "Does God Exist?" and "Is it possible to prove that God exists?" seriously. In addition, there are writers who accept the notion that the question of whether a single transcendent God exists is an important one, but who differ in multifarious ways from the main lines of the Christian theological tradition. In this group, we can mention Spinoza, Hume, Mill, and such recent figures as A. J. Ayer and Anthony Flew. The literature emanating from the Christian tradition, and its critics, is thus vast and contains a host of ingenious approaches to this central issue.

Still, even to narrow the boundaries of the question in this way is insufficiently precise. There are problems within Christianity itself that must be disposed of before the question, "Does God exist?" is susceptible to cogent argumentation. In particular, a crucial issue that must be resolved is whether the Christian God is a single being. I will mention two famous controversies that challenge this presupposition. Both are still living issues for contemporary theologians, even though their origins can be traced back to the third and fourth centuries C.E. Like Judaism, Christianity is a religion whose main precepts are found in documents that are regarded as divinely inspired. In the case of Christianity, these canonical writings comprise the Old and New Testaments. Because of divergent interpretations of those texts the question of whether God is a single entity has been for centuries now the subject of disagreement within Christian theology. Let us look at the sources and the nature of the dispute in order to refine our question, "Does God exist?" even further. It may be that we can detour around the most treacherous obstacles to arrive at an interpretation that all parties can accept.

SOME FURTHER SHAPING: TRINITARIANISM AND UNITARIANISM

Shortly after the canon of the *New Testament* had been agreed upon, a dispute arose about whether what was called "the Godhead" is complex, and in particular whether one of its supposed components, Jesus, is identical with God. In early Christian communities it was frequently said that God had incarnated himself as Jesus, thus assuming the form of a human being. The three synoptic gospels (Mark, Matthew, and Luke) and the later Gospel according to St. John give overlapping, though somewhat different, descriptions of Jesus' ministry, death by crucifixion at Golgotha, and his subsequent resurrection. But they all agree that God assumed a human shape for reasons mostly connected with the relief of original sin and the possibility of salvation for mankind. The identification of Jesus with God is based on these canonical materials. Jesus says, for example, "I and the Father are one" (John 11:31).

This outlook ran into difficulties with other compelling readings of Scripture. There are numerous places in the Gospels where Jesus distinguishes himself from God, whom he often refers to as the Father: "for I am not alone, but I and the Father that sent me" (John 8:16–17); "And Jesus said, Father, forgive them for they know not what they do" (Luke 23:34). Perhaps the most dramatic passage in which Jesus discriminates himself from God occurs when he is being crucified. He cries out: "My God, my God, why hast thou foreseken me?" (*"Eli, Eli, lama sabachthani?"*) (Matt. 27:46). Some theologians interpreted such passages to mean that Jesus was identifying God as an independent power whose authority is greater than his own. He also sometimes refers to himself as "the Son." Furthermore, there are references to the Logos or Word which indicate that besides Jesus and God there is a separately existing entity later to be called "The Holy Spirit." (See, for example, "In the beginning was the Word" [John 1:1] and "The Word became flesh, and dwelt among us" [John 1:14].) It thus seemed to many acolytes that there was not one transcendent divine being, but three: God, the Holy Spirit, and Jesus.

Such interpretations of the Bible were puzzling to those exegetes who wished, on the one hand, to maintain the autonomy and cohesiveness of a single God, and, on the other, to recognize the differing roles ascribed in Scripture to the Holy Spirit and to Jesus. Two views attempting to accommodate these somewhat conflicting aspirations were developed by Sabellius (fl. 230 C.E.) and Arius (fl. fourth century C.E.). According to Sabellius, there is a single entity, God, that manifests himself in three different ways, as Father, Son, and Holy Spirit. In his view there are not three independent beings (autonomous persons) composing the Godhead. Instead, there is just one being – God – who manifests himself in different forms, depending on his purposes and the contextual situation. The question that arises here is: "What is meant by 'manifest'"? The conceptual problem is how can something retain its autonomy and integrity while exhibiting seemingly incompatible properties. One might think by way of analogy of collections of molecules of H_2O. At room temperatures such collections take a liquid form, at 0° Celsius they become a hard, cold, opaque substance, and at 100°C. they turn into a vapor. Water, ice, and steam have different properties; yet they are essentially the same substance (note this word) since all of them are composed of H_2O. So it is with God. He is one and the same substance, but he plays different roles: as Jesus, a human being who suffers and dies for mankind, as the Word, an avatar that becomes flesh, or as the Father, the transcendental creator of the universe.

Christianity is sometimes described as an "historical" religion. It specifies that at a certain moment, whose temporal coordinates can pretty well be defined as occurring between 7 B.C.E. and 33 C.E., God manifested himself in the form of a human being, Jesus. The basis for this historical account lies in the scriptural materials mentioned above. But they are complex and lend themselves to different interpretations. As a consequence of such different construals, two divergent views about the nature of the Godhead arose in early Christianity, the first due to Sabellius and the second to Arius. Both wished to preserve the notion that God is a single entity. Sabellius did this by arguing that the apparently different persons comprising the Godhead are all identical, that is, that they are merely different phases of God, the Father and Creator. Arius adopted a different solution. He argued that though Jesus was indeed a divine being he was of a lesser order than the Father. This solution allowed for the singularity of God and his distinction from Jesus. Arius appealed to some of the passages I have just cited in support of this interpretation. Some of his followers went even further and denied the divinity of Jesus, contending that he was a prophet, divinely inspired to be sure, but essentially a human being. Both the Sabellian and the Arian accounts are thus variants of a "Unitarian" interpretation of Scripture. The orthodox Catholic view, based on subsequent Councils, differs from both. It is Trinitarian. It contends that although there is one unique *substance* that constitutes the Godhead, it is composed of three autonomous *persons*. The distinction between the concepts of a substance and a person are key to this construal. In later councils, both Sabellianism and Arianism were declared to be heresies, that is, interpretations that were inconsistent with the fundamental teachings of the Church. In what follows, I shall try to develop a reading of both doctrines that will satisfy the requirement that the question, "Does God exist?" is a query about a single transcendent entity.

MONOPHYSITISM

There is another major controversy in the history of Christianity that occasions problems for the thesis that God is a single being. This is a problem that developed in part through the identification of Jesus with God. The issue is whether Jesus is human or divine. As we have seen above, this problem had resonances in the interpretations of Sabellius and Arius, but it is essentially a different issue. The problem arose because it was presupposed by all parties that the properties of being human and being divine are incompatible. The major argument to this effect was derived from an ancient literary tradition which held that all divine beings are immortal, even though in some cases they are indistinguishable in appearance and behavior from humans. Contrariwise, humans are mortal. The distinction occurs, for example, in the Odyssey. It will be recalled that Calypso offers to confer immortality on Odysseus if he will remain forever on the island with her. But the contrast also runs through the later religious literature as well. Hence, nothing can be both human and divine at the same time. It thus seemed to theologians that they either had to abandon the thesis of Incarnation, in which God became a human being, or the notion that God – as Jesus – had expired on the cross.

The conflict essentially centered around what was on the cross when Christ died. Was it human or divine? Either answer led to a paradox or at least to a position that was inconsistent with Scripture. According to the Gospels, Jesus suffered and died for mankind. His death was designed to ameliorate the effects of original sin and to lead to the possibility of salvation for some human beings. This is the conception of Jesus as Savior. It requires that his suffering and death be real. This interpretation is called "the Soteriological thesis." The term is derived from the Greek "Soter" (or "Savior.") The Gospels also hold that God as Creator of the Universe is immortal. On this view, it follows that neither God nor Jesus died on the cross, since what was on the cross was not a human being. The object that was crucified appeared to be, but was not, human. What appeared to be a dead body was a phantasm, a visual illusion.

In order to avoid the paradox of reading Scripture as maintaining that Jesus was both mortal and immortal – i.e., both human and divine – two groups developed differing theories stressing that Jesus had only one nature. According to one such view he was divine and according to the other he was human. These were called the Phantastiastae and the Phthartolatrae, respectively. The Phantastiastae, wishing to defend the divinity of Jesus, held – as the name indicates – that Jesus did not really die and therefore what was on the cross was a phantasm, a mere figment of the imagination. The Phthartolatrae (the name in Greek means "worshippers of the corruptible") were driven by the soteriological thesis and held that Jesus really suffered and died. Though differing about Jesus' nature, the two views had something in common. Each agreed that Jesus could not be both human and divine. To claim that he could be both was to embrace a contradiction. So each tried to interpret the nature of Jesus in a way that was logically consistent. But despite such efforts, each encountered an enormous difficulty in reconciling its position with the actual pronouncements about Jesus in the Gospels. According to those canonical documents it is true that Jesus really did suffer and die and it is also true that he was divine. The dilemma could thus be traced back to Scripture itself. Nonetheless, each side argued its case vigorously while refusing to impugn the Gospel accounts.

The conflict between these factions eventually became severe and led to riots and violence. After more than two centuries of such turbulence the Church decided in 451 C.E. to hold a council in Chalcedon to decide the issue. The outcome was an official declaration to the effect that Jesus is both fully human and fully divine, and that the relationship between these characteristics is a mystery. It justified this decision by appealing to what is said about the dual nature of Jesus in Scripture. It also declared both forms of monophysitism to be heretical. The orthodox view today is still the view enunciated at Chalcedon, namely that Jesus is both fully human and fully divine. Here is a key excerpt from the text of the decision:

> that Christ is true God and true man, according to the Godhead begotten from eternity and like the Father in everything only without sin; and that after his incarnation the unity of the person consists of two natures which are conjoined without confusion, and without change, but also without rending and without separation.

A SOLUTION

We thus have two sets of views that seem to challenge the thesis that God is a single entity: the orthodox Trinitarian view of the Godhead, and the orthodox view that Jesus has two natures, one of which is human. But as difficult as this challenge is, I believe there is an interpretation consistent with Scripture that can meet it. This solution is to be found in a resolution passed at the Council of Nicea in 325 C.E. Nicea argued against Arius that the Son was of the same substance as the Father, and that the Son was neither created nor subordinate. This is the famous doctrine of the consubstantiality of Father and Son that since the Council of Constantinople of 381 has been the orthodox creed of the Catholic

Church. It is also the position adopted by the many Protestant denominations that are members of the World Council of Churches. In effect, the Nicean Creed supported the singularity of God by its contention that the Father and the Son were of the same substance. This is consistent with the position that the Father, the Son, and the Holy Spirit are different persons. But as such they are not independent entities whose substance differs from that of the Father. The doctrine of personhood was designed to meet the Sabellian thesis that God's manifestations did not involve different persons, and the doctrine of consubstantiality was designed to counter the Arian view that Jesus was a subordinate being. In this orthodox tradition, then, we find justification for our claim that the word "God" in the question, "Does God Exist?," refers to a single being. This interpretation of one of its key words thus leads to a significant narrowing of the question.

"EXISTS"

But we are still not ready to look at the arguments pro and con. As I mentioned at the outset of the chapter the words "God" and "exists" have been the sources of confusion about the meaning of the question. We have now, I believe, obtained sufficient clarification about the meaning of "God." It is a term that will be understood to refer to one and only one transcendent being. But we still have to avoid some of the complications raised by "exists" before the question is clear enough to be susceptible to incisive argumentation.

"Exists" is indeed a difficult word. From a standpoint of traditional grammar it seems to be a predicate like "melt," or "shine." "Does God exist?" looks very much like "Does gold melt" or "Does gold shine?" Yet a little logical analysis will show that this superficial resemblance is misleading. Consider the following sentences:

1. Some tigers growl.
2. Some tigers do not growl.
3. Some tigers exist.
4. Some tigers do not exist.

"Some tigers growl" means roughly the same as "There exists something that is a tiger and growls."

"Some tigers do not growl," by parallel reasoning, means roughly the same as "There exists something that is a tiger and does not growl."

"Some tigers exist," by parallel reasoning, should thus mean: "There exists something that is a tiger and exists."

"Some tigers do not exist," by parallel reasoning, should thus mean the same as "There exists something that is a tiger and does not exist."

Obviously sentences three and four in the above list cannot mean what parallel reasoning would suggest. Nobody who wishes to say such things as "Dinosaurs do not exist," or "Some tigers do not exist," means to be asserting both that Dinosaurs do and do not exist, or that tigers do and do not exist. Such contradictions arise only if we interpret "exists" to be a genuine predicate in the way that "growl" is. Now it is clear that if a polytheist were to affirm that "Some gods exist," and if one accepted the consequences of parallel reasoning, that person would be understood to mean that "There exists something that is a god and exists." And again by parallel reasoning, if an atheist were to say "Some gods do not exist," that utterance would mean "There exists something that is a god and does not exist." But this last sentence states that something that is a god exists and does not exist, and that is a flat contradiction. Clearly, an atheist who wishes to deny that there is a god would not intend to assert a contradiction in saying what he or she does. It follows that "exists" is not a true predicate in the way that "growl," or "shine" is. So we shall need to interpret "exists" as having a different function in language. It is one of the glories of modern mathematical logic to have shown what that function is by developing a new type of grammar.

A full account of this grammar is not possible here, but it is possible to illustrate how radical and profound it is. Consider the sentence: "All horses are animals." According to conventional grammar, the word "horse" is the subject of the sentence, and the word "animal" is its predicate. The whole sentence is in categorical form. But translated into this new grammar the sentence would read: "If anything is a horse it is an animal." The words "horse" and "animal" have both become adjectives, and the sentence has become a hypothetical rather than an apodictic sentence. (The reasons for treating it as a hypothetical sentence are too complex to be described here.) Mathematical logic thus distinguishes surface grammar from a deeper logical grammar that captures the "real meanings" of the sentences it analyzes. According to this deeper grammar, "exists" is not a predicate but a "quantifier." The word "all" in the sentence "All horses are animals" is also a quantifier. In this respect, it functions like such words as "There exists," "any," "anything," "anyone," "some," "none," "there is," "there are," and "at least one."

On the assumption we are speaking about a Judeo-Christian God of infinite capacity, the sentence "God exists" is analyzed in modern logic as: "Something is omniscient, omnipotent, and benevolent." An atheist who asserts: "God does not exist," would not be contradicting himself but would be saying "It is not the case that anything is omniscient, omnipotent, and benevolent." Note that in these translations the word "God" does not function as a subject term but as a complex predicate, that is, "being omniscient, omnipotent, and benevolent." "Exists" is not a predicate but a quantifier. In terms of conventional grammar, it functions as an indefinite pronoun, that is, as the words "something" and "anything" do in everyday English. Since the time of Kant the notion that "exists" is not a predicate has been thought to constitute a refutation of the ontological argument. Though I agree that "exists" is not a predicate, I will argue below that the tradition is wrong in this interpretation. Still, concurring that "exists" is not a predicate, we still have not shown what the question, "Does God exist?" means. To obtain that result we shall have to dig deeper into the grammar of "exists."

Suppose we are talking to a lad who has just read a book about dinosaurs. He might ask his teacher: "Do dinosaurs exist?" The question looks a lot like "Does God exist?" But there is a difference. "Do dinosaurs exist?" probably means something like, "Do dinosaurs still exist?" or perhaps "Are there any dinosaurs alive today?" But "Does God exist?" doesn't mean: "Does God still exist?" or "Is God alive today?" (The philosopher, Frederich Nietzsche, 1844–1900, once said: "God is dead," but he clearly did not mean that God had just died or was alive earlier in the year.)

"Does God exist?" is thus palpably less straightforward than the question about dinosaurs.

Suppose, however, that a boy had just been reading a detective story by Sir Arthur Conan Doyle. He might wonder: "Does Sherlock Holmes exist?" A girl named "Virginia" once asked her father whether Santa Claus exists. Neither youngster meant "Is Holmes alive today?" or "Does Santa Claus still exist?" If the questions were interpreted in those ways, the children would be asking whether Holmes and Santa Claus had lived at an earlier time and were now possibly defunct. But it is obvious that "Does God exist?" does not presuppose that God had a previous life that might have come to an end in the recent past. So, then, what does the question mean? I suggest that "Does Sherlock Holmes exist?" and "Does Santa Claus exist?" should be given a different, non-temporal interpretation. I think that they mean something like "Is Sherlock Holmes a fictive character?" and "Is Santa Claus a mythical being?" Such questions are designed to find out whether a living, hirsute creature uses a sleigh pulled by reindeer to deliver presents at Christmas time and whether Holmes is a human being who lives in London. "221B Baker Street" is a current address in London but were the premises ever occupied by a flesh and blood detective named "Sherlock," or was Holmes simply a figment of Conan Doyle's lively imagination? Thus, the questions asked by the children presuppose a contrast between fictive, mythical, or imaginary beings and real human beings, the sorts of creatures that could be counted in a national census. So by analogical reasoning the question, "Does God exist?" should be construed to mean: "Is God a fictive or mythical entity, a product of human imagination, or is He real?" What is meant by "real" in this usage is also complicated. It clearly does not mean that God had parents, that he attended high school and college, and so forth. As J. L. Austin pointed out, "real" gets its meaning from its contrasting terms, such as "fictive," "legendary," "mythical," and so on. In a colorful phrase, Austin said that in such cases it is "the negative use that wears the trousers." Following Austin, then, I suggest that "Does God exist?" gets its meaning from these contrasting concepts. One asking the question wishes to know whether God is real or mythical. In my opinion, this is also what Anselm and other proponents of the ontological argument had in mind.

As I emphasized in the first chapter, science deals with matters of fact. Many persons believe that, in principle, science can solve all factual problems. The question, "Does God exist?" clearly raises a question of fact. According to our narrowed question, it asks: "Is there a unique personal spirit who created the universe and who is omnipotent, omniscient, and benevolent?" Posed in this form, the question is now clear enough to be susceptible to cogent argumentation. Under this interpretation, it represents a challenge to science. Can any scientist or indeed any person tell us, definitively, whether or not there is such a being. I say that no one can. But now to see why, let us turn to the arguments pro and con.

THE ARGUMENTS

There are many reasons why people believe in the existence of a singular transcendent being of the sort just described. Some of these reasons are personal. They may arise from a unique, powerful psychological experience that these individuals cannot explain but which they are sure has put them into direct contact with the supernatural. Ecstatic experiences described by mystics, such as St. Teresa of Avila, fall into this category. Scholars refer to such reports as "arguments from revelation." Or again, someone may think that to decide whether or not God exists is very much like trying to decide whether to buy homeowner's insurance. The cost of such coverage is weighed against the likelihood, usually remote, that one's house will burn down. A home is an expensive item and possibly prohibitive to rebuild if a catastrophe occurs. So one invests in insurance to protect against a traumatic event. In the same way one may argue that it is better to bet on the existence of God than on his non-existence. If God exists one has the prospect of salvation. If one is mistaken not much has been lost. So it is prudential to bet on the more felicitious option. The French philosopher, Blaise Pascal (1623–1662), argued for this position. It is known as "Pascal's Wager." Three centuries later William James arrived at a similar view, and nowadays it is widespread. There are still other reasons for believing in God, among them the "The Moral Argument." Immanuel Kant contended that there must be a transcendent God on the ground that such a being is necessarily presupposed in the operations of practical or moral reason. The list of reasons goes well beyond those I have mentioned. No doubt all such arguments or views have played prominent roles in the history of religious belief. Nonetheless I shall exclude them from consideration here. I do so because they are tangential to a set of arguments that have been central to philosophical debate since the time of Plato. And it is these that I shall concentrate on.

Philosophically, the most important have been – and still are – the ontological argument, the cosmological argument, and the argument from design. In Chapter 5, I shall be discussing the question, "Where did the universe come from?" and in that connection I shall deal with the cosmological argument. In order to avoid repetition I shall therefore bypass it here. This leaves us with the ontological argument and the argument from design. But they will provide plenty of meat to chew on. Both are not only among the most widely discussed proofs for the existence of God in the history of Western thought but each represents a sharply contrasting philosophical approach to understanding reality. The ontological argument is a special case of the rationalist position that pure reason can attain substantive truths about the world. It is an argument that has been propounded by some of the greatest philosophers of all time – Descartes, Spinoza, Leibniz – all rationalists. Its model is mathematics. The design argument is a product of empiricism, the notion that all knowledge about matters of fact is based on sense experience. Its model is science. It has proved attractive to philosophers such as David Hume, William Paley, A. E. Taylor, Robert Clark, Teilhard de Chardin, and to many scientists.

Much of the ongoing debate in philosophy from Descartes to the present is based on the rationalist/empiricist distinction. It has issued in two great intellectual streams. The former attempts to deduce facts about the world through the exercise of reason. The latter contends that the only way of understanding the world is by observation and experiment.

The two arguments are thus exemplars of two opposing ways of trying to grasp the nature of reality. The ontological argument attempts to prove on the basis of reason alone that God exists. No appeal to experience is made or needed according to its proponents. It is thus an *a priori* argument. The argument from design begins from the notion that nature is orderly and infers that God is the creator of such order. It is the observation that nature is not chaotic that initiates the search for the sorts of regularities that are called "scientific laws." The design argument is thus *a posteriori*. To investigate these contrasting ways of answering the question, "Does God exist?" is in effect to explore the nature and limits of rationalism and empiricism in a particular application. The arguments are thus important examples of the power and limitations of these contrasting approaches to existential matters. I shall focus on them in part because they involve such important ramifications, and in part – indeed to a great extent – because they are of interest in their own right.

THE ONTOLOGICAL ARGUMENT

The argument has different formulations in such seventeenth-century writers as Descartes, Spinoza, and Leibniz. But its classic and most interesting presentation occurred much earlier in the *Proslogion* of St. Anselm (c. 1033–1109), who was Abbot of Bec and later Archbishop of Canterbury. In the *Proslogion* the argument takes two different forms, the first attempting to prove that God exists and the second that God *necessarily* exists. Nearly all philosophers, from Kant to the present, have claimed that the first version is fallacious, on the ground that existence is not a property. But many hold that the second version is a valid proof. We shall thus divide our discussion to accommodate these differing interpretations. Each is what logicians call an "indirect argument." This is a unique form of argumentation that attempts to show that starting from a certain premise, for example, that God does not exist, the line of reasoning leads to a falsehood. It follows that the negation of the original premise is true, namely that God exists. Here are Anselm's own words, as translated by E. R. Fairweather (*The Library of Christian Classics*, 1956).

Version one (from *Proslogion*, chap. 2: God Truly Is):

> And so, O Lord, since thou givest understanding to faith, give me to understand – as far as thou knowest it to be good for me – that thou dost exist, as we believe, and that thou art what we believe thee to be. Now we believe that thou art a being than which none greater can be thought [*aliquid quo nihil maius cogitari possit*]. Or can it be that there is no such being, since "the fool hath said in his heart, 'There is no God'"? (Psalms 14:1; 53:1). But when this same fool hears what I am saying – "A being than which none greater can be thought" – he understands what he hears, and what he understands is in his understanding, even if he does not understand that it exists. For it is one thing for an object to be in the understanding, and another thing to understand that it exists. When a painter considers beforehand what he is going to paint, he has it in his understanding, but he does not suppose that what he has not yet painted already exists. But when he has painted it, he both has it in his understanding and understands that what he has now produced exists. Even the fool, then, must be convinced that a being than which none greater can be thought exists at least in his understanding, since when he hears this he understands it, and whatever is understood is in the understanding. But clearly that than which a greater cannot be thought cannot exist in the understanding alone. For if it is actually in the under-standing alone, it can be thought of as existing also in reality, and this is greater. Therefore, if that than which a greater cannot be thought is in the understanding alone, this same thing than which a greater cannot be thought is that than which a greater can be thought. But obviously this is impossible. Without doubt, therefore, there exists, both in the under-standing and in reality, something than which a greater cannot be thought.

In order to help determine whether this line of reasoning is cogent, I will lay out the argument in a more perspicuous form.

1. What a person understands exists in his understanding.
2. It is one thing for an object to exist in the understanding and another for it to exist in reality.

3. An example: When a painter considers beforehand what he is going to paint, it exists in his understanding. When he has painted it, it exists in his understanding and also exists in reality.

4. The Lord (God) is a being than which none greater can be thought.

5. That than which a greater cannot be thought cannot exist in the understanding alone.

6. For if it exists in the understanding alone, it can also be thought of as existing in reality, and this is greater.

7. Therefore, if that than which a greater cannot be thought exists in the understanding alone, this same thing than which a greater cannot be thought is that than which a greater can be thought.

8. But this is a contradiction.

9. Therefore, there exists, both in the understanding and in reality, something than which a greater cannot be thought.

As I mentioned earlier, this is an indirect argument that leads to a contradiction (premise 8). Since all contradictions are falsehoods, the pattern of reasoning that precedes (8) entails the conclusion (9). Note the use of the passive voice throughout the argument. Anselm carefully avoids making the positive claim that the Lord (God) is the greatest conceivable being. Such a statement would be blasphemous, since it would imply that a finite human being can fully comprehend God's infinite nature. Anselm is thus framing this proposition in a deliberately negative way that leaves it open whether God exists. Therefore a proof is apposite. There are some premises in the argument that might be challenged – for example, that what the fool hears he understands; that what he hears exists in his understanding; and that he is convinced that a being none greater than which can be thought exists in his understanding. But note – and this is an important point – the argument does not mention that existence is a property (in the parlance of modern logic, that "exists" is a predicate). What it does say is *that to exist in reality is greater than to exist in the understanding alone.* The question is: "What does Anselm mean by 'greater'?"

The philosophical tradition – and especially that based on mathematical logic – has interpreted Anselm to mean that "greater" denotes a property, "existing in reality," and it is the possession of this property that makes God "greater" than a being that exists in the understanding alone. But I think that this is a misconstrual of what the argument actually says, since it never mentions that existing in reality is a property. This traditional interpretation also fails to capture a distinction that the argument presupposes. On this latter point, it is clear that Anselm is trying to answer the kind of question that Virginia asked about Santa Claus: namely "Is God just a fictive being, a mythical character, or is he real?" The text makes this clear. As he says: "Or can it be that there is no such being, since 'the fool hath said in his heart, "There is no God"'?" Anselm wishes to prove that God is not merely a figment of the imagination. His use of the term "greater" has nothing to do with whether existing in reality is a property or not. It is rather his way of affirming that God is not simply a conceptual entity. His choice of "greater" to express this contrast is perhaps unfortunate. It has surely misled hundreds of philosophers. But if the argument is understood as presupposing a distinction between mythical and real beings, this confusion disappears.

But to say this is not to say that the argument is not fallacious. It is fallacious. It rests on a subtle equivocation that runs through the entire train of reasoning. For example, one finds it in the sentence: "Therefore, if that than which a greater cannot be thought is in the understanding alone, *this same thing* than which a greater cannot be thought is that than which a greater can be thought" (my italics). It can perhaps be best illustrated by considering Anselm's painter example. He says: "But when he has painted *it* he both has *it* in his understanding and understands that what he has now produced exists." I have italicized the two occurrences of "it" in the preceding sentence. They pick out different objects – the first occurrence refers to an actual physical object, a painting, the second to a mental entity, the painter's conception of what he wishes to paint.

Anselm is assuming that the object that exists in the painter's understanding before he has painted anything *is the same object* that will exist in reality after he has painted it. (I call attention to his use of the words "the same thing" in the sentence quoted above.) He is using "it" and "the same thing," equivocally. What the painter has in mind is an idea or

97

perhaps a visual image of what he wishes to paint. When he has finished the painting, what exists is nothing mental. It is a physical object that has a determinate size and can be hung on a wall. The mental object cannot be displayed in a museum. The two objects are thus not identical. So the object – something than which a greater cannot be thought – that exists in the understanding is *not* the same object that exists in reality. The fallacy is equivalent to the following argument: Nothing is colder than ice. I have nothing up my sleeve. What I have up my sleeve is therefore colder than ice. This argument contains an equivocation on "nothing." Anselm's argument contains a similar equivocation on "it." It conflates a conceptual entity with something that is non-mental – whether that be a painting or a Divine Being. The argument is invalid and thus does not prove that God exists. A proof is a valid argument whose premises are known to be true. Being invalid, the ontological argument proves nothing.

Before leaving this topic, it is worth pointing out that many critics of the argument have failed to notice that they have unconsciously committed the same fallacy in their objection to Anselm's reasoning. They have assumed that "it" denotes the same object that exists in the mind and presumably exists in reality. Their objection assumes that Anselm cannot distinguish between something that exists in the mind and something that exists in reality because existence is not a property. If it were, then presumably they would agree that the same object would be greater. But this is to presuppose that it is the same object that one is speaking about. Kant may well have been the first philosopher to have made this mistake. In the *Critique of Pure Reason* he writes:

> By whatever and by however many predicates we may think a thing – even if we completely determine it – we do not make the least addition to the thing when we further declare that this thing *is* (p. 505).

Like Anselm, Kant is using "it" to refer both to what we think is and to what *is* (exists). As he puts it, "even if we completely determine *it* – we do not make the least addition to *the thing* when we further declare that this thing is" (my italics). If we ask what is "the thing" Kant is referring to, we can see that his reasoning incorporates the same fallacy as Anselm's original argument. To the list of invalid arguments that includes Anselm's first version of the ontological argument we can thus add all those arguments that assume that if existence were a property Anselm would have been right.

THE ONTOLOGICAL ARGUMENT CONTINUED

Version two (from *Proslogion*, chap. 3: God Cannot Be Thought Of As Non-existent):

This version is a very different argument. It turns on the distinction between contingency and necessity, already described in Chapter 1. There the distinction applied to statements. In this context it is applied to objects. In effect, Anselm is saying that there is a difference between an object whose existence is contingent, that is, one that depends for its existence on something else, and an object whose existence is unconditioned. The latter is thus a being whose existence is necessary. It does not come into existence through the causal agency of anything else, nor does it go out of existence through such an agency. In neither coming into nor going out of existence it is thus immune to the ravages of time, which is a way of saying that it is eternal. Only one such entity satisfies these conditions and that, according to Anselm, is God. Here, in his own words, is how he arrives at this conclusion.

> And certainly it exists so truly that it cannot be thought of as non-existent. For something can be thought of as existing, which cannot be thought of as not existing, and this is greater than that which *can* be thought of as not existing. Thus, if that than which a greater cannot be thought can be thought of as not existing, this very thing than which a greater cannot be thought is *not* that than which a greater cannot be thought. But this is a contradiction. So, then, there truly is a being than which a greater cannot be thought – so truly that it cannot even be thought of as not existing. And *thou* art this being, O Lord our God.

Again, I should stress that this is an indirect argument. The reasoning is very compact. To make it less terse, I shall reformulate it.

1. It is possible to think of something that now exists as not existing. Example: I am working on an assembly line in Detroit. Metal and plastic components were collected at an earlier time by other employees, and are now being assembled by a lengthy process. I stand at the end of the line, and perform a final operation. Something that did not exist two days ago – an automobile – now exists. I can easily think of it as non-existent. In that case, I would be thinking of the parts before they were assembled. It is thus sensible, and on this occasion even true, to say that it is possible to think of the automobile as not having existed at a previous time. That it did not exist at a particular time and now exists is what it means to say that it is a *contingent* entity. In a somewhat parallel vocabulary, one can also say that the statement "This car did not exist two days ago" is a contingent statement.

2. Generally speaking, if a given locution is meaningful, its antonym will also be meaningful. Since (1) indicates that the term "contingent" is meaningful, its polar term "necessary" is also meaningful. It is thus possible to speak meaningfully about an entity which cannot be thought *not* to exist. We shall say of such an entity that it necessarily exists. An example: the number five. One cannot imagine that it does not exist.

3. God is that than which a greater cannot be thought.

4. Something can be thought of as existing which cannot be thought of as not existing.

5. This is greater than something that *can* be thought of as not existing.

6. By (4) and (5): If that than which a greater cannot be thought can be thought of as not existing, this very thing than which a greater cannot be thought is not that than which a greater cannot be thought.

7. But (6) is contradictory.

8. Therefore there exists a being that cannot be thought of as not existing, and this is God. (This is another way of saying that God is a necessary being or that the statement "God exists" is necessarily true.)

This argument is stronger than the previous version. It contains no obvious fallacies and no doubt this explains why it has been defended by various writers. In particular, it is free of the equivocation on "it." It does not state that necessary existence is a property of God. Its key is the premise that something that *cannot* be thought of as *not* existing is greater than something that *can* be thought of as *not* existing. So the question that arises here is what is meant by "greater." "Greater" is not being used in this context, as it was in the previous argument, to discriminate fictive or mythological entities from real ones. The contrast that is being drawn is between contingency and necessity. A being that cannot be thought not to exist is greater than one that can be thought not to exist.

But now we must ask: "Is this a sensible distinction?" I believe that the answer is "yes." Here is a story in support of this answer. John is now thirty years old. He has never worked a day in his life. He is a bachelor who lives at home with his parents. They support him, paying for his clothes, food, and entertainment, and ask for nothing in return. He is thus totally dependent for his existence on their largesse. He is a dependent being. His brother, Bill, is twenty-eight. He is a mechanic who works for an auto-repair shop. He works an average of forty-eight hours a week. He is well paid. He is not married and lives in a small home that he has bought. He sees his parents regularly but does not demand or receive money from them. In comparison with his brother, Bill is an independent being. He supports himself. To say this, of course, does not mean that he does not receive funds from others. He is paid a salary by the company for which he works. So judged by *absolute* criteria he is not totally independent. Still, the comparison between him and his brother is important; it illustrates the difference between a dependent and an independent existence.

Anselm, of course, wishes to say something even stronger. He wishes to say that God is a being whose existence depends on nothing whatsoever. If God had been brought into existence by some other being, or by some set of factors, then God would not – in this strong sense – be a wholly independent being. And if something could cause God to exist then his existence would be conditional and not absolute. But if God is a being than which none greater can be thought, then he must be a being whose existence is totally independent of any causal agency. This is then another way of saying that God is eternal. There has never been a time when he did not exist and there will never be a time when he ceases to exist. If either option were conceivable then God would not be a being than which none greater can be thought. To say, then, that he is a being satisfying this description is to say that he necessarily exists.

Norman Malcolm has argued, in a brilliant essay, that this version of the ontological argument is a genuine proof. Here is what he says in this connection.

> What Anselm has proved is that the notion of contingent existence or of contingent non-existence cannot have any application to God. His existence must either be logically necessary or logically impossible. The only intelligible way of rejecting Anselm's claim that God's existence is necessary is to maintain that the concept of God, as a being a greater than which cannot be conceived, is self-contradictory or nonsensical. Supposing that this is false, Anselm is right to deduce God's necessary existence from his characterization of him as a being a greater than which cannot be conceived.
>
> "Anselm's Ontological Arguments," pp. 141–162

Many philosophers have agreed with Malcolm. If as a group they are right, the argument does constitute a proof that God necessarily exists. Though I find Malcolm's reasoning compelling, I have a serious reservation about the argument that he does not consider. This is particularly strange since the point I will be making is one that Wittgenstein might have made; and since Malcolm was one of the most profound exegetes of Wittgenstein's work one might have expected him to have noticed it as well. Wittgenstein says:

> Doubting has certain characteristic manifestations, but they are only characteristic of it in particular circumstances. If someone said that he doubted the existence of his hands, kept looking at them from all sides, tried to make sure it wasn't "all done by mirrors", etc. we should not be sure whether we ought to call that doubting. We might describe his way of behaving as like the behavior of doubt, but his game would not be ours.
>
> On Certainty, p. 255

In saying that doubting has characteristic manifestations but only in particular circumstances, Wittgenstein is calling attention to the limited nature of such conduct. He is saying that extreme behavior, such as he describes, is not a case of doubt. He is also making a linguistic point when he says that "we should not be sure whether we ought to call that doubting." If behavior is wildly aberrant it does not fall within the spectrum of recognized communal activity. As such – and this is his message with respect to the situation he has described – it is not a case of doubting and we would be misusing language to call it "doubting." Every word has parameters that determine its proper use. If behavior exceeds those parameters it is no longer to be described in customary terms even if, as Wittgenstein puts it with respect to the case above, "we might describe his behavior as *like* the behavior of doubt." However, to stress that it is not a case of doubting, he adds: "but his game would not be ours."

My query with respect to the second version of the ontological argument is based on Wittgenstein's insight that we cannot meaningfully use such terms as "contingent" and "necessary" apart from the circumstances that determine their normal use. In the example I gave about John and Bill, and on the assumption that the terms "contingency" and "necessity" refer to circumstances involving dependence on others, these words are playing their normal roles. We can say of John that he is a dependent person – that is, that his existence is *contingent* on support from his parents. With Bill, it is otherwise; his existence is not contingent on their support. But note, we also pointed out that to say this is not to say that Bill's existence is not contingent on anything. He has a job and is paid a salary and that allows him to live an independent life. The difficulty with Anselm's "proof" is that it treats God as a being whose existence depends on nothing at all. But to claim this, in my judgment, is to misuse the notion of "dependence." In its normal employment it has a significant use only in a given context, for example, in which there is a contrast between someone who is and someone who is not dependent on others. But it is not possible to conceive of a someone who is in no way dependent on anything for his or her existence.

I can put this point in the traditional language of philosophy. "Contingent" and "necessary" are normally taken as excluding one another. Nothing can be both at the same time. But in describing a being as "contingent," we must appeal to the normal circumstances in which this term is used. In my reconstruction of Anselm's proof, I gave such an example, stating that "This car did not exist two days ago" is a contingent statement. The use of "contingent" in that context was appropriate; it fit the circumstances described. I deny that an example could be given of anything whose existence did not depend on *some* conditions or factors. But if this is right, then to speak of a being whose existence is non-contingent has stretched ordinary speech beyond its sensible application.

In the light of this last remark, we should pause here for a moment to summarize where we now stand with respect to the question, "Does God exist?" We have seen that Anselm presents two different arguments that purport to prove that God exists. The first, for the reasons adduced above, is invalid and does not establish that conclusion. According to some philosophers, the second version of the argument is a proof. Norman Malcolm, for example, claims that the only way it can be shown to fail is to show that the concept of God (as a being none greater than which can be conceived) is either self-contradictory or nonsensical. Malcolm contends that it is neither. In response to this challenge, I argued that if "necessary" is used as Anselm and Malcolm propose, that is, to refer to a being that depends for its existence on nothing at all, this is a misuse of the term "dependence" and accordingly that the concept of God is nonsensical. If I am right, then the second version fails as well. But I must also admit that my argument depends on premises that are open to challenge, for example, whether "depends on nothing at all" is always context dependent. More generally, the issue, as I see it, ultimately hinges on whether three propositions that are key elements of my opposing argument are true. The first is whether "non-dependence," as used in this particular context, means the same as "necessarily exists." The second is whether "dependence" is being misused by Anselm and Malcolm. The third is whether a misuse of "dependence" is a species of nonsense. I know no way of proving that any one of these three propositions is true, let alone that all are. My conclusion is that Anselm's second proof cannot be shown to be either valid or invalid, and that based on his reasoning, the question of whether God necessarily exists is undecidable.

THE ARGUMENT FROM DESIGN: BACKGROUND

This is an argument that flourished in the eighteenth-century Enlightenment, deriving its persuasive power from the great achievements in science that occurred a century earlier. Galileo, Descartes, and Newton were scientific geniuses, but they were also thoughtful philosophers, with similar metaphysical views about the natural world. Each believed that nature operated according to mechanical laws that were susceptible to exact mathematical expression. All of them were experimentalists as well as theorists; but they differed in how much emphasis and importance they placed on experiment. Descartes is especially interesting in this connection. Despite carrying out ingenious experiments in optics, he believed that the high road to reality lay in mathematics. As distinct from his two coevals, he thought that by means of reason alone one could deduce facts about the world, including demonstrating that God existed. Like Anselm he therefore proffered a variation of the ontological argument to this effect.

The argument from design differs from any a priori argument in deriving its support from the observation of nature, and accordingly is a posteriori. It thus had special appeal for those thinkers with an empirical bent. The Enlightenment was dominated by intellectuals – Hume is a stellar example – who were especially impressed by the cosmological theories of Newton. Hume said at various times that he wished to be the Newton of philosophy. Indeed, his first and greatest work, *A Treatise of Human Nature*, published in 1739, is subtitled: *Being an Attempt to Introduce the Experimental Method of Reasoning Into Moral Subjects*. Probably no other philosopher before him had thought that Newton's methods would help to resolve moral questions.

His *Dialogues Concerning Natural Religion* is generally agreed to be the finest treatise in dialogue form written in English, and more than half of its twelve parts are devoted to the argument from design. The issue that was central for an Enlightenment figure like Hume was: "To what degree can the appeal to observational data produce compelling evidence that a single, transcendent God exists." The impact of modern science is evidenced in all of his most important writings. That the design argument would therefore be of paramount importance for him is not surprising.

The history of the argument is closely connected with Newton's career and accomplishments. He was, of course, a formidable mathematician who developed (possibly contemporaneously with Leibniz) the differential and integral calculi. But he was also an experimentalist who investigated, among other things, the behavior of light when reflected from and refracted through prisms. His experimental talents were impressive, but his real genius lay in formulating mathematical theories that explained hitherto mysterious observational data, from optical phenomena to the movements of celestial bodies.

Newton thought that the material world was wholly deterministic and ran according to quantifiable scientific laws. He compared the physical world to a watch that when wound up would run thereafter according to the principles of mechanics. The watch analogy was much discussed by subsequent philosophers, among them Hume and Paley, and is one of the examples appealed to by supporters of the design argument. Newton recognized that mechanical devices do not start up by themselves. They need to be turned on. What puzzled him was: "If the world is like a watch what initiated its first movements?" He believed that science could not answer the question, but was confined to explaining how the watch ran once its various components, such as wheels and gears, began to turn. In the end he decided that the only plausible answer required the existence of a being *ex machina* (outside of the machine) that gave the world its original propulsion – and this was God. Newton did not regard this account as a *proof* of the existence of God. It was rather a posit that was demanded to account for the motions we all observe.

Impressed by Newton, proponents of the design argument took an additional step. They felt they needed to prove, rather than assume, that the world (or, as they sometimes said, the universe) was a machine. They thought that if they could demonstrate that it was a machine, it would follow by easy steps that it needed an artificer to set it into motion – and this was God. Their view thus depended on producing observational data that the world was an artifact. Much of the argument about the cogency of the argument depends on this point. What sort of evidence would prove that they are right? We shall discuss the matter in a moment.

HUME'S *DIALOGUES CONCERNING NATURAL RELIGION*

It is generally agreed that the *Dialogues Concerning Natural Religion* contains the most comprehensive, detailed, and incisive discussion of the design argument. It consists of a debate between three intellectuals, each of whom represents a certain philosophical position. The three speakers are Demea, Cleanthes, and Philo. Demea is an exponent of orthodox Christianity, a rationalist, in the philosophical tradition of Descartes and Leibniz. In part IX, for example, he advances a complicated argument that conflates three different a priori arguments: the ontological proof, the cosmological proof, and the argument from the principle of sufficient reason (first propounded by Leibniz.) He is opposed by Cleanthes and Philo, who are both empiricists. Hume never speaks for himself. Most commentators believe that Demea's rationalistic views are not Hume's and that it is either Cleanthes or Philo who best represents the author. But it is a tribute to the subtle literary quality of the book that scholars are almost equally divided about whether it is Cleanthes or Philo who most accurately expresses Hume's views about the existence of God.

There are good reasons why Hume apparently felt it necessary to hide his own opinions. In the *Dialogues* some of the most compelling arguments, usually propounded by Philo, support a form of agnosticism or even atheism, and Hume may have worried about the negative reaction the work might precipitate if made available to the public. It was written in the early 1760s and although Hume did not die for another fifteen years, he refused to publish it during his lifetime (this was finally accomplished by his nephew three years later and only after Hume's close friends Adam Smith and William Strahan refused to support the project). There is still another factor. Though Hume was much impressed by the achievements of science, he was also a skeptic. Not a mitigated skeptic but a radical one who felt that certainty about matters of fact is unattainable. In the *Treatise of Human Nature* Hume's skepticism manifests itself in his treatments of causality, personal identity, our knowledge of the external world, induction, and the role of reason in moral conduct. On this last point, he says: "Reason is and ought to be a slave of the passions." As Richard H. Popkin has shown in his magisterial study, *The History of Skepticism From Erasmus to Spinoza*, Hume felt that the maxims that science depends on – such as the principle of the uniformity of nature – directly lead to skeptical doubt when pushed beyond facile acceptance. Popkin's interpretation of Hume's general philosophical stance thus explains why it is difficult to decide between Cleanthes – an empiricist and yet a devout believer – and his able opponent, Philo, who is also an empiricist and yet a radical skeptic. Each captures one facet of an uneasy tension within the author.

Before looking at the argument itself, as debated by the three central characters in the *Dialogues*, I should say something about the term "natural religion," that appears in the title. Natural religion or natural theology is a comparatively late development in the history of religion. It is essentially a product of the new scientific age. It confines its discussion of religion to what can be proved on the basis of reason. "Reason" is used broadly in this context to mean any form of rational argumentation. Natural religion thus excludes any attempts to establish the existence of God by revelation, faith, or dogma. Its findings are therefore subject to the same canons of logic and evidence as are employed in the support or refutation of any proposition of science. Hence, anyone whose religious beliefs depend on natural religion must regard them with the same open-mindedness that a scientist would exhibit with regard to any statement about the natural world. In the *Dialogues*, Cleanthes and Philo willingly commit themselves to following these precepts.

THE ARGUMENT ITSELF

It is Cleanthes who introduces the argument. He says:

> Look round the world, contemplate the whole and every part of it:
> you will find it to be nothing but one great machine, subdivided into
> an infinite number of lesser machines, which again admit of subdiv-
> isions to a degree beyond what human senses and faculties can trace and
> explain. All these various machines, and even their most minute parts,
> are adjusted to each other with an accuracy which ravishes into admir-
> ation all men who have ever contemplated them. The curious adapting of
> means to ends, throughout all nature, resembles exactly, though it
> much exceeds, the productions of human contrivance – of human
> design, thought, wisdom, and intelligence. Since therefore the effects
> resemble each other, we are led to infer, by all the rules of analogy, that
> the causes also resemble, and that the Author of nature is somewhat
> similar to the mind of man, though possessed of much larger faculties,
> proportioned to the grandeur of the work which he has executed. By this
> argument a posteriori, and by this argument alone, do we prove
> at once the existence of a Deity and his similarity to human mind and
> intelligence (p. 15).

The argument attempts to establish two things: the existence of a deity,
and his similarity to "human mind and intelligence." The overall line of
reasoning to demonstrate these conclusions is complex. The supporting
grounds it offers for these two propositions differ, though in fact they
tend to overlap in the course of the debate. Sometimes the debate is
directed toward the existence of God, at other times – and to a considerable extent – it concerns his nature. The contention that God exists is supported by the assertion that the universe is a machine. There is a second
step in this connection. Since all machines are artifacts they are not self-
generated, but need an artisan to bring them into existence. God is the
craftsman who fashioned the world, and since the product exists, he
therefore must exist. (The notion that God is such an artificer comes very
close to the orthodox Christian doctrine that a single transcendent entity
is the creator of the universe.)

The proposition that God is an intelligent being is supported by the thesis that the world exhibits the kind of order found in such devices as ships and watches, and that the creation of such artifacts requires skill and know-how. It is an underlying assumption of the design argument that only a knowledgeable technician could produce objects of this degree of complexity. The essential move here is that any investigation of the world discovers that it involves a "curious adapting of means to ends", that is, that it has a discernible order and is not simply a chaotic assemblage of bits and pieces. Cleanthes asserts that such an adaptation exists throughout all nature, that is, that the vast machine that is the world (or the universe) is subdivided into a number of lesser machines. The evidence in favor of the adapting of means to ends is that all these machines, and their most minute parts, are adjusted to each other with incredible accuracy. As he says:

> Consider, anatomize the eye, survey its structure and contrivance, and tell me, from your own feeling, if the idea of a contriver does not immediately flow in upon you with a force like that of a sensation. The most obvious conclusion, surely, is in favour of design ... Who can behold the male and female of each species, the correspondence of their parts and instincts, their passions and whole course of life before and after generation, but must be sensible that the propagation of the species is intended by nature? Millions and millions of such instances present themselves through every part of the universe, and no language can convey a more intelligible, irresistible meaning than the curious adjustment of final causes (p. 25).

I do not find these particular examples to be well chosen. Hume was, of course, a man of his time, and the science of biology in the eighteenth century was pre-Darwinian. Cleanthes' assertion that the propagation of animal species is the result of design is not convincing to the modern reader whose knowledge of the role of DNA in natural selection results in an opposite conviction. So later I shall try to supply some better examples to bolster his case. But first some comments about the kind of argument he is offering.

110

Cleanthes tells us that the design argument is based on "the rules of analogy," and that the argument is a posteriori. All analogical arguments are indeed a posteriori, but not all a posteriori arguments are analogical. Without pursuing the difference here, we should explain what Cleanthes means by "the rules of analogy." Consider the following situation. In the past whenever we have seen smoke and have investigated its source we have found fire. It is plausible from this frequent conjunction of observations, and especially when there are no perceived exceptions, to infer that fire causes smoke. Now suppose we see smoke in the distance but for various practical reasons cannot get to its source. It is plausible to believe that the smoke *in this particular case* has also been caused by fire. This is analogical reasoning. It states that the new case of smoke resembles past cases of smoke. So even though we cannot observe the cause of the smoke in this instance it is reasonable to believe that it is caused by fire. The analogy is between past cases of smoke, and their origins, and a new case of smoke and its origin. Because all cases of smoke resemble one another, the principle that Cleanthes invokes – that similar causes have similar effects – justifies the inference that this present case of smoke is caused by fire.

This is an argument based on past experience and that is why such reasoning is said to be a posteriori. It is logically possible, of course, that the new case of smoke may have a different genesis than anything observed in the past. So the inference from past correlations to a new conjunction of events (fire producing smoke) is not a necessary truth. The conclusion is probable only. Yet the reasoning is sound, since the more frequently cases of smoke and fire are found to be correlated, the higher is the probability that the inference about any new case is true.

In the design argument, Cleanthes is asserting that in the past whenever we have observed a machine we have also observed that it had a designer or artificer. In this case, he argues, because the world is a machine, and even though we are not able to observe its origin (it is like the new case of smoke mentioned above), it is highly probable that it was created by a Designer – and this, of course, is God.

The argument depends on two assumptions: (1) That the world is a machine, and (2) That in the past all machines have been created by designers. The argument in favor of (2) recalls Newton's notion that the world is like a watch. Suppose an anthropologist exploring a desert area in Asia should come across a watch lying on the sand. It would be obvious to him that some sentient being had made (and possibly lost or abandoned) that object. Watches, unlike dunes and rocks, are not produced by a fortuitous combination of sand and wind. They are artifacts, manmade objects, that require the application of intelligence and the ability to manufacture such complex components as wheels, gears, and springs. Almost all scholars agree that (2) is true and, indeed even more generally, that all artifacts – whether they are machines or chairs and tables – require human effort and skill to bring them into existence. That robots can perform such functions does not militate against the point. They can be regarded as extensions of human ingenuity. So this part of the design argument survives any reasonable challenge.

It is premise (1), that the world (or the universe) is a machine, that Philo and Demea question. Much of the debate thus turns on the issue of whether there are observable data that would make it persuasive that the world is a machine. As we have seen, some of the examples Cleanthes offers in support of this proposition are outmoded from the standpoint of modern genetics, and tend to weaken his case. Let us put ourselves in his shoes and try to help him by updating his approach.

Take a wristwatch. How does it work? Nowadays such watches do not require winding; they are battery operated. The batteries provide an electrical current that causes the components to run in an orderly way. The device is thus governed by the laws of electro/mechanics. Its behavior is totally predictable once we know its purpose, what its components are made of, and how they relate to one another. Now take something that does not seem to be an artifact – say an oak tree. It begins as an acorn and with the passage of time eventually becomes a full-fledged tree. What causes its growth? The answer is that certain physical laws, known in great detail by botanists, can fully explain this development. These laws apply to fluids that provide nourishment for the tree. When rain falls, water is picked up by its roots, is absorbed by cells, and nutrients are transferred through the cell membrane to other parts of the organism.

The movement of these energy-containing liquids is governed by the laws of hydraulics. The tree is a hydraulic pumping station. It contains the equivalent of pumps, pipes, and valves. Its growth and development are totally explicable by mechanical principles.

Starting with this account, we can generalize, but this time using more examples. The tree will drop leaves on the ground, and these will eventually turn into compost that supports the growth of other foliage, and an insect population. These in turn have important ecological effects. There is thus a close interrelation between various ingredients in nature such that, as Cleanthes puts it, its "minute parts are adjusted to each other with an accuracy which ravishes into admiration all men who have ever contemplated them." Without rain the tree will not grow, without leaves that fall there will be no grass, and without grass, insects will not survive. There is thus a causal chain in nature that results in the adaptation of its parts to one another. It is these sorts of examples that support Cleanthes' remark that there is in nature a "curious adapting of means to ends," an adaptation that is similar to the ways in which the components of a watch are adapted to one another in order to measure time. These examples lend weight to Cleanthes' contention that the world (the universe) is one great machine and that it is subdivided into a number of lesser machines.

One can generalize even further. We know that physical science is committed to the exploration of nature. But this, as we pointed out in Chapter 1, is not a random process. Scientists search for regularities in the behavior of natural phenomena that allow for the development of scientific laws. These laws frequently describe how the operations of mechanical devices, such as levers, pulleys, inclined planes, pumps, pipes, and valves affect the behavior of such phenomena. That such laws apply to the natural world indicates that from a scientific standpoint the world – and its various parts – are nothing but machines. The very existence of science, according to this point of view, thus supports Cleanthes' position that the world is a machine. Many scientists today would agree, but would be reluctant to take an additional step, that is, to acknowledge that this complex machine must have an artificer. But, according to

Cleanthes, if they were consistent this is the only conclusion that they could draw. It is the design argument, he insists, that justifies such a step.

THE ISSUES

As just mentioned two issues are at stake in the *Dialogues*: they concern the existence of God and his nature. With respect to both topics, Philo and, to a lesser extent, Demea, are on the attack, and Cleanthes is put in the position of countering their thrusts. The dialectic that ensues is intricate and moves in a sinuous fashion from speaker to speaker. It is this interplay between the characters that gives the work much of its dramatic quality. Here we can only touch on some main themes. On the question of whether God exists, Demea is on Cleanthes' side. Both agree that there is such a divinity. They also concur in defending what is often called a Judeo-Christian conception, namely that God is a transcendent being of infinite wisdom, power, and goodness. Philo is evasive on both points, though at the end of the book, he will admit, surprisingly, that "the cause or causes of order in the universe probably bear some remote analogy to human intelligence," thus ultimately siding with Cleanthes. For commentators, Philo's recantation in Part XII has proved to be one of the most puzzling features of this work, since for most of the dialogue he has argued, as a skeptic, against this conclusion. He does assert that insofar as the analogy holds at all it leads to what he calls the unwanted consequences of *anthropomorphism.* He means by this term that if one assumes that God has a mind similar to that of man it will follow that he is not omniscient or all powerful, but is sometimes confused in the way that humans often are, is a limited being who learns by trial and error and who may well have bungled the creation of this world or others, and so on. Philo's sarcasm reaches a fever pitch in the following passage:

> But were this world ever so perfect a production, it must still remain uncertain whether all the excellences of the work can justly be ascribed to the workman. If we survey a ship, what an exalted idea must we form of the ingenuity of the carpenter who framed so complicated, useful, and beautiful a machine? And what surprise must we feel when we find him a stupid

mechanic who imitated others, and copied an art which, through a long succession of ages, after multiplied trials, mistakes, corrections, deliberations, and controversies, had been gradually improving? Many worlds might have been botched and bungled, throughout an eternity, ere this system was struck out; much labour lost, many fruitless trials made, and a slow but continued improvement carried on during infinite ages in the art of world-making. In such subjects, who can determine where the truth, nay, who can conjecture where the probability lies, amidst a great number of hypotheses which may be proposed and a still greater which may be imagined? (p. 36).

Despite the pessimism of these remarks, Philo agrees with Cleanthes that the only kind of argument that can be used to establish whether God exists (as well as establishing something about his nature) must be a posteriori. Like Cleanthes, he is thus a committed empiricist. With respect to this matter, both stand against Demea, a rationalist. Demea also holds an independent position. He claims – against Philo and Cleanthes – that God's *nature* is mysterious and cannot be apprehended by human beings. For Demea there is a huge gulf between attempts to prove God's existence and attempts to understand his nature. He thinks the former is possible by a priori arguments but that no form of reason can accomplish the latter. Cleanthes and Philo accuse him of misrepresenting the orthodox position, and indeed of being a mystic, skeptic, or atheist. Here is how Cleanthes responds to Demea's self-proclaimed orthodoxy.

It seems strange to me, said Cleanthes, that you, Demea, who are so sincere in the cause of religion, should maintain the mysterious, incomprehensible nature of the Deity, and should insist so strenuously that he has no manner of likeness or resemblance to human creatures. The Deity, I can readily allow, possesses many powers and attributes of which we can have no comprehension; but, if our ideas, so far as they go, be not just and adequate and correspondent to his real nature, I know not what there is in this subject worth insisting on. Is the name, without any meaning, of such mighty importance? Or how do you mystics, who maintain the absolute incomprehensibility of the Deity, differ from sceptics or atheists, who assert that the first cause of all is unknown and unintelligible? (p. 28).

115

THRUST AND PARRY

I shall say no more here about the dispute about God's nature that plays such a vital role in the *Dialogues*. As I mentioned at the beginning of the chapter, my main focus is on the question raised by those three little words: "Does God exist?" In Hume's text, the controversy about God's existence is intense and is carried on mostly between Philo and Cleanthes. It is true that Demea participates, but because he offers a priori arguments neither of the other personages takes him seriously. The real debate is waged within the parameters of empiricism. It is what science can tell us about the transcendent that is at stake, and Demea has nothing to say about this issue. So the question is: "Can one prove, even if only with some degree of probability, that God exists on the basis of data derived from the careful observation of the natural world?" There is, in my judgment, an objection advanced by Philo to the design argument that goes to the heart of that question. He contends that the design argument *is not an argument from experience at all*, and hence that it fails to provide any evidence in favor of God's existence. Here is what he says:

> When two species of objects have always been observed to be conjoined together, I can infer, by custom, the existence of one wherever I see the existence of the other; and this I call an argument from experience. But how this argument can have place where the objects, as in the present case, are single, individual, without parallel or specific resemblance, may be difficult to explain. And will any man tell me with serious countenance that an orderly universe must arise from some thought and art like the human because we have experience of it? To ascertain this reasoning it were requisite that we had experience of the origin of worlds; and it is not sufficient, surely, that we have seen ships and cities arise from human art and contrivance (p. 20).

We can explain what Philo means by comparing and contrasting three cases of analogical reasoning, one of them sound, the other two unsound. Probably the simplest way to do this is by means of sketches:

Sound Analogical Reasoning

S = smoke	S' = a new case of smoke
--------------------	--------------------------
F = fire	F' = (unobserved fire)

Version 1: The Design Argument (unsound)

G = any world (or universe)	G' = our world
--------------------	--------------------------
H = any deity	H' = God

Version 2: The Design Argument (unsound)

C = watch	C' = world
--------------------	--------------------------
D = watchmaker	D' = God

As Philo explains, an argument from experience depends on two things: first that we have frequently observed a correlation between events F and S (e.g., between cases of fire and smoke) and, second, that new cases of S are *similar* to previously experienced cases of S. When we see a case of S' (a new case of smoke), but cannot reach its source, we can infer by the "rules of analogy" that S' will be caused by F' (i.e., fire). It is thus past experience that justifies this inference. In the case of the design argument, Philo points out that although we have experienced correlations between watches and their artificers, we have never experienced any correlation between artificers and worlds. Therefore the experienced correlation between F and S that sound analogical reasoning requires is lacking in the relationship between H and G. This is what he means when he says: "To ascertain this reasoning it were requisite that we had experience of the origin of worlds; and it is not sufficient, surely, that we have seen ships and cities arise from human art and contrivance." In short, we have no experience of worlds being created and hence there is no reason, *based on experience*, to believe that this world has been created by an Artificer.

But there is an additional problem with the argument. If the dark patch we now see in the sky is not smoke then it would be a mistake to assume its cause is fire. So the design argument depends on showing that the world (or the universe) is similar enough to ordinary machines, such as ships and sewing machines, to justify the inference that it has a designer as its source. Philo also attacks this assumption. As he says: "But how this argument can have place where the objects, as in the present case, are single, individual without parallel or specific resemblance, may be difficult to explain." He is emphasizing that the world (or universe), unlike a watch, is unique. But if so how can it be compared with objects that are not only not unique but whose creation is witnessed over and over again. Thus, the argument fails on two counts. It fails to establish a genuine causal link between designers and worlds, and it fails to show that the world is similar to those artifacts whose creation we have frequently observed.

Cleanthes' rebuttal to Philo is clever and compelling. He says:

Suppose, therefore, that an articulate voice were heard in the clouds, much louder and more melodious than any which human art could ever reach; suppose that this voice were extended in the same instant over all nations and spoke to each nation in its own language and dialect; suppose that the words delivered not only contain a just sense and meaning, but convey some instruction altogether worthy of a benevolent Being superior to mankind – could you possibly hesitate a moment concerning the cause of this voice, and must you not instantly ascribe it to some design or purpose? Yet I cannot see but all the same objections (if they merit that appellation) which lie against the system of theism may also be produced against this inference.

Might you not say that all conclusions concerning fact were founded on experience; that, when we hear an articulate voice in the dark and thence infer a man, it is only the resemblance of the effects which leads us to conclude that there is a like resemblance in the cause; but that this extraordinary voice, by its loudness, extent and flexibility to all languages, bears so little analogy to any human voice that we have no reason to suppose any analogy in their causes; and consequently, that a rational,

wise, coherent speech proceeded, you know not whence, from some acci-
dental whistling of the winds, not from any divine reason or intelligence?
You see clearly your own objections in these cavils, and I hope too you see
clearly that they cannot possibly have more force in the one case than in
the other (p. 23).

In this reply to Philo, Cleanthes is parrying both of the thrusts his
opponent has made. With respect to the point that we have no experience
of worlds being created by gods, Cleanthes argues that we have no experience of a voice such as that he describes. It is thus a unique case, in that
respect no different from the world (or the universe). Yet that it is a
singular voice does not preempt our recognizing it as emerging from an
intelligent being. The fact that the world (or the universe) is equally
singular does not debar our recognizing that it is a product of intelligent
design. The example neutralizes Philo's contention that we need to have
experienced a correlation between designers and worlds for the argument
to go through.

But it is his response to the second point that is even more important.
He is arguing that the voice has effects which make it *similar* to the effects
we hear when we are exposed, as we sometimes are, to a human voice
emerging from a dark place, and cannot see its source. Because the voice,
later determined to be that of a human being, utters sounds that are intelligible, we can, before seeing the speaker, correctly infer that those sounds
emerge from a rational entity. Likewise in the case of the extraordinary
voice we can make a comparable judgment because its effects are similar
to those of a human voice coming from an invisible source. With these
comments Cleanthes is countering Philo's assertion that the universe is
not similar to an artifact. His point is that we can recognize similarity of
structure between two objects or events even where one of them differs
radically from the other. The analogy between the extraordinary voice
and the human voice is exactly like that between the universe and a watch.
The design hypothesis allows us to infer that something unique in our
experience is similar to something that we observe on a daily basis.

Embedded in Cleanthes' example is a proposition that he does not
make explicit, but it is what makes his response to Philo so compelling: *that*

similarity or resemblance is a matter of degree. If this proposition is true – and in my judgment it is – it means that we cannot determine for any arbitrarily selected group of As and Bs whether they are similar to one another. We cannot say, for example, that children in general resemble their parents, even if we specify the particular respect in which they might do so – such as being tall or short, interesting or dull, intelligent or not, and so on. To determine whether two things are similar or not requires that we look at the particular case. But such cases run a gamut from instances where similarity is obvious, or where a lack of similarity is obvious, to those cases where one cannot decide one way or the other. Does Johnny resemble his father or his mother or neither? The dispute may be irresolvable. One can imagine interminable arguments within a family about the question. The positive arguments will emphasize particular features, and the negative arguments will point out that they are insufficient to establish the resemblance. Clearly the truth of any statement to the effect that A is similar to B will depend on the particular case, and it will also depend on the individual observer. As John Wisdom pointed out many years ago in his paper, "Gods," one man's weedy plot of land is another man's carefully tended garden. To an important degree, whether A is similar to B depends on one's point of view and the emphasis one will give to certain features of whatever object is under discussion.

From Philo's perspective the world (or universe) is not similar to an artifact. From Cleanthes' perspective it is. The latter sees order and regularity in the world and the former does not – or at least does not with the same implications. We are thus dealing with a particular case. With respect to this case these two visions of the world are incommensurable. A third party, such as the present writer, cannot adopt both perspectives because they are incompatible; and if one carefully examines the reasonings of their respective proponents about design, one cannot determine which of them is right. Is the world a machine or is it not? Since we cannot decide that in general any two things resemble one another, even in a particular respect, and since the arguments in this particular case are equally powerful, one must suspend judgment about the answer. I conclude that the design argument does not resolve the question, "Does God exist?"

SUMMARY

This chapter has focused on the question, "Does God exist?" Because the question can be – indeed has been – given various interpretations, I began by refining it to make it precise enough to be susceptible to cogent argumentation. It is thus eventually interpreted to mean: "Is there exactly one transcendent, all powerful, all wise and benevolent being who is the creator of the universe?" This is, indeed, how the philosophical tradition that began with early Christian theologians and came down to the present time has understood the query. In the lengthy history of the subject there have been innumerable arguments pro and con on this issue, including appeals to ecstatic personal experience, faith, tradition, and so forth. I set all of these approaches aside in order to consider two historically important arguments based on reason: the ontological argument and the argument from design.

The earliest and probably most famous formulation of the ontological argument is found in St. Anselm's *Proslogion*. This is a work that was written at the end of the eleventh or at the beginning of the twelfth century. Norman Malcolm has argued that the *Proslogion* contains two closely resembling but nonetheless differing versions of this argument, the first attempting to demonstrate that God exists, and the second that he necessarily exists. Following Malcolm, I also have distinguished between these versions and considered them independently. The philosophical tradition, beginning with Kant, has almost unanimously considered the first version invalid on the ground that the argument assumes that existence is a property. Developments in modern logic show that existence is not a property, and I concur with this point of view. However, my analysis of the argument indicates that Anselm is not making this assumption, but rather that the purpose of the argument is to distinguish mythical or fictitious beings from real ones. I concluded that the traditional interpretation of the first version is thus misguided. Nonetheless, I find that the argument is fallacious, but for a different reason. It assumes that the item that exists in the mind of a person who holds that God is a being none greater than which can be conceived is the same item as that which exists in reality. The conception that a painter has in mind before he begins to paint is not, as Anselm assumes, the same item as the physical painting itself. The latter can be hung on a wall while the former cannot. This version of the ontological argument assumes that the mental conception and the physical painting are identical, thus committing the fallacy of equivocation. Hence the argument fails.

The second version of the argument is completely different. It is not formally invalid. Malcolm argues that the version is a valid proof. He claims that the only intelligible way of rejecting Anselm's claim that God's existence is necessary is to maintain that the concept of God, as a being a greater than which cannot be conceived, is self-contradictory or nonsensical. I agreed with his assessment, but then attempted to show that the concept is nonsensical, and accordingly that the argument does not go through. However, my counter-argument depends on whether three propositions that play key roles in my rebuttal are true: first, that "non-dependence" in this context means the same as "necessarily exists;" second, that "dependence" is misused by Anselm and Malcolm; and third, that such a misuse of "dependence" is a species of nonsense. But I admitted that I cannot prove that any one of these three propositions is true, let alone that all are. I therefore concluded that since I cannot show that the proof is either valid or invalid, the question of whether God necessarily exists is – at least on the basis of Anselm's reasoning – undecidable.

The remainder of the chapter deals with the argument from design, as presented by Cleanthes in David Hume's *Dialogues Concerning Natural Religion*. This argument is essentially a product of the seventeenth-century scientific revolution. Galileo, Newton, and Descartes, among its greatest figures, all believed that the natural world operates according to mechanical laws that are susceptible to exact mathematical expression. According to their common outlook, the natural world (or universe) is a complicated machine and like all artifacts can be brought into existence only by an artificer or designer. This is of course God. Unlike the ontological argument, which attempts to deduce God's existence (or necessary existence) by a priori reasoning, the argument from design is a posteriori. It attempts to assemble observational evidence in support of the proposition that the world is a machine. It is expected that such evidence will establish two things: the existence of God and his similarity "to human mind and intelligence."

The issue is debated by three intelligent speakers, each representing a well-known philosophical position. They are Demea (a rationalist) and Cleanthes and Philo, both of whom are empiricists, and who are, accordingly, committed to the canons of scientific evidence. The main debate thus takes place between the latter personages and turns on the issue of whether there is empirical evidence that proves, even if only with some degree of probability, that God exists and is similar to the human mind. Philo, a skeptic, contends that the evidence is weak and indeed that the argument is based on a faulty analogy. His attack is rebutted by Cleanthes, a believer, who argues both that the argument is sound and that observational data establishes that the universe is similar to a machine.

My assessment of their dispute is that it ultimately turns on the issue of whether the universe is similar to such artifacts as watches and ships. I argued that this issue is, as a general matter, undecidable; and therefore that the question whether any A is similar to any B is only resolvable in particular cases. But such cases run a gamut, from instances where similarity is obvious, or where a lack of similarity is obvious, to those cases where one cannot decide one way or the other. The question is thus whether the universe is similar or similar enough to the kinds of artifacts we find in daily life. From Cleanthes' perspective it is, and from Philo's perspective it is not. The arguments that these antagonists present about the existence of God I find equally powerful, and concluded therefore that the design argument does not lead to a resolution of the question. Since this is also the verdict I reached earlier with respect to Anselm's second ontological argument, my ultimate assessment is that both of these important arguments are indecisive with respect to the question, "Does God exist?" Either there is such a transcendent being or there is not, so the issue is clearly factual. But no decisive answer is possible. We thus have another example of a factual question about which we must suspend judgment.

4

DID MY GENES MAKE
ME DO IT?

I turn now to another irresolvable factual dispute: the free will problem. It is one of the oldest, most complicated, and most intractable of philosophical challenges. Though its origins are lost in the mist of time, it has footings in early Greek thought about fate, in the Judeo-Christian conception of God, in Enlightenment debates about whether punishing criminals is ever justified, and in our own time in the sciences devoted to human behavior. Despite such diverse origins and conceptions, all of these differing views are united by a central question: Is all human comportment determined by antecedent factors, including one's genetic makeup, so that no one can choose or act differently from the way that he or she does? For example, if one believes, as many do, that an omniscient and omnipotent God has created the universe according to a preconceived plan, it is obvious that he will know from the moment of creation how the future will play out; and if this is so, that no events, including those comprising human choice and conduct, could have been different from the way they were or are. And if that is the case, it seems to follow that the belief in freedom of choice and action is an illusion.

Science has added a recent, compelling thrust to this ancient religious dilemma. As empirical evidence continues to accumulate it is plausible to believe that all animal behavior is severely constrained by genetic factors. Here the argument is that small, invertebrate, segmented animals, such as ants and spiders, behave in ways that are determined by their constitutional make-up, and that human conduct is subject to a similar influence. Despite the differences in intellectual and linguistic capacities between insects and humans, it would seem that the genetic component in behavior is overwhelming. It is now commonly argued that because everyone's behavior is determined by his or her genes, all of our actions, including criminal and anti-social ones, are beyond our control. So this is the problem: Are freedom of choice and action possible for human beings? As we shall see, the conundrum, traditionally called "the free will problem," is exceedingly complex, and crucially involves as a minimum such notions as fate, predictability, determinism, causality, and responsibility. Historically, there have been many different responses to this question. We shall focus on three of the most important, two of which argue that there is freedom of choice and action, and the other, which, basing its opinion on psychological and genetic evidence, denies that there is. Each of these approaches is highly persuasive, but as one commentator has recently stated: "Almost no philosophical issue has been so widely debated as the free will problem, and yet no generally accepted solution to it has been reached." I agree with this remark, but think that something even stronger can be said. I will conclude after a detailed examination that the problem is irresolvable.

THE COMMON-SENSE VIEW

I will begin by describing what I will call "the common sense view of freedom of the will." In speaking of such an everyday or ordinary "view," I hasten to add a caveat. It is doubtful that most persons have "views" in the sense in which philosophers use that term. It is true, of course, that non-philosophers have beliefs, some of them well-informed and well-argued, about all sorts of things. But there is a difference. The philosopher is primarily interested in arriving at a position on a given topic that is carefully formulated, logically consistent, and rationally justifiable.

This position may take the form of an explicit argument or a well-formed theory. Whichever it is, it must be exposed to his or her peers to see whether it can withstand critical analysis and counter-examples. The convictions of most people do not belong to the public domain in this sense, although of course whenever anyone expresses an opinion in the presence of others it may well be subject to debate. I do not want to dwell on this difference. I mention it only to make the point that ordinary persons in the course of their daily, practical lives, do advance firm judgments about specific human actions. Among these is the proposition that those who commit crimes should in general, though not always, be held responsible for their actions. Such a notion is part of a broader outlook that is not an explicit theory in the philosophical sense just mentioned. It is rather a non-technical, diffuse, mostly latent collection of assumptions and presuppositions that are held by non-specialists. Nonetheless it is coherent enough so that it represents a characterizable response to the free will problem. That there is such a conception is important for the ensuing discussion, since it represents what might be designated as "The Default or Standard Position." The philosophical accounts – some of which are quite paradoxical – can only be appreciated for what they are when seen against the background of this common sense point of view. I shall therefore begin by describing five of its major provisions.

1. It presupposes that during the course of their lives, and even on a daily basis, human beings *generally* have options to choose and act differently from the way they in fact do. It also modifies this principle to make allowances for special circumstances. These include cases of compulsion and constraint, cases of madness, psychosis or severe neurosis, cases where there are practical limitations on behavior (I cannot, even if I wish to, run one-hundred meters in fewer than nine seconds), and cases of certain inevitabilities in life (i.e., each of us will eventually die). The concept of fate is of special interest in this connection. Some persons believe that something they call "fate" inexorably determines what has happened in the past and what will happen in the future. Obviously those who believe in fate do not accept the common-sense point of view since it holds that at least some of the time each of us can choose or act differently from the

way we do, and fatalists deny that this is ever possible. This tenet thus denies that each of us is fated.

2. We can also safely say that it embodies a distinction between choice and action. Choice is a mental phenomenon, whereas action is not. Choice is also frequently identified with what philosophers call "the will," that is, a kind of mental set that may involve deliberation and a willingness to act. Moreover, this common-sense outlook posits a close connection between choice and action (one first decides to buy a new pair of shoes and then does it. If one doesn't buy the shoes then, all other things being equal, it is assumed that one has changed one's mind). This point of view also presumes that choice involves autonomy, that is, the independence that an agent has to make his or her own decisions. It thus holds that if a human being were hypnotized what that individual would choose to do would not stem from his or her own desires and interests. Many of us have witnessed live performances in night clubs or theatres where persons are hypnotized and then directed to act as animals or as clowns, that is, in ways they would never normally behave. They appear to heed only the communications of the hypnotist and respond in an uncritical, automatic fashion, ignoring all aspects of the environment other than those pointed out by the hypnotist. Such subjects can become temporarily deaf, blind, paralyzed, hallucinated, delusional, or impervious to pain or to uncomfortable body postures. In such circumstances, they cannot act differently from the way they are programmed to act. In the technical parlance of philosophy, this would amount to asserting that the hypnotized person's *will* is not free and that one's "choices" would really be those of the mesmerist. If choice is not free in such a circumstance, then the hypnotized person's actions will not be free either. Or again, the common-sense view holds that if one were under the influence of certain drugs, one's choices would differ from those that one would normally make, and that in such a contingency one's conduct would also be affected. This is another way of saying that one's will is affected by these drugs.

3. It also recognizes two different ways in which choices and actions may be unfree. To simplify the discussion we shall speak here only of

actions, but the same analysis applies to choices. Unfree actions may be *compelled* or *constrained*. Compulsion and constraint are relationships that hold between two or more entities. They differ in that compulsion consists in an entity or a group of entities forcing another or some others to do something, whereas constraint is just the opposite. It involves preventing movement. If a group of singers pushes a bashful member forward to take a bow that is a case of compulsion. But if the group prevents the individual from stepping forward that is constraint. In these instances, human agents force others to do or restrain from doing something. But both concepts also apply to non-human relationships. A neurotic man's need constantly to wash his hands is a case of compulsion where no other person is forcing him to act as he does. Even though he knows that his hands are clean his actions are dominated by internal psychological factors over which he has no control. Why he engages in what psychiatrists call "anankastic behavior," is, of course, a complicated matter and we shall consider some explanations of this obsessive/compulsive phenomenon later in discussing John Hosper's essay on the freedom of the will.

Constraint may occur both where human agents are involved and where they are not. Suppose some burglars enter a home and tie up the owners. Though the victims might choose to leave or wish to call the police they cannot. Their bonds constrain them from acting according to their choices and wishes. A man held up at gunpoint by a robber is also constrained. The robber has limited his options. It is true that the man might choose to run rather than giving up his wallet, but neither is a course of action that he would normally choose to follow. The example is thus a case in which an agent prevents another from doing what that individual wishes to do. There are, of course, many examples of constraint by non-human forces. An avalanche that buries a skier and prevents him from moving would be such an instance.

4. Unlike certain philosophical and biological theories we shall be considering below, common sense does not have a fixed opinion about the influence that genes have on human behavior. It does, of course, accept the scientific judgment that the behavior of "lower order animals,"

such as ants, mites, flies, and spiders, is entirely determined by their genetic backgrounds; but it wavers when it comes to higher order animals. Think of the interminable arguments one finds in families about whether dogs can feel guilt or shame. It is even less apodictic with respect to human beings, although with respect to certain individuals, such as those who are palpably insane, it would probably agree that "it is all a matter of genes."

5. It also attributes a certain "belief" to most persons. That is, it assumes that the vast majority of human beings *act as if* most of the time they believe that genuine alternatives are open to them in terms of choice and behavior. This "belief," if I can so designate it, is deeply internalized and only becomes overt when situations involving extreme behavior or compulsion or constraint challenge it. It presupposes that normally, and without reflection, one just chooses to do something and then does it. This is why I have said that it does not constitute an explicit theory in the way that the philosophical conceptions we shall be considering do. It is less self-conscious and much more unwittingly motivated. And yet because some sort of belief schema is challenged when persons are subjected to constraint or compulsion we are, I submit, justified in speaking of it as a proto-philosophical response to the free will problem. That response, put summarily, is the "view" that sometimes each of us is free to choose and act differently, and sometimes each of us is not. As a sub-case of this open-textured outlook, it says much the same about the genetic role in human conduct. It is this mixture of heterogeneous and often incongruous elements that one of the philosophical doctrines will challenge, and that two will accept, though with the proviso that it is too diffuse and insufficiently developed to constitute the kind of articulate explanation which a philosophical account must provide.

THREE PHILOSOPHICAL THEORIES

We shall call the three philosophical theories to be discussed below, *Hard Determinism*, *Indeterminism*, and *Soft Determinism*, respectively. Each of these differs from the common-sense view in important ways.

Hard Determinism holds that no persons (or for that matter animals) are *ever* free to choose or act differently from the way they do, and some versions claim that this is largely due to the genetic influence on behavior. Both Indeterminism and Soft Determinism offer specific explanatory accounts about the nature of causation and scientific laws, which are topics that most persons of common sense never think or speculate about. Indeed, it is one of the signs that the inquiry has become technical that these notions are selected as being of central importance. They also disagree about the role played by genes in human conduct. In philosophy, the notion of fate is given diverse interpretations. It is part and parcel of Hard Determinism; is taken seriously by Indeterminism with respect to the physical component in human action but is considered inapplicable to choice; and is rejected by Soft Determinism. These various divergencies will be explored in greater depth as we examine these doctrines. Let us then begin with a view in which fate and determinism are at least intertwined and sometimes even identified.

HARD DETERMINISM

Hard Determinism is the thesis that whatever happens is inevitable and unavoidable. The thesis applies to choice and to action. Neither the choice anyone makes nor the action that follows from it could be otherwise than it is. It is thus a view that denies in the strongest possible way that the human will is free. It is a complicated philosophical conceit that rests on specific interpretations of five main concepts: *fate, determinism, causality, predictability,* and *responsibility*. The doctrine can thus only be appreciated when this interrelated group of concepts is fully understood. I shall therefore begin my account with a discussion of these crucial notions.

Fate

Fatalism is the doctrine that the pattern of all happenings is fixed in advance in such a manner that no animate being (human or animal) can change it. A contrast is thus drawn between an overwhelming power, *fate,* and the helplessness of those subject to its dictates. The overwhelming power may consist of a particular divinity (*Yahweh* in the Old Testament) or of a group of gods (in Greek literature, *Moiroi*), or of Nature itself. Such words as *destiny*, *lot*, *portion*, and *doom* also turn on this contrast. Each, with a slightly different emphasis, suggests that a certain outcome in life is inevitable. Some of these concepts, for example *doom*, imply a negative or unfortunate outcome. Others are more neutral. In everyday discourse, they are often used interchangeably: "Poverty was his fate (destiny, lot, portion) in life." Fate is often personified in ancient mythologies – so that there are depictions or legends of goddesses who spin out the destiny of each individual. In early Germanic mythology there are three such supernatural beings, the Norns. Some sources name them "Urd," "Verdandi," and "Skuld," words that are thought to mean "past," "present," and "future." The threads that are spun by these divinities contain written information, something like a primitive version of DNA, that spells out the destiny or lot that each person will inherit in life.

Determinism

Determinism not only has lengthy historical and religious antecedents, but is heir to differing interpretations, such as we find in Indeterminism and Soft Determinism. For the moment let us confine ourselves to three versions that appear in variants of Hard Determinism, and that for purposes of clarity I shall designate as A, B, and C. A identifies determinism with fate, whereas B and C do not, but nonetheless are equally necessitarian. B is the doctrine that all occurrences, whether mental or otherwise, are the products of antecedent causes, usually identified as environmental, psychological, social, or genetic. C is the idea that all events are governed by natural laws and that such governance is necessitarian in character. Both Indeterminism and Soft Determinism reject A, B, and C. They both deny that all occurrences are fated, for example. But they offer different reasons for rejecting B and C. The Indeterminist maintains that mental events are exempt from causality and natural laws, whereas the Soft Determinist agrees with the Hard Determinist that all events are subject to such governance, while at the same time denying that causality and natural laws imply inevitability. With these discriminations noted for future reference, let us now return to Hard Determinism.

Having discussed the concept of fate above, I will make no further reference to it here. Instead, my concentration will be on B and C. B, as just mentioned, is the notion that all occurrences in nature, whether mental or otherwise, are the products of antecedent factors or causes. This conception, which asserts that causes *rigidly* determine their consequences, is interesting and complex. It depends on two subordinate theses: (1) that every event has a cause, and (2) that a given effect will necessarily follow an initiating causal event provided that all other things are equal. In effect this second thesis expresses a *ceteris paribus* condition, that is, the provision that a certain effect will invariably follow an antecedent happening only if no intervening causes are operative.

Although Hard Determinism is often associated with religious approaches, it also claims that B is the doctrine that best captures the motivating principles of scientific research. In this respect, it points out that scientific inquiry presupposes that every happening is produced by antecedent factors, and that when these causal antecedents are the only operative factors, they will rigidly determine the effects that follow. According to the Hard Determinist, even if investigators do not know the cause of a certain happening, say a malady such as amyotrophic lateral sclerosis, every investigator will operate on the assumption that it must have a cause and that in principle such an initiating occurrence can be discovered. The search for a necessary cause in science is important, the Hard Determinist affirms, because it is tied to what counts as a proper explanation. When we know the cause of a particular event we know *why* it happened and to know that is to explain the event. Moreover, the Hard Determinist emphasizes, B applies equally to physical and mental events. It is assumed that such mental states as depression, anxiety, fear, or jealousy are each caused by something; and it is one of the duties of the scientist to discover what this something is. In such cases, the search is for a causal explanation. But such a search presupposes the rigidity of the relationship between cause and effect. If this were not invariable, we would have no explanation as to why the consequence (say a particular disease) is produced by its antecedents. B thus rests on two main tenets: the principle that every event has a cause and a *ceteris paribus* clause.

Causality

Let us spell out, in a little more detail, the role played by causality according to Hard Determinism. Suppose that two persons are playing billiards. One of the players, taking his turn, will use a cue stick to hit a ball. The action of the stick occurs before the ball is struck and is the cause of the ball's forward movement. This train of events thus begins with a single antecedent event – the movement of the cue stick. On the assumption that no intervening factor or set of factors is involved (e.g., that the surface of the table is not extremely sticky or that the ball will not shatter when hit) the initiation of the cue stick is the cause of the ball's advancement. In the circumstances described the ball will necessarily move forward. If it does not then some other factor or group of factors must be present that prevents it from doing so.

The causal relationship in this case can be generalized. To say for any case that X is the cause of Y requires that three conditions be satisfied. First, X must be antecedent to Y. A cause can never temporally follow its effect. In the case just described, X is the movement of the cue stick and Y is the movement of the ball. "Antecedent" thus means the same as X's *occurring prior in time* to the occurrence of Y. Second, X and Y must be *juxtaposed*. This condition is designed to rule out cases of coincidence, for example that a whistle blowing at noon in San Diego is the cause of persons leaving their offices for lunch in San Francisco; and third, X and Y must be *constantly conjoined* (i.e., to say that fire causes smoke implies that when the former occurs the latter will always occur.) Necessity thus arises from this tripartite causal relationship provided that no intervening factors are present. When these three conditions and the *ceteris paribus* clause are satisfied X will invariably produce Y.

Some varieties of Hard Determinism identify Determinism with natural laws. (They represent the C conception.) They assert that everything that happens falls under the scope of a law of nature, and accordingly that any particular happening will follow an inexorable course. It is assumed, of course, that such preordination occurs only if the *ceteris paribus* condition is satisfied. Both human choices and the actions that follow are thus necessitated on this view. I shall discuss this interpretation of Determinism now in its application to physical or material occurrences and then later and in more detail its treatment of mental events. In physics there are many types of laws, of which causal laws are a species. All physical laws are principles that are formulated on the basis of conclusive evidence or tests and are held to be universally valid. To say that a law is universally valid does not mean that at every moment some event is taking place in accordance with that law but rather that at all times and places when the law applies to an event or a set of events, it will hold without modification. If there were no objects in the universe Galileo's Law of Falling Bodies would not apply to anything. Or if no bodies in the universe were freely falling then predictions based on the law would require modification. But since there are such bodies in outer space the law does apply to them as originally formulated. In such cases, a body acting in accordance with that law will traverse a particular distance in an exactly specifiable period of time.

Many physical laws are not causal laws. The principle of the lever states that equilibrium is obtained when two weights vary inversely to their distances from a fulcrum. Invariable relationships of this type do not assert a sequence in time and hence are not examples of causal order. Ohm's Law is another instance. It affirms that an electrical current is equal to the potential difference divided by the resistance. It does not assert a relationship between a prior event and a subsequent one but rather indicates that certain invariable relationships hold between measurable quantities. When events follow a temporal direction in which invariant relationships obtain between sets of occurrences, we have a causal law. It is the notions of direction and invariance that Hard Determinism fixes on. The claim is then made that, where events fall under the scope of causal laws, and where the *ceteris paribus* condition is satisfied, no alteration in the order of events is possible and hence that freedom of action does not exist.

Predictability

According to the Hard Determinist the ultimate aim of science is to arrive at a true theory of the world. The question is: "How can one tell when any theory is true?" and to that the answer is: "When it is able to make predictions that are verifiable." Let us return to Galileo for a moment. He predicted, from the law of falling bodies, that if the acceleration of a freely falling body is constant, the path of a missile fired from a cannon would be a parabola. This surprising conjecture was later verified by firing projectiles at sea level. Such tests required modifications in the hypothesis because of air resistance and variations in the speed at which different projectiles were propelled from the weapon. But even with these accommodations the flight patterns were close to being parabolas.

One should distinguish verifiable hypotheses from those that are not. By "verifiable," as the philosopher Karl Popper has emphasized, scientists also mean that in principle such predictions are falsifiable. The point applies especially to fate. The notion that whatever happens must happen does not have falsifiable consequences, since no matter what happens it can be said to be fated. One cannot even in principle describe an observation that would disprove the hypothesis, and accordingly the thesis cannot be a scientific truth. The distinction can be brought out by another example. Suppose one puts forth the claim that all human beings are mortal. If we should find a man who is three hundred years old does this show that the assertion is mistaken? Not necessarily, since he may die at the age of 400. To formulate a verifiable theory requires that it be sufficiently specific to be falsifiable. So if we modify the prediction that all men are mortal to say that no man will live to be more than 400 years and then find a man who is known to be 500 years old the hypothesis will have been shown to be false. It is thus a meaningful scientific conjecture, even if false. A true causal law cannot, of course, be falsified, but nevertheless it is falsifiable in principle. In the case of the Law of Falling Bodies, one can imagine conditions that would contravene the law. Freely falling bodies would be observed acting in ways not predicted by the law.

The impossibility of falsification is the basic objection to the thesis that every event is fated. According to that doctrine, we cannot conceive of an avoidable occurrence, and therefore even in principle the claim is not falsifiable. Hence, it cannot be a scientific law. This means that the concept of fate must ultimately be abandoned by any theorist who argues that Hard Determinism is the view that best captures the scientific method.

Still, this outcome does not deter a defender of that position. The concept of fate can be excluded from a revised version of Hard Determinism. Nonetheless the doctrine can still be defended on the ground that because scientific laws do give rise to accurate predictions, freedom of choice and action do not exist. The argument leading to that conclusion is simple: If one knows all the antecedent factors that produce a certain effect, and if those factors fall under the scope of a scientific causal law, the effect will be predictable with one hundred percent accuracy. And if that is the case, its occurrence is inexorable. Choice and action are subject to a similar analysis. They are the consequences of antecedent factors and, being predictable, are inevitable. Accordingly, freedom with respect to such happenings is not possible. The concept of accurate prediction is thus a powerful weapon in the armory of Hard Determinism.

Responsibility

The final component in Hard Determinism is its rejection of personal responsibility. This point of view is a consequence of the preceding argument about the accuracy of prediction. Once again, the argument is direct and simple. The Hard Determinist holds that if human choice and behavior are accurately predictable it follows that, like all events, they must be produced by causal antecedents. Assuming that no intervening factors are present, the contention is that if a man's choices and behavior are accurately predictable, he could not have chosen or acted otherwise; and if not he is clearly not free. This conclusion thus runs counter to the common-sense view, which holds that at least some of the time most of us are free to choose and act differently from the way we do. It also has important implications for moralists, politicians, and jurists. If the Hard

Determinist is right it makes no sense to hold anyone responsible for his or her actions. In everyday life we do not hold a rock responsible if it falls off a cliff in a heavy storm and injures someone. We do not do so – at least in part – on the ground that the rock could not have avoided doing what it did. Its actions were dictated by irresistible forces. The argument is thus that if the rock could not have helped doing what it did, neither could a criminal who is motivated by social or environmental conditions over which he has no control. We do not punish or blame the rock and therefore by parallel reasoning we should adopt a similar stance toward the criminal. The Hard Determinist point of view, including its attitude toward responsibility, can be supported by powerful arguments. Let us now consider two of these, the first based on psychological/social factors and the other on genetic considerations.

TWO ARGUMENTS IN FAVOR OF HARD DETERMINISM

A psychological argument

As pointed out above, the doctrine we are calling "B" is a specific version of Hard Determinism. It maintains that all events, whether mental or physical, are the products of antecedent factors or causes that rigidly determine their effects. I shall concentrate on it because in the philosophical literature it is the most widely espoused form of Hard Determinism, and it has widespread support in the social sciences and biology. In psychology the view is found in various forms of behaviorism and psychiatry. Rather than attempting to survey all such variants, I shall focus on an argument generated in a paper by a philosopher, John Hospers, that relies on psychiatric (especially Freudian) concepts. Hospers' essay, "What Means This Freedom?" was first published in 1961 and has appeared in various collections since. It has reached the status of a classic because of its compelling (and to some, unsettling) argument that the actions of countless numbers of criminals and of all neurotics should be exempted from responsibility. But it is not just its application to such individuals that commentators have found to be controversial. It can be interpreted as applying to human beings in general. This extension rests on the idea that all human beings are motivated by unconcious psychological factors that rigidly compel their behavior. The conclusion reached via this analysis is that no one can choose or act otherwise, and accordingly that freedom of the will is an illusion. Hospers arrives at this judgment via a series of deepening steps.

Here is how his argument begins:

> There are many actions ... for which human beings in general and the courts in particular are inclined to hold the doer responsible, and for which, I would say, he should not be held responsible ... his behavior was brought about by unconscious conflicts developed in infancy, over which he had no control and of which (without training in psychiatry) he does not even have knowledge. He may even *think* he knows why he acted as he did, he may *think* he has conscious control over his actions, he may even *think* he is fully responsible for them; but he is not. Psychiatric case-books provide hundreds of examples. The law and common sense, though puzzled sometimes by such cases, are gradually becoming aware that they exist; but at this early stage countless tragic blunders still occur because neither the law nor the public in general is aware of the genesis of criminal actions. The mother blames her daughter for choosing the wrong men as candidates for husbands; but though the daughter thinks she is choosing freely and spends a considerable amount of time "decid-ing" among them, the identification with her sick father, resulting from Oedipal fantasies in early childhood, prevents her from caring for any but sick men, twenty or thirty years older than herself. Blaming her is beside the point; she cannot help it, and she cannot change it. Countless criminal acts are thought out in great detail; yet the participants are (without their own knowledge) acting out fantasies, fears, and defenses from early childhood, over whose coming and going they have no con-scious control (pp. 26–27).

In this quotation, Hospers is arguing against one of the tenets of the common-sense view. He remarks that the law and common sense have been culpable in failing to recognize that the behavior of *many* human beings is motivated by unconscious psychological factors over which they have no control and for which they therefore should not be held responsible. At least three points of interest can be elicited from this citation. (1) The argument presupposes a theory about the roles played in human behavior by the unconscious and the occurrence of childhood traumas. This is a doctrine that is still widely espoused by psychiatrists and psychologists, though not necessarily in the form originally developed by Freud, and accordingly must be taken seriously. (2) Hospers asserts that it is not merely some criminal but also some non-criminal actions that should be exempted from responsibility. In this connection, he cites the case of a young woman who thinks she is freely "deciding" whom to marry, but whose "decisions" are determined by "Oedipal fantasies" of which she is unaware. (3) According to Hospers, most of the persons he is speaking about suppose that they are free to behave otherwise. But this is an illusion, and it is this claim that supports his rejection of the common-sense belief in freedom of the will.

This complex train of reasoning does not yet constitute an endorsement of Hard Determinism. Hospers at this stage of the essay cautiously restricts the scope of his remarks to "countless" criminal actions and to specific cases of idiosyncratic behavior. However, as the essay continues he broadens its thesis to include *all* cases of neurotic behavior. He does so in the course of explaining what he means by "responsibility." He writes:

> There is still another criterion, which I prefer to the previous ones, by which a man's responsibility for an act can be measured: the degree to which that act can (or could have been) *changed by the use of reasons*. Suppose that the man who washes his hands constantly does so, he says, for hygienic reasons, believing that if he doesn't do so he will be poisoned by germs. We now convince him, on the best medical authority, that his belief is groundless. Now, the test of his responsibility is whether the changed belief will result in changed behavior. If it does not, as with the compulsive hand washer, he is not acting responsibly, but if it does, he is. It is not the use of reasons, but their *efficacy in changing behavior*, that is being made the criterion of responsibility. And clearly in neurotic cases no such change occurs; in fact, this is often made the defining

characteristic of neurotic behavior; it is unchangeable by any rational considerations (pp. 31–32).

In this passage the set of individuals who should not be held responsible for their actions is broadened to include neurotics. They are defined as those whose behavior cannot be changed by rational considerations. This is so because they are "acting out fantasies, fears, and defenses from early childhood, over whose coming and going they have no conscious control." So now the set of those who should be exempted from responsibility has been widened to include all neurotics, as well as "countless criminals," and some "normal" persons, such as the young woman who is trying to decide whom to marry. But even such an extension of the total class of those exempted from responsibility does not entail the B version of Hard Determinism. To arrive at that position requires another step which Hospers, with some trepidation, ultimately takes. This is the thesis that, as he puts it, even "the so-called normal person is equally the product of causes in which his volition took no part." The theory of unconscious motivation is thus true of everyone. Even those who are regarded as normal are subject to unconscious drives over which they have no control. So the conclusion to be drawn from Hospers' steadily deepening analysis is that nobody can choose or act otherwise, and hence that no one is ever free. The outcome of this train of thought is thus Hard Determinism – just as some of Hospers' critics have contended. The following passage supports their interpretation:

> But one may still object that so far we have talked only about neurotic behavior. Isn't non-neurotic or normal or not unconsciously motivated (or whatever you want to call it) behavior still within the area of responsibility? There are reasons for answering "No" even here, for the normal person no more than the neurotic one has caused his own character, which makes him what he is. Granted that neurotics are not responsible for their behavior (that part of it which we call neurotic) because it stems from undigested infantile conflicts that they had no part in bringing about, and that are external to them just as surely as if their behavior had been forced on them by a malevolent deity (which is indeed one theory

on the subject); but the so-called normal person is equally the product of causes in which his volition took no part. And if, unlike the neurotic's, his behavior is changeable by rational considerations, and if he has the will power to overcome the effects of an unfortunate early environment, this again is no credit to him; he is just lucky (p. 34).

We can summarize Hospers' argument as follows:

1. Countless criminals and some normal persons are motivated by unconscious conflicts in infancy over which they have no control. Psychiatric case books are replete with such examples.
2. This is also true of all neurotic individuals, who are defined as those whose behavior cannot be changed by rational considerations.
3. So-called "normal persons" are equally the products of causes in which their volitions played no role.
4. Therefore, the behavior of all persons is motivated by unconscious factors over which they have no control, and accordingly no one is ever free to act otherwise.

Although Hospers does not argue that such unconscious factors can be explained as actions initiated by the genes, this is a plausible extension of his view. We shall discuss such an amplification in the next section. The conclusion to be drawn from this line of reasoning is that those who think they have conscious control over their actions, and even think they may be fully responsible for them, are deluded. Hospers' aim is to rid human beings of such self-deception by convincing them that the B version of Hard Determinism is true.

A genetic argument

According to some biologists, Hospers' psychiatric approach, with its emphasis on the unconscious, is a primitive, folk-theoretical account that modern science has rendered obsolete. Instead, they assert that it is one's genetic makeup that determines what they call "basic human behavior." Their arguments are admittedly less sweeping than Hospers', being confined to basic behavior, but nonetheless they provide strong support for the B version of Hard Determinism. For these theorists it is the genes that are responsible for such behavior: they are the causes of intelligence, aggression, alienation, and achievement, *inter alia*.

I will now turn to one such argument, recently advanced by the noted biologist S. J. Singer. It can be found in chapter 6, "Behavior and the Genes," in his book, *The Splendid Feast of Reason*.

Singer begins by accepting the nature/nurture distinction, that is, the idea that human behavior falls into two incompatible classes: innate or learned. As an alternative to these familiar notions, he introduces a somewhat different terminology in which "basic" or "fixed" behavior is contrasted with "environmentally influenced" or "malleable" behavior. His view also crucially relies on a principle of evolutionary development. This is the idea that animals can be classified as more or less primitive, depending on the degree of complexity of their nervous systems. Bacteria stand at one end of this scale and human beings at the other. He argues that scientific evidence strongly supports the inference that the behavior of living beings at the lower limit of this series is primarily determined by fixed genetic programs. In this connection he cites the migrations of birds and the organizational powers of ants (and will provide more detailed examples later). In contrast, the behavior of animals with more intricate nervous systems, such as human beings, exhibits less reliance on genetic makeup and more on environmental influences. But that such malleable behavior exists does not imply that the genetic component in human behavior is negligible. Quite the contrary. It is the main determinant of basic behavior (a concept to be discussed in greater depth below), and again the scientific evidence for which is strong.

Singer thus categorically rejects the Enlightenment idea – primarily stemming from John Locke – that the human mind is an empty receptacle in which the genetic contribution to behavior is non-existent. In this respect, his view anticipates Steven Pinker's in *The Blank Slate: The Modern Denial of Human Nature* (2002). Locke says: "How does the human mind become imprinted with knowledge? To this I answer in one word, 'Experience'." Singer's view is that the biological evidence runs counter to this position. It shows that *basic* behavior in human beings is governed by genetic factors. They determine what an individual is *able to learn*. Here is a passage that concisely expresses his point of view:

> The evidence supports the view that each individual's genetic makeup greatly influences, from the cradle to adulthood, his or her capacities for the learning of behavior. To account for the evidence from behavioral studies of identical twins ... one must conclude that the genes largely determine what an individual is *able* to learn, what one selects from experience to retain or emphasize, and how one transforms such selective learning into basic kinds of behavior. Furthermore, recalling the genetic diversity that is inherent in the human species, this view therefore means that each individual brings a different genetic background to bear on what one learns, what one comes to believe, and how one learns to behave. In this scenario, the essential roles of the environment and of learning are not so much to determine an individual's basic behavior, but rather to influence the extent to which the more or less fixed genetic potential of that basic behavior is realized and specifically directed. In this view, there is no way that Ronald Reagan, however his early environment might have been rearranged, could have become another Albert Einstein; on the other hand, without proper infant nutrition, a decent family life, and a good education, all acquired by nurture, it is highly probable that Albert Einstein would not have fully achieved his own genetic potential (pp. 86–87).

Obviously the distinction between basic and environmentally conditioned behavior is key to Singer's theory. It is pretty clear what he means by environmentally conditioned or malleable behavior. That most Americans speak English and that most Brazilians speak Portuguese are behaviors learned in particular contexts and through interactions with other persons living in comparatively localized areas. They are palpably the outcome of environmental influences. But what does he intend by "basic" behavior? Clearly he does not wish this concept to mean the same "as behavior governed by genetic factors." If it did, his contention that basic behavior is motivated by one's genetic makeup would be trivial, a definitional truism. (Singer will eventually lay out the data in support of their logical independence.) It is thus evident that his aim is to put forth a verifiable scientific theory about human behavior. We can elicit some clues about what constitutes basic behavior from the preceding paragraph, and using this material and some other, we can explain why "basic behavior," and "behavior governed by genetic factors," do not mean the same thing. It will be helpful to start with some examples he gives.

He thinks that I.Q., well-being, achievement, stress reaction, social closeness, alienation, aggression, control, harm avoidance, absorption, and traditionalism are examples of basic behavior. Some of these notions are technical and are used by psychologists in multiple personality questionnaires. Without trying to determine what each of these means, let us take one feature that is part and parcel of everyday discourse, namely I.Q., or intelligence. Using it we can explain why Singer's characterization of basic (as distinct from malleable) behavior is not trivial. The answer turns on another distinction, that between dispositions and occurrences. In effect, Singer is offering a dispositional account of basic behavior. A disposition is the inclination, tendency or power of anything to act in a certain manner under certain circumstances. Some common examples of dispositions: fragility, flammability, solubility.

Take "solubility," for example. To say that sugar is soluble means that if a specific quantity of sugar were put into a particular kind of liquid it would dissolve. "Dissolving" is an event that occurs at a particular time and place. For example, if one puts a teaspoon of sugar into a cup of coffee at 9 A.M. on a given Tuesday it will quickly dissolve. But solubility is not an occurrence. Sugar sitting in a bowl is not dissolving. Thus to say that sugar is soluble means that if it were subjected to a certain procedure it would dissolve. Solubility is thus the capacity (or disposition) of a substance to act in a certain way in specifiable circumstances. The resulting action (say, dissolving) is an occurrence.

For Singer basic behaviors are dispositional. To say that a particular man, John Smith, is intelligent is to attribute an aptitude to him. It means that in specifiable circumstances, such as when taking an examination, he will do well. His intelligence is a potentiality that is manifested in a performance, and a performance is an instance of learned (environmentally conditioned) behavior. Without appropriate training it is doubtful that Smith would be successful. But unlike his performance his intelligence is not an occurrence or a happening. If Smith were suffering from an illness, he might not pass the examination. But such a failure, given the extenuating circumstances, would not entail that he is not intelligent. It would be like trying to dissolve sugar in ether or chloroform – it just will not work. But that does not entail that sugar is not soluble. You just have to start with the right liquid. This is roughly the case that Singer mentions with respect to Einstein. He points out that without proper nutrition, a decent family life, and a good education, it is highly probable that Einstein would not have fully achieved his own genetic potential. That potential is a disposition; and it is that sort of propensity that Singer characterizes as basic behavior.

Given the distinction between basic and non-basic behavior, what is the evidence that basic behavior is driven by genetic factors, and accordingly that the two concepts are logically distinct? Singer begins his answer by citing evidence about animal behavior. Out of many possible examples, he chooses two to discuss in detail. The first involves the cuckoo bird – and because of the length of the passage I shall bypass it here. The second concerns the behavior of spiders. Here is a key paragraph:

As a second example of the genetic control of a complex behavior, consider the construction of spider webs. Many of us have no doubt been fascinated at one time or another watching a spider build a gorgeous web. Those species of spiders that spin webs rely on them completely for their food supply, so these webs are not just a casual artistic display; they have been refined during evolution by the processes of natural selection to enable these spider species to survive. The spinning of webs is not learned. If spiders are raised from birth in isolation from other spiders and are then released into the wild on reaching maturity, they proceed immediately to construct that species' characteristic webs. The first web is already perfect. The information for web spinning is therefore innate in these spiders. It must somehow be encoded in their genes. This genetic program includes the structural features of web spinning, such as the extraordinary properties of the several kinds of spider silk proteins that make them so suitable for producing ultra-thin threads of great tensile strength and appropriate elasticity and the special body parts (the silk glands and the spinnerets) involved in the spinning process. But I am not here concerned so much with the material components of web spinning, remarkable as they are, as I am with the spinning operations themselves. These operations in their most highly evolved forms constitute an astonishing feat of engineering know-how, but no spider ever had to go to MIT to learn how to do it. (For those interested, some of the almost incredible details are collected in several sources listed in my notes.) (pp. 88–89)

The heart of Singer's argument in the preceding citation is contained in five brief sentences:

The spinning of webs is not learned. If spiders are raised from birth in isolation from other spiders and are then released into the wild on reaching maturity, they proceed immediately to construct that species' characteristic webs. The first web is already perfect. The information for web spinning is therefore innate in these spiders. It must somehow be encoded in their genes (p. 89).

Singer is pointing out that if all behavior is either innate or learned (where these are exclusive categories) and if spiders are raised in conditions where they cannot learn from other spiders, then it follows that their capacity to spin specific types of webs is innate. This is a very tight, highly compelling piece of reasoning. And it is that argument that is then transferred to the human case. It will thus follow that *all* basic human actions are genetically determined. Here, in his own words, is the evidence that Singer advances to support this conclusion:

Particularly informative have been behavioral studies carried out on human twins. Twins are of two kinds, fraternal and identical. The former arise from an infrequent event: two independently fertilized eggs are nearly simultaneously implanted in a woman's uterus and produce two separate embryos that come to term at the same time. Fraternal twins are thus genetically different, equivalent to any other two siblings born at different times to the same mother and father. Consequently, fraternal twins can be of different sexes and may look no more alike than any other two siblings. Identical twins in contrast, arise from a single fertilized egg when, on relatively rare occasions in early embryonic development, the single embryo splits into two and each embryonic fragment goes on to develop fully. (If this process occurs too late in embryonic development and is incomplete, Siamese twins result.) As a consequence, identical twins have identical genetic endowments, which are, of course, reflected in their same sex and nearly indistinguishable physical features.

Identical twins therefore permit a kind of natural experiment: namely, one can observe and compare the basic behavioral characteristics of two humans whose genetic constitution is identical but who, if they were reared apart from a very early age, have been subjected to different sets of environment influences. The basic behavioral characteristics of identical twins reared apart, presumably under significantly different conditions, can be compared with those behaviors of other identical twins reared together, presumably under closely similar conditions. If the environment is the primary influence on behavior, then the behaviors of any two identical twins reared apart should on average be quite significantly different; with twins reared together, the behaviors should be much more similar. By contrast, if genes are the primary influence, then identical twins reared apart should show strongly correlated behaviors that are not significantly different from the correlated behaviors of other such twins reared together. This enables us to explore the relative behavioral influence of genes and of the environment – of nature and nurture.

Careful scientific studies along these lines have been carried out, particularly by the Minnesota Center for Twin and Adoption Research, which was established in 1979. T. J. Bouchard and his colleagues summarized much of this excellent work in 1988 and 1990. Because quantitative measures of behavior, such as IQ tests for intelligence, are controversial, the investigators generally used several accepted tests for each behavior measured. What is more, even if the absolute value of a behavioral measurement such as IQ is controversial, when it is used as a relative measure of behavior between two groups of individuals, as in the twin studies, it has significance.

147

The results were clear. The average correlation for a behavioral measure between mature identical twins reared apart was generally quite high, ranging between 0.5 and 0.7 for a given behavior. (A correlation value of 1.0 represents a perfect correlation; 0.0 is a complete absence of correlation, such as we observe on average with any two randomly chosen individuals.) For a physical attribute such as fingerprint details, the correlation value was 0.97, close to 1.0, as expected. For IQ, the correlation was 0.7 to 0.8, a quite large value. Even more remarkable, however, the average correlation for almost all basic behaviors measured for mature identical twins reared together was not significantly different from the average correlation for identical twins reared apart. Hence, no environmental influence was detectable. In addition to IQ, a wide range of psychological, personality, and other behavioral characteristics, such as well-being, social potency, achievement, stress reaction, alienation, aggression, and traditionalism, were measured for the identical twins, with much the same results.

The comparison between identical and fraternal twins reared apart or together was also revealing. The average correlation coefficients for several behavioral characteristics were about half as large for fraternal twins as for identical ones who were reared either apart or together. Given that two fraternal twins have 50 percent genetic identity, compared to 100 percent for two identical twins, this value of half is consistent with a primary genetic role in determining these behaviors. Reinforcing this inference, fraternal twins reared together showed no greater correlation coefficients for these behaviors than did fraternal twins who had been reared apart; a significant environmental influence on these behaviors was thus not detected (pp. 93–95).

This argument exactly parallels the argument about spiders. The main difference between the two cases, as Singer emphasizes, is that nurture plays a greater role in the overall behavior of humans than it does with spiders. But with respect to fixed components of behavior, the genetic programs are equally strong. We may summarize Singer's view as thus supporting the B variant of Hard Determinism. His formulation of this view can be expressed in one sentence: *All basic human behavior is wholly determined by genetic factors.* It is our genes that are ultimately responsible for our propensities to choose and do. Accordingly, freedom of the will does not exist at the level of basic human action. I submit that this is a powerful, highly compelling addition to Hospers' psychological version of Hard Determinism.

INDETERMINISM

Let us now move on to the second of the three philosophical theories that in their differing ways provide challenges to the common-sense view. A common name for it is *Indeterminism*. Like the other philosophical doctrines, it is a cluster of views that have an ancient lineage. I shall concentrate on one – the most recent – often called "Action Theory." But all of the variants jointly possess a set of principles which justifies the use of a common appellation for them. Here is a list of the main ones:

1. There is a fundamental, irreducible difference between mind and matter.
2. Causality holds with respect to all material (or physical) events.
3. To say that causality holds with respect to material events means that, all other things being equal, those events are strictly determined by antecedent forces.
4. Accordingly, freedom of action does not exist in the material (or physical) world.
5. This is the world the physical sciences have traditionally explored.
6. The mental domain (which includes decisions, choices, intentions, etc.) is exempt from the causal nexus and is thus the locus of free will.
7. Insofar as the physical sciences are dedicated to discovering causal laws, their investigative activities do not apply to this domain.

It is clear from this list of maxims that Indeterminism represents a compromise between the common-sense view and Hard Determinism. It agrees with common sense that human beings can sometimes choose freely. But it also accepts the Hard Determinist principle that where causality applies freedom does not exist. This principle is genuinely philosophical in the sense that it depends on a specific, technical analysis

149

of causation. According to that analysis causality gives rise to necessity. Indeterminism also accepts this analysis. It thus differs in this respect from the common-sense outlook which is pre-philosophical and does not think or speculate about the nature of causality. In accepting the principle that where causal continuity obtains freedom does not exist, Indeterminism also concurs with Hard Determinism that no physical phenomena are exempt from causal laws. Classical indeterminists have thus generally accepted both 4 and 6. In doing so, they have assumed that every free action is divided into a mental and a physical component. This leads to a puzzle. If a physical event is the effect of a mental act it is difficult to see why the two are not causally related. And if they are it would seem that freedom is impossible. It is this dilemma to which Action Theorists will offer a solution. We shall examine their arguments to this effect below.

I will not offer a detailed, historical survey here of the many versions of Indeterminism that have been held by past philosophers. But a brief review of a few important precedents may help make a complex doctrine like Action Theory easier to understand. The idea that mind and matter are irreducibly different can be traced back to Plato, of course; but his is not a full-fledged specimen of Indeterminism since it lacks most of the causal features described in the preceding list. Probably the main modern source of this doctrine is to be found in two important works by Descartes: *Discourse on Method* (1637) and *Meditations on First Philosophy* (1640). According to Descartes, the difference between physical and mental phenomena is that the former have "extension," that is, length, and hence occupy a specific locus in space-time. But mental phenomena – ideas, wishes, decisions – are not extended. They have neither mass nor bulk and are not marked off by spatial or temporal boundaries. The distinction rests on a powerful intuition. If we ask: "How long is an idea?" or "How much does a thought weigh?" we can appreciate the contrast that motivates the Cartesian philosophy. This opposition is captured by item 1 on the list.

Descartes also held, possibly as a consequence of that provision, that mental phenomena are private and physical phenomena are public. Much of the subsequent epistemological literature has agreed with this judgment and, like him, has often expressed the private/ public opposition as an "internal/external" contrast. Mental phenomena are said to be internal and physical phenomena are said to be external to the mind. Mental phenomena are thus subjective in a way that physical objects are not. Descartes believed, and here he was again influential, that each human being has direct access to his or her own thoughts, feelings, and sensations, and hence cannot be mistaken about their existence. In contrast, access to the external world is always *indirect* (since it is filtered through each person's subjective sensations) and therefore that mistakes about the existence of physical objects are always possible. (This distinction is the source of the persistent problem of our knowledge of the external world.) Since the time of Descartes, his "two worlds doctrine" has frequently been taken to imply that scientific inquiry is limited to investigating the behavior of physical objects. In his superb *A New History of Philosophy*, Wallace I. Matson explains why the Cartesian philosophy has given rise to this implication:

> Descartes intended to reconcile the new mechanical philosophy with the traditional religious interpretation of the world by separating two spheres of reality in such a way that science would be supreme and unchallenged in the one, theology in the other. Body, including the human body, is unthinking extended substance, the proper subject for scientific physical investigation. Mind or soul, unextended thinking sub-stance, lies entirely outside the sphere of physical investigation. There can be no conflict between science and religion because the combatants are to be kept separate – only except that theology would have the last word, since God is the source of everything, body and mind alike, and the only substance in the strict sense of that which can exist no matter what else does or does not (p. 330).

Matson has put his finger on the essential point. As he says, for Descartes "Mind or soul, unextended thinking substance, lies entirely outside the sphere of physical investigation." Nearly all the

151

post-Cartesian variations of Indeterminism, including Kant's, incorporate this principle, adding the further stipulation that where causality obtains there can be no freedom. The intuition that underlies this stipulation is powerful. From a scientific perspective the world is a mechanical object. If one knows its structure (as defined by physical laws) and the antecedent events that precede a particular event, the effect produced by such a causal sequence is wholly predictable. Accordingly, that train of events could not be otherwise. When this notion is generalized, it follows that freedom is not possible in the physical world. With various, sometimes important, qualifications, this is the picture of Indeterminism that Descartes bequeathed to his successors.

One of the most prominent of these in the twentieth century was C. A. Campbell. In a paper, "Is 'Freewill' a Pseudo-Problem?" (1966), Campbell provided a vigorous and compelling defense of Indeterminism. He argued both that "causal continuity" and freedom are incompatible, and that it is only in the mental domain that freedom exists. The following passage contains an excellent summary of his position:

> Let us put the argument implicit in the common view a little more sharply. The moral "ought" implies "can." If we say that A morally ought to have done X, we imply that in our opinion he could have done X. But we assign moral blame to a man only for failing to do what we think he morally ought to have done. Hence if we morally blame A for not having done X we imply that he could have done X even though in fact he did not. In other words, we imply that A could have acted otherwise than he did. And that means that we imply, as a necessary condition of a man's being morally blameworthy, that he enjoyed a freedom of a kind not compatible with unbroken causal continuity (p. 119).

It will be noted that Campbell's argument ends with a curious remark. It begins with a reference to the common-sense view and describes one feature that is unquestionably part of that everyday outlook. This is the notion that ordinary persons attribute moral responsibility to an agent only if he could have done otherwise. This is why they withhold blame from psychotic or profoundly neurotic persons. But at the end of this passage Campbell attributes a maxim to the common-sense view that does not belong to it. This is his comment that persons of common sense believe that causality is inconsistent with free will. As I pointed out above, the common-sense view is non-technical in character and accordingly proffers no thesis about causality at all. The notion that causality and freedom are inconsistent is therefore not part of common sense. That Campbell defends this thesis is thus further evidence that he is advocating a philosophical theory, in this case a traditional Cartesian form of Indeterminism. But shortly after his essay was published in 1951, a new form of Indeterminism appeared on the philosophical scene that was to be called "Action Theory." Nearly a half-century later it is still one of the most widely espoused forms of moral philosophy.

ACTION THEORY

Among the philosophers who have held variants of this doctrine are William Dray, *Laws and Explanation in History*, 1957; G. E. M. Anscombe, *Intention*, 1959; Stuart Hampshire, *Thought and Action*, 1959; H. L. A. Hart and A. M. Honoré, *Causation in the Law*, 1959; and Anthony Kenny, *Action, Emotion and Will*, 1963. Unquestionably the most important modern statement of the view is to be found in A. I. Melden's *Free Action*, 1961. I shall quote from it below. Action Theory in these various hands, and especially in Melden's, has made new, highly significant contributions to Indeterminism. It holds, for example, that human actions (e.g., the decision to open a book or to go out for dinner) are not to be analyzed into two distinct components – a mental event and a physical event – that are causally connected. This is a special way of expressing principle 6 in the above list, that is, the Cartesian point that the human mind is exempt from causality. However, Action theorists also disavow some views that were crucial for Descartes – for example, that matter and mind are substances. They believe that the concept of substance is an outmoded holdover from Greek and medieval philosophies, often having a religious tint, and that the radical distinction they wish to make between mind and matter does not depend on this older supposition. But at the same time the overall conclusion that Descartes draws – that the universe is dualistic – is congenial to them. In turn it is probable that Descartes would have welcomed their form of dualism even if it differs in important respects from his original formulation.

Two later, more direct founts of Action Theory are Arthur Schopenhauer's *Die Welt as Wille und Vorstellung* (1819) (translated as *The World as Will and Idea* in 1883–1886) and Wittgenstein's *Philosophical Investigations* (1953). The first is a form of Cartesianism, the second is not. Both of these documents are sources of the notion that human actions are not to be analyzed into causally connected components. In *The World as Will and Idea*, Schopenhauer says:

> The act of will and the action of the body are not two different states objectively known, connected by the bond of causality; they do not stand in the relation of cause and effect, but are one and the same thing.

> vol. 1, p. 100

This passage contains affirmations that were to become the foundation stones of Action Theory. These are that an act of will and the action of the body are not two different states or entities but are one and the same thing, and that an act of will and the action of the body are not causally related. We can add a third statement to this pair that also plays an important role in Action Theory. This is the idea that human actions are to be explained by proffering reasons rather than causes. Reasons are tied to purposive action, causes are not. We shall see below why they regarded these three propositions as justifying their contention that the human mind and its various activities stand outside of the causal order.

Schopenhauer's comment also greatly influenced Wittgenstein. In *Philosophical Investigations*, Wittgenstein is thinking of his famous predecessor when he writes:

> "Willing" is not the name of an action; and so not the name of any voluntary action either. And my use of a wrong expression came from our wanting to think of willing as an immediate, non-causal bringing-about.

A misleading analogy lies at the root of this idea; the causal nexus seems to be established by a mechanism connecting two parts of a machine.

p. 613

To this remark he quickly adds:

One imagines the willing subject here as something without any mass (without any inertia); as a motor which has no inertia in itself to overcome.

p. 618

In these characteristically compressed passages, Wittgenstein is making three points that were also to be incorporated into Action Theory: that "willing" is not the name of an action; that it is not an autonomous component of an action; and that to think of it as a massless action is to fall heir to a conceptual error based on a misleading analogy. The analogy consists in presupposing that willing functions in the human psyche in much the same way that a gear does when it turns a spindle. Both the gear and the spindle are independent parts of a machine. They are causally related, since the former produces a rotating motion in the latter. But to transfer this model to the mind is a mistake. The error consists in attributing mechanical powers to something that is non-mechanical. Since mental events lack mass, there can be no such thing as a "massless gear" or a "massless spindle." To suppose that a decision, say, causes a physical action, such as one's opening a book, is a second mistake. The relationship between the decision and the physical movement must be analyzed differently. In 1949, in *The Concept of Mind*, Gilbert Ryle was to call such an error "A Category Mistake." In his terminology the mistake lay in conceiving of mental events as "para-mechanical" forces. His point was that a conceptual model, illustrating how one mechanical part affects another, is misplaced when applied to decisions and the physical acts that follow.

Action Theory is thus "a battle against the bewitchment of our intelligence by means of language" (to use a famous phrase of Wittgenstein's). It is our language that seems to force a certain causal model on our ways of thinking about human action. Here is an example of how the model works.

While driving a car, one decides to make a left turn at the next corner. One does this – so the model insists – by first making a mental decision and then engaging in a physical action to carry it out. The decision consists in an exercise of the will. It is a mental act that initiates a causal process. That process is completed by a physical action, in this case extending one's arm out an open window. According to this highly intuitive analysis, the total act of signalling thus consists of two autonomous or independent occurrences, an act of will and a succeeding physical movement, that are causally connected.

Action theorists – following the suggestions made by Schopenhauer and Wittgenstein – claim this analysis is profoundly mistaken. As Melden states:

> In raising one's arm one signals – there is only one occurrence – for one does not raise one's arm in order to signal in the way in which one turns the ignition key in order to drive one's car out of the garage and onto the road. In the latter case two things are being done, one following the other; in the former one and only one occurrence is taking place.
>
> *Free Action*, p. 214

If the traditional view were correct, Melden and his colleagues argue, the human mind would be susceptible to causation in just the way the mechanical world is, and accordingly freedom of choice and action would be impossible. Action theorists are thus committed to all seven of the principles in our preceding list, plus at least one other – that a human action does not consist of separate components that are causally connected. So what is their counter-argument to this seemingly obvious analysis? Here is Melden's explanation:

> But is it possible, in general, to define action as bodily movement or happening plus desire? Only if we can understand what a desire is without invoking the concept of an action. Is this possible? Only if in our account of the action of raising one's arm, we do not invoke any desire to do, for example, the desire to notify others that one is about to make a turn. Or, if we do this, only if we go on to explain a desire to do in terms of a desire together with some feature of the desire which does not involve a reference

to doing at all – in which case the desire to do would then be 'reduced' to some sort of occurrence called 'a desire' having a feature that could be described without reference to any doing at all. Now what sort of a thing called a 'desire' could this possibly be? Here is one suggestion: the desire is a desire for something, for example, food that one will get if such-and-such things take place. Let us then see if it is possible to "explain" the desire *to do* in terms of a desire *for* something. In our example, this then is the situation: One is hungry; food is around the corner, so one notifies others that one is about to make a turn in order to get food; one desires to do what is needed in order to get the food; but to say that one desires *to do* these things can be explained or elucidated simply and solely in terms of the presence of a certain occurrence called the desire *for food*. On this suggestion, the notion of desiring to do is elucidated in terms of the logically prior notion of a desire for something (p. 118).

As Melden points out, a desire always requires an object. There cannot be a desire without there being something desired. So when one makes a left turn at the corner because one desires food, one is describing an entire action. The desire cannot be separated logically from its purpose or aim. The model that is being rejected presupposes that there can be, as it were, a "bare" desire and that this can independently be distinguished from the physical action that is presumably causally connected to it. But action theorists like Melden and company say – and here they are following Schopenhauer – that "the act of will and the action of the body are not two different states, connected by the bond of causality, but are one and the same thing." In rejecting the causal model, they are thus affirming that the tie between desire, decision, intention, etc. and a so-called physical act, such as extending one's arm, is "logical" and not "contingent." A desire and what it is a desire for is just like the relationship between being a husband and being married. In referring to someone as a husband, one is not giving a description of two separate entities – being a husband and being married – but to one thing, namely a married male. So it is with a human action, such as a desire, a choice, an intention, a decision, an opinion, a judgment. To say, for example, that one has made a choice entails that the content of the choice must be specified. It is logically impossible to describe a choice without describing its objective. So it will always be a choice to hire so and so, or to subscribe to this magazine rather than that, and so forth.

This account has two important consequences. First, it explains why the genes do not initiate choices and decisions; and second, why one must speak of reasons rather than causes in describing mental phenomena. It should by now be clear that genes are components of the physical world and accordingly that the role they play in conduct is causal. But to say this is to say they have no application to choice, decision-making or intention. They do play a generating role in various maladies, schizophrenia, for example. But persons suffering from schizophrenia do not have control over their anti-social or self-destructive actions, and accordingly insofar as their behavior stems from their genes, it does not fall within the purview of free action. Moreover, such behavior is not intentional or purposive; it is not initiated for any reason and is not aimed at any end. Being beyond the control of its proprietors it is determined by physical antecedents and hence is not a case in which the will is freely exercised.

An example may help make the point clearer. In deciding to turn left at a corner, one may signal by extending an arm. Various sorts of physical processes unquestionably accompany the raising of an arm. Let us suppose that there is an increase in vascular pressure in such a case. This increase may be one of the necessary conditions for an arm to rise and in that sense it can be described as one of the causes of such an event. But the decision to signal a turn was not the cause of one's arm's rising. The decision to signal and the raising of one's arm were one unit. Accordingly a causal relationship that connects two independent entities was not operative in such a circumstance. Hence the conclusion of Action theorists that one's genetic makeup is not a factor in free action.

This analysis thus leads by natural steps to the question: "What counts as an explanation of an action?" It is true that many different locutions, including causal talk, may be used in speaking about human actions. One might ask: "What caused him to signal for a left turn?" or "What impelled him to signal for such a turn?" and so on. But these locutions, Melden and his cohorts argue, are somewhat lax ways of speaking about one's purpose or aim or goal in signalling. And here the answer, they say, ultimately requires a reason: "He signalled *because* he wanted to make a left turn, and he wanted to make such a turn *because* he wanted to get something to eat." With all mental concepts, such as intending, deciding, desiring, and judging we must invoke purposive language in order to explain what was intended, decided, and desired. The desire *to do*, according to Melden, is thus to be explained as the desire *for* something. In contradistinction, the world of events that are susceptible to causal continuity is a mechanical world in which purpose plays no explanatory role. This is why, according to Indeterminists, there is an irreducible gulf between the mental and the material.

We can arrive at an interesting assessment of Action Theory if we consider it from an historical perspective, especially one that carries us back to Aristotle. In Chapter 1, I wrote the following about Aristotle:

> He thought that the basic question any theory should answer is: "Given that every object, whether man-made or natural, has a unique constitution (or essence) what is its special purpose or function?" Thus, as Aristotle saw it, a scientific investigation should uncover the essential purpose that any entity belonging to the natural world is designed to serve.

Aristotle has been widely criticized by commentators for failing to see that the natural world, the world investigated by science, is a kind of machine, operating according to mechanical laws. In that world the concept of purpose plays no role. The "why question" has been replaced by the "how question." Action theorists agree with this criticism of Aristotle. They regard the causal order as applying only to the world of matter, and that is a world exempt of purpose. But they have nonetheless been influenced by his vision, only they have transferred it from the natural order to the realm of the mental. It is here, they assert, that purpose plays a substantive role. They have thus reversed an Aristotelian conception that dominated Western philosophy from the time of the ancient Greeks to Galileo. Like Galileo they removed teleology from nature; but unlike the mechanically oriented science of the mind that Galileo's successors pursued, they reinstituted it within the realm of action.

Action Theory thus allows for freedom of choice *and* action. Hence it differs from all versions of Hard Determinism in denying that every physical action is necessarily part of a causal series. Raising one's arm in the process of signaling is a physical action, they agree, but it is not part of any causal sequence. Unlike traditional forms of Indeterminism it thus does not regard all physical occurrences as belonging to the mechanical world. The sharp cleavage between mental and physical happenings that Descartes, Kant, and C. A. Campbell draw is thus rejected. In this respect, Action Theory represents a new movement in Western philosophy. What is retained from traditional Indeterminism is the notion that where causality exists there can be no freedom.

SOFT DETERMINISM

Let us now consider a third philosophical position, Soft Determinism, that embodies much of the common-sense outlook but is dissimilar from it in at least one important way – in its analysis of causation. As we have emphasized throughout this chapter, common sense does not engage in much reflection about causation. In this respect it diverges from the philo-sophical accounts we have already considered and likewise from Soft Determinism, which like its philosophical congeners, depends on a tech-nical, subtle analysis of causation. Soft Determinism is thus a sophisti-cated theory that agrees with many things that Hard Determinism and Indeterminism say about causality. It concurs with the former that causal-ity applies to all events, whether mental or physical, and with the latter that freedom of choice and action exist. In opposition to these theories it holds that causation does not give rise to compulsion or constraint or indeed to any form of necessity, such as fate; and it also differs from them in main-taining that determinism (causality) and predictability are compatible with free will. For this reason, it is sometimes called "Compatibilism."

Soft Determinism has a long history. It can be traced back at least to the writings of St. Augustine (354–430 C.E.) for example. It is also found in some of the scholastic theologians, and becomes a prominent view in such seventeenth- and eighteenth-century writers as Hobbes and Hume. I will deal here with what is perhaps its most detailed and compelling formulation. This is an article that appeared just before the Second World War in a collection entitled, *University of California Publications in Philosophy*. Although the name of its author is not given, the paper is known to have been written by the late Paul Marhenke, who was at that time Professor of Philosophy at Berkeley. I will therefore refer to it as Marhenke's essay and will speak about Marhenke's views, opinions, and so forth in discussing it. (The essay is listed in the Bibliography under 'University of California Associates'.)

Marhenke begins by distinguishing between freedom and constraint/compulsion. He says:

> I am free when my conduct is under my own control, and I act under constraint when my conduct is controlled by someone else. My conduct is under my own control when it is determined by my own desires, motives, and intentions, and not under my control when it is determined by the desires, motives, and intentions of someone else ... Freedom, therefore, implies the existence of alternatives, any one of which I could have chosen had I so desired; compulsion implies the removal of one or more of these alternatives ... The restriction of an alternative is always effected by means of a command, regulation, ordinance, or law. Where there are no parking laws, for example, I can park my car anywhere along the street and for as long as my fancy pleases ... Even if I have no intention of violating the law, I am still constrained by it, because it prevents me from acting contrary to its provisions. My conduct is free ... only so long as my actions are not determined by a "must."

In this citation, Marhenke states that it is *always* commands, injunctions, ordinances, or laws that restrict freedom of choice and action. On this construal, one's freedom is limited by the actions of other human beings. It is they who formulate and implement the rules and regulations that reduce or eliminate alternatives. That constraint and compulsion are *always* the creations of human agency is an assumption that many philosophers, including C. A. Campbell, have challenged. They point out that a variety of inorganic causes – drugs, illnesses, natural catastrophes, and accidents – can affect human choice and behavior. From their perspective, Marhenke is not giving a correct diagnosis of the free will problem. It does not arise simply through human intervention, but also through the impact of inanimate events on choice and action. The objection is important because it challenges the solution that Marhenke will ultimately propose. Whether it undermines it will depend to a great extent on whether the Humean analysis of causation he adopts is accepted as cogent. That is a complicated matter that we shall consider in due course, but first let us see how Marhenke sets up the free will problem.

In his view, the issue arises via a two-step confusion. The first consists in confounding,

> the concept of compulsion (or constraint) with the concept of determination (or causation). The traditional formulation of the problem of free will assumes without question that compulsion, constraint, necessitation, determination, and causation are all synonymous. If the problem is to be solved, this assumption must be challenged. Our task, therefore, is to show that compulsion, constraint, and necessitation are not identical in meaning with determination and causation.

The second step is closely connected with the first. It consists in explaining *why* intelligent persons confuse determination (causation) with necessitation. The conflation arises through a failure to recognize that the concept of *law* is ambiguous: that it sometimes refers to *prescriptions*, such as parking or speeding laws, and it sometimes refers to *descriptions*, such as the law of falling bodies. These two kinds of laws have different properties. All prescriptions are the products of human activity: they include rules, regulations, commands, and orders. But all natural laws are descriptions of causal regularities. Prescriptions enjoin (restrict, compel, necessitate) behavior; but natural laws do not constrain or compel anything. The idea that causality involves necessity is thus a conceptual mistake. It was David Hume who first recognized that this is so, and Marhenke's argument that determinism and freedom are compatible ultimately depends on that account.

Its main point is worth repeating. It is that causality never entails necessity. Here, in summary form, is the argument that Hume gives in support of this conclusion. All scientific laws, he maintains, are generalizations based on past experience. Galileo's law of falling bodies is a case in point. It is the product of many observations conducted over a vast period of time. Despite the wealth of such evidence, is it *absolutely certain*? The answer, Hume says, is no. It is no because past experience is not an infallible guide to the future. It is thus *possible* that next year or in times yet to come the behavior of bodies will diverge from what it has been in the past. Perhaps the real law of falling bodies is cyclical. It may be that bodies have fallen at different times in the distant past, and only in accordance with Galileo's formula, $s = \frac{1}{2}gt^2$, for the past three or four millennia. In the future, they may revert to their earlier behavior. So we cannot know on the basis of past observational data that Galileo's formula is necessarily true.

Those who attribute certitude or necessity to scientific laws fail to understand that they differ intrinsically from logical or mathematical theorems. The latter are necessary; they hold come what may. Hume claims that they are tautologies and never get beyond the linguistic level to the world of fact. Knowledge about matters of fact, he argues, is not merely linguistic or conceptual: it ultimately derives from the kind of evidence that the senses provide. All causal laws are based on such data. But no amount of observational support is sufficiently strong to entail certainty about matters of fact. Because that is so all causal relationships, including the regularities we call "laws," are contingent. To say they are "contingent" is to say they are not necessary, that is, that their negations are logically consistent or that it is possible to describe or imagine circumstances in which such laws would fail. It follows from this Humean analysis that scientific laws never give rise to necessitation. In the essay from which I have quoted, Marhenke assumes rather than expressly articulates this principle, but it is the real basis for his distinction between prescriptive and descriptive laws. He is, in effect, presupposing that all natural laws are contingent. His argument thus reduces to the contention that natural laws are descriptive in character and that the causal regularities they describe are probable only.

Marhenke's proposed solution to the free will problem is thus that when these two conceptions of law are distinguished the problem simply vanishes. This resolution of the problem is buttressed by an additional argument he advances which holds that the concept of "the will" applies only to living organisms, such as human beings, and not to inanimate objects, such as planets or molecules. Items of the latter sort do not have a "will" or indeed any form of consciousness, and hence the antecedent events that affect them do not eliminate any of their alternatives. As he says, the laws of planetary motion do not force the planets to follow eliptical orbits, since a planet, not being conscious, cannot have the desire to travel differently from the orbit specified by those laws.

Clearly his solution depends on his thesis that causal laws are descriptive, and as such do not constrain or compel any form of behavior. In order to feel the full force of his position, I shall quote him at length.

> Formulas that make predictions possible are known as *laws*. Thus Kepler's laws enable astronomers to predict the future positions of the planets when their positions at a given instant are known ... The law of falling bodies not only fails to state that a given body is now falling from the position P; it does not even state that there are falling bodies. Similarly, Kepler's laws convey no information either about the present positions of the planets or about their number, nor do they even assert that there are planets. Laws merely express regularities of connection between physical quantities and properties. If they are interpreted as making assertions about the physical world, their import is hypothetical. Thus, the law of falling bodies may be taken to assert that if a body falls from position P, then the distance it falls increases as the square of the time. That the body falls from the position P can be ascertained only by observation. But once we have ascertained this fact by observation, we are not dependent on future observation for our knowledge of the future positions of the body. Its future positions can be calculated by means of the law ...
>
> We revert now to the concept of determination, since it was for the sake of clarifying its meaning that we undertook to analyze the concept of law. The considerations that generate the problem of free will, we may recall, make no distinction between determination, causation,

compulsion, and constraint. Determination and causation are, indeed, identical concepts. "A determines B" and "A causes B" are identical propositions. Thus we say, indifferently – that is, without intending a difference of meaning – that the increase in the temperature of an iron rod *causes* an increase in its length or that an increase in its temperature *determines* an increase in its length. When we inquire into the meaning of determination (or causation) we must ask ourselves: "Under what circumstances do we regard these statements as being true?" The answer to this question is implied in our analysis of the concept of law. We say that an increase in the temperature of an iron rod determines an increase in its length when the increase in length can be calculated or predicted. And this calculation can be made when we have a law that connects the increase in length with the increase in temperature. Determination therefore means predictability by means of a law. In general, we say that A determines B when B can be calculated or predicted, given A. And B can be predicted, given A, when we have a law that connects the properties of B with those of A. Hence, determination does not mean compulsion. The increase in temperature does not compel the increase in the length of the iron rod. When we say that A compels B, we imply that A and B have desires and volitions, and are therefore conscious organisms. The notion of compulsion is obviously inapplicable to the iron rod that is being heated by a flame. The flame does not desire the iron to expand, and the iron neither complies with any such desire nor does it resist any intentions of the flame. Neither the iron nor the flame is conscious, hence they are alike incapable of desire or volition.

The confusion between determination and compulsion seems to be explained by the fact that we speak of the determination of B by A whenever A and B are connected by a law. The laws of nature, it might be said, hold without exception; they cannot be transgressed. Hence, when A and B are connected by a law, the happening of B is necessitated whenever A has happened. The iron rod cannot avoid expanding when it is being heated, because its failure to do so would involve the violation of one of nature's laws. The law prescribes what the iron must do when its temperature is increased.

We have only to state the assumptions of this argument in order to expose the fallacy on which it rests. The argument assumes that human and natural laws have something in common, namely the fact that they are both prescriptions ... It is this assumption that constitutes the fallacy. For human laws are rules of conduct, constraining conduct by the threat of penalties for violations of the rules. They prescribe the things one ought to do and and prohibit the things one ought not to do. In short, they are imperatives. But natural laws are not imperatives and they have nothing in common with human laws except the name ... Natural laws do not prescribe the happenings that ought to take place; they describe the happenings that do take place. The law of falling bodies describes how bodies actually fall; it does not prescribe or command how they ought to fall ... We are, therefore, victims of a confusion of ideas when we say that the planets are forced or compelled by the laws of planetary motion to follow elliptical orbits, or that the manner in which a body falls is constrained or necessitated by a law. Compulsion, as we have seen, presupposes the existence, or at least the possibility, of desires and intentions, which seek the realization of actions incompatible with the actions performed under compulsion. A planet, not being conscious, could not have the desire to travel on any orbit incompatible with the orbit specified by the laws of planetary motion.

The difference between a natural and a human law, to sum up, is the difference between a description and a prescription. A description is either true or false; a prescription is neither. A prescription can be obeyed or disobeyed; a description can neither be obeyed nor disobeyed. A prescription is a constraint on action; a description can by its very nature never encounter opposing desires.

As this long discussion makes plain, Marhenke's way of dealing with the free will problem amounts to "dissolving" it. The dissolution consists in showing that the problem is an artificial creation generated by conceptual confusions. Among these are the failure to distinguish compulsion from causality and prescriptions from descriptions. The dissolution of the problem is completed when it is recognized that the concept of the "will" does not apply to inanimate entities. The idea that the flame compels an iron bar to expand is a mistake that rests on the indefensible supposition that the bar does not wish to expand. To think in this way is to fall heir to the "pathetic fallacy." It is the error of attributing thoughts and desires to inanimate objects.

The key move in Marhenke's approach is that causal (descriptive) laws do not mandate or force anything to happen. In this respect they differ from the regulations and ordinances generated by human beings. Consider the law of falling bodies as an illustration. It does not compel or force any entity to fall. Its import is hypothetical. It states that *if* a body is freely falling it will take a specific amount of time to traverse a certain distance. A person may intervene in the course of nature, by dropping a body, and if that happens its subsequent course is predictable. But the law does not compel the person to drop the body or to do anything else. No natural law compels or restrains anything, and hence has no effect on what any human being desires or wishes to do. The upshot of the argument is that causality, determinism, and predictability are perfectly consonant with freedom of choice and action.

The intuition that lies behind this outlook is a profound and compelling one. Consider the following example. A psychiatrist may come to know a patient's psychological makeup very well. He may thus be able to predict when that person will commit a violent crime. The psychiatrist is thus invoking a psychological law which states that given such and such antecedent factors any human being will behave in such and such a fashion. But from the fact that the psychiatrist, using such a generalization, can predict a particular case of behavior, it does not follow that his knowledge and the prediction based on it compel that person's actions. They stem from the patient's desires, intentions, and volitions. In Marhenke's view the patient could have chosen and acted otherwise.

This analysis, as I mentioned earlier, is espoused by many theologians. They argue that God's foreknowledge is consistent with human freedom and responsibility. Even though God created the cosmos according to a detailed plan, and therefore knew from the moment of creation that Adam and Eve would later sin, their culpability was not caused by him. The fact that God created the kinds of personalities that Adam and Eve possessed does not entail that he caused them to behave as they did. Their actions stemmed from their characters. All of us are subject to influences that produce the different sorts of persons we are. So from the mere fact that a particular character was formed by antecedent events, including genetic influences, it does not follow that its possessor does not have free will. That the characters of Adam and Eve were produced by God does not therefore entail that God compelled them to do anything. Their sin was not God's but theirs. This theological analysis is thus a form of compatibilism; it holds that foreknowledge and predictability are consistent with choosing and acting otherwise.

Does it, however, meet the challenge issued by C. A. Campbell and by many other philosophers, who assert that if God created Adam and Eve, instilling in them the dispositions to sin, they could not have acted otherwise and therefore were not free? I think it does. Let us see how Marhenke would deal with this objection.

He is unquestionably correct in holding that the "will" is a concept that applies only to living organisms; and accordingly that the concepts of freedom of choice and action do not apply to planets and iron bars. But since Adam and Eve were not inorganic entities, this response does not meet Campbell's objection. Marhenke is also correct in saying that God did not pass any law or regulation that compelled Adam and Eve to behave as they did. In giving them the intelligence, desires, and volitions they possessed he was at the same time giving them the capacity to choose and to act otherwise. That he could predict that they would sin is thus not inconsistent with their having free will. Marhenke's view is, then, that even in the case of the Creator, the possession of divine foreknowledge does not entail constraint or compulsion. But this response, as good as it is, is still insufficient to quell the nagging worry that if one has a certain kind of character one could not act otherwise. We therefore need a stronger line of defense. This, in my opinion, is to be found in Hume's theory. According to it causality is a *contingent* relationship. To say that A causes B, where this relationship is subsumed under a natural law, is not to say that B *must* occur. It is always possible that any prediction based on a natural law will turn out to be false. It is thus always possible that fire will not cause smoke or that one's inability to handle stress will not result in violence. Therefore, causality must be differentiated from any form of necessitation. Hume's analysis is ultimately the basis for Marhenke's thesis that freedom and determinism are compatible. In my opinion, it is a good answer to Campbell's challenge.

THE PROBLEM OF EVIL

The preceding considerations bear on a closely related issue – the problem of evil. In the *Dialogues Concerning Natural Religion* (Part X) Hume calls it "Epicurus' Old Questions," and states that they are "yet unanswered." The problem is a complex logical/moral/theological issue, and it is especially acute for those who believe in the Judeo-Christian concept of God. In their view God is an infinite being. He is omniscient (all-wise), omnipotent (all-powerful), and benevolent. The problem that this conception generates stems from the seemingly obvious fact that evil exists in the universe. If God is omniscient, he could have designed a cosmos devoid of evil; if he is omnipotent, no force could have prevented him from bringing about such a situation; and if he is benevolent, he would have produced a world which is wholly good. But if he possesses these attributes why then is there evil? That is the classical problem. Some theologians have concluded from this set of premises that God cannot be at once omniscient and benevolent. A detailed exploration of this dilemma would take us into deep waters. We shall therefore restrict our discussion to an aspect of the problem, that is, to the narrower question of whether the attributes of omniscience and benevolence are compatible.

At the end of his essay Marhenke addresses this more limited problem and claims to solve it by means of the distinction between determination and compulsion. He writes as follows:

> The problem may be stated in the form of four hypothetical propositions. (1) If God is good, then man is a free agent. (2) If man is a free agent, then God is not omniscient. (3) If God is omniscient, then man is not a free agent. (4) If man is not a free agent, then God is not good. From these four propositions theologians have drawn the conclusion that God cannot be at once good and omniscient. This conclusion will not follow if any of these propositions are false. And since (1) is equivalent to (4) and (2) is equivalent to (3) the conclusion will be false if either (1) or (2) should turn out to be false. It is not difficult to show that proposition (1) is true. If man were not a free agent, God would not be justified in

meting out rewards and punishments for his actions, as He does, and He would therefore not be good. But proposition (2) is false. The thesis that God is not omniscient is supposed to be a consequence of the hypothesis that man is a free agent. If this thesis can be established at all it can only be established on the hypothesis of the indetermination of man's voluntary actions. Propositions (2) and (3) depend for their plausibility on the confusion between freedom and indetermination. On the supposition that man's voluntary actions are not determined, God would be unable to predict them if, like mundane scientists, He depended upon a knowledge of laws. If He is not so dependent (and there is no reason to suppose that He is), the indetermination of voluntary actions is no hindrance to his foreknowledge. For it follows from the law of excluded middle that in the instance of every one of my actions I either do A or I do *non*-A. If God has access to the truth, He can know which one of these alternatives is true. We conclude therefore, theologians to the contrary, that God's goodness is not incompatible with His omniscience.

Marhenke's solution is familiar; it is analogous to the claim that a psychiatrist who can predict a patient's behavior does not compel such behavior. God's omniscience is another example. His foreknowledge does not entail that human beings are not free or that he has caused them to act in ways that are morally reprehensible. Freedom thus allows for the possibility of both evil and predictability. The supposition that omniscience and goodness are inconsistent properties thus depends on the false belief that if man is a free agent God cannot foresee his choices and actions, including those that are evil. Once it is seen that omniscience does not entail compulsion or constraint the problem is resolved. His goodness and omniscience are then seen to be compatible. The resolution of the problem thus depends on accepting this thesis; and it in turn depends on accepting Hume's claim that causality never gives rise to necessity.

SUMMARY

In this chapter we have compared and contrasted three philosophical theories, measuring them in the process against a somewhat diffuse common-sense outlook about freedom of choice and action. Our contention throughout has been that common sense does not take a well thought-out, logically defensible position with respect to this issue. Philosophers have been sensitive to this liability and have tried to rectify it by developing theories about human action that are consistent and compelling. The three main philosophical accounts that we have considered are obviously inconsistent with one another. Hard Determinism, for example, holds that freedom and causality are incompatible, that is, wherever causality obtains, freedom is necessarily excluded. The Hard Determinist also maintains that causality holds universally. It follows from this conjunction of theses that nobody is ever really free to choose and act otherwise. Indeterminism accepts the claim that causality and freedom are inconsistent, but it disagrees with the Hard Determinist thesis that causality has no exceptions. It holds that causality does not apply to mental phenomena and accordingly that the mind is the locus of free will. Soft Determinism agrees to some extent with both of these theories. It accepts the Hard Determinist position that causality is universal, and the Indeterminist notion that freedom of choice and action exist. It dissents from both of these accounts, however, in holding that even where causality obtains freedom is possible. Its argument for this judgment is that causality (determination) must be distinguished from compulsion or constraint; and it supports this assertion with a Humean analysis of causation.

What inference should the uncommitted observer draw from this multilateral disagreement? My answer, as an independent observer, is that because these views are logically incompatible, and because each is so well-argued and convincing, none of them is an obvious choice to replace philosophically untutored common sense. We are thus left without any good options. We cannot decide between these compelling philosophical alternatives and we cannot rest content with the liabilities of common sense. My conclusion is that the issue is unresolvable. We can thus add to the list of unanswerable questions we have identified in this book still another – whether freedom of the will really exists.

5

WHERE DID THE UNIVERSE
COME FROM?

After having investigated a number of irresolvable problems, each of which has its own difficulties, we now confront what is perhaps the deepest of them all: "Where Did the Universe Come From? And What Is It Expanding Into?" The query arises because most ordinary persons understand the universe to be the totality of whatever exists. If they are right, the universe includes all of space and time, and possibly even such invisible things as God, souls, spirits, dark energy, and dark matter. The question is a profound one because it encompasses most of the other controversial matters we have investigated in this book – post-mortem survival, the existence of God, and the problem of evil, among them. It is also a challenging issue in its own right. If the universe is identical with the sum of what there is, nothing can be "outside" of it, so there can be nothing it could have come from or enlarge into. Yet, according to current astronomic orthodoxy it is rapidly and inexorably inflating. Moreover, if string theory is correct, there are multiple universes.

Non-scientists find it hard to understand these claims. What, for example, could the universe be expanding into? The question is an ancient one. The Italian philosopher, Giordano Bruno, posed it shortly before he was burned at the stake in the Campo Dei Fiori in Rome in the year 1600. Furthermore, although nobody doubts that there is at least one universe, most human beings find it incomprehensible that there is – or even that there could be – more than one. "Uni" – a fragment of the locution – clearly expresses singularity, as does the entire expression. Such synonyms as "cosmos" and "totality," as well as such adjectives as "catholic," "generic," and "whole," support this interpretation. From the perspective of everyday discourse it seems obvious that when cosmologists speak about multiple universes they are using the term in a special way.

The issue that results from these divergent interpretations is profound; it is essentially whether there is a pre-technical outlook that is deeper, more primitive, and conceptually prior to any description of reality that science can advance. Some eminent twentieth-century philosophers, including G. E. Moore, have defended such a position. They hold that common sense, in certain important respects, is absolutely correct in what it asserts. Thus, when ordinary speakers refer to the universe, implying by such usage that there cannot be more than one, they cannot be mistaken. So whether in the end the expert will have to defer to the non-specialist about whether there may be many universes is thus an interesting issue. But it is so complex we cannot explore it here. Instead, we shall now turn to three different attempts to answer the question. These come from science, theology, and philosophy, respectively.

A SCIENTIFIC ACCOUNT

Almost any book about modern astronomy is likely to be obsolete by the time it is published, including this one. With respect to string theory the remark is certainly apposite. It has generated an enormous, abstruse literature about the origin and future of the universe, much of which reads like science fiction. It is thus difficult for the average person to sort out what is strictly scientific from what is mere speculation. For example, many recent books produced by credible investigators speak about the possibility of human beings tunneling through black holes to parallel universes by means of time machines. In such visionary schemes causality is obliterated and all sorts of paradoxical consequences are possible – for example, meeting your parents before you are born.

Despite such recent, extravagent speculations, there are some theories that most professionals accept (although at least in one case with severe qualifications, as we shall see below). Among them are Einstein's special and general theories of relativity, and Hubble's Law. Each of these has had momentous implications. This is notably true of general relativity, which has revolutionized modern scientific thinking about gravity and space/time. Indeed, Frank Shu has described it as "one of the most beautiful artifacts of pure thought ever produced." It rests on three assumptions. The first is that the universe is homogeneous (i.e., the same everywhere at any instant in time); the second is that it is finite but lacks edges or boundaries; and the third is that it is static, that is, that its large-scale properties do not vary with time.

The second assumption – that the universe is finite – is now commonly challenged, and the third assumption, that it is static, has turned out to be mistaken. Nonetheless, even with these qualifications general relativity is a mainstay of contemporary cosmology. Max Tegmark is one of the investigators who has contested its thesis that space is finite. He writes:

> How could space not be infinite? Is there a sign somewhere saying "Space Ends Here – Mind the Gap"? If so, what lies beyond it? In fact Einstein's theory of gravity calls this intuition into question. Space could be finite if it has a convex curvature or an unusual topology (that is, interconnectedness). A spherical, doughnut-shaped or pretzel-shaped universe would have limited volume and no edges. The cosmic microwave background radiation allows sensitive tests of such scenarios (see "Is Space Finite?" by Jean-Pierre Luminet, Glenn D. Starkman and Jeffrey R. Weeks; Scientific American, April 1999). So far, however, the evidence is against them. Infinite models fit the data, and strong limits have been placed on the alternatives.
>
> "Parallel Universes," p. 42

The contravening evidence for the third assumption is based on a phenomenon that is commonly observed on earth. When a train approaches a bystander, its whistle sounds both louder and higher than it does after it has passed. That is the Doppler Effect, and it applies to any form of motion. It is not only true of sound but also of light. When viewed through a prism, light from an approaching object is shifted toward the blue end of the visible spectrum, and toward its red end when reflected from a receding object. This shift parallels the change in sound just mentioned.

Hubble's Law, named after the American astronomer, Edwin P. Hubble (1889–1953) is an application of the Doppler Effect to galactic phenomena. Before Hubble's findings, physicists from Newton to Einstein considered the cosmos to be static. What Hubble showed, contra the received opinion, was that it was motile and that its rate of movement is quantifiable. The equation he formulated (Hubble's Constant or Law) states that velocity = H × distance. What this algorithm means is that the greater the distance a galaxy is from a given frame of reference the faster it is receding. On the basis of telescopic evidence, Hubble claimed that all visible galaxies, except the Milky Way, exhibit the red shift and hence are moving away from the earth at a rate defined by his law. Unquestionably, the most important implication of this finding is that the universe is expanding. The symbol H denotes the rate at which the expansion is occurring. Hubble's original value for H (as of 1929) was 93 miles per second per one million light years. This estimate was later refined using more precise measurements. The current figure places the value of H as between 9.3 and 18.6 miles per second per one million light years.

Galaxies estimated by independent calculations to be the most remote exhibit the largest red shift and are judged to be moving away from the earth at a rate approaching the speed of light. (According to Einstein's special theory nothing can exceed the speed of light. This result is another constant that most cosmologists accept.) At its present rate of expansion, the universe is projected to be twice its present size in about twenty or thirty billion years. Another important consequence of Hubble's Law has been to provide an estimate of its age. The figure generally agreed upon is that it originated ten to twenty billion years ago. In current astronomical treatises almost all scenarios, from the origin of the universe to its ultimate demise, are based on the assumption that the Doppler Effect is universal. If this assumption should turn out to be mistaken most of modern cosmology would have to be tossed into a dustbin.

However, as far as we know, no reputable scientists have ever challenged Hubble's Law. The stories they tell about the universe, and which frequently differ in detail, begin with this finding as a rock-solid datum. Therefore up to a certain point there is a consensus about the overall nature of the cosmos, whose basis is Hubble's Constant and its uncontroversial implications. Let us therefore track that narrative as far as we can. It will tell us a lot about the early history of the universe and its future development. Once disagreement sets in the story becomes more diffuse and speculative. Shortly after we reach that boundary we shall turn to those disciplines where conjecture is the norm: to theology and philosophy.

THE SCIENTIFIC STORY

The consensual scientific narrative begins with an obvious point. Plainly, if the universe is expanding, then it must have been smaller in the past. This, of course, means that its galaxies and stars must have been closer together at one time than they are now. (Incidentally, it should be understood that by "now" one means that we are seeing these distant objects as they were eons ago. Light from some remote objects may have taken millions of years to reach the earth; so we are observing those entities as they were in the distant past. It is thus not even certain that some of them still exist.) A central problem in determining how much smaller the universe must have been at an earlier period is whether the rate of cosmic expansion has been uniform. Until recently this was thought not to be the case. In the early 1980s, for instance, it was asserted that the rate of expansion was slowly and steadily diminishing. This was believed because of the effect of gravitation on the galaxies and other supernal bodies. As these enormous entities move apart gravitational forces restrain their motions. It was thus expected that the tendency for the universe to expand would begin to diminish, thus affecting the rate of expansion, and ultimately leading to a massive contraction. The situation as so described was taken to be something like throwing a baseball into the air. As it leaves the player's hand it is traveling at a comparatively high speed, but as it climbs higher into the air, the earth's gravitational pull will gradually retard its forward movement and eventually will bring it down. The information provided by Hubble that the universe is expanding, it was generally agreed, had to be modified due to the gravitational effect on its components. However, more recent observations suggest that gravitational attraction is not sufficiently powerful to produce such a contraction. It is now (as of 2004) believed that the universe will continue to expand forever. But that gravitation plays a fundamental role in the development of galactic structures is still the received opinion.

The story continues with another widely accepted postulate. Newton had discovered that gravitation weakens as the distance between contiguous bodies widens, and he was able to quantify the diminution that occurs. This was expressed in his so-called inverse square law and it has been used by physicists and astronomers since the seventeenth century to calculate the orbits of the planets and the motions of asteroids, stars, and galaxies. The law implies, for example, that when the distance between objects is doubled the gravitational attraction between them drops to one quarter of its original value. Thus, if the earth (say) were relocated 186 million miles from the sun, rather than its mean actual distance of 93 million miles, it would be subject to twenty-five percent of the sun's pull that it now experiences. The algorithm is simple: square the distance and invert the total. Thus, twice the distance $2^2 = 4$ leads to a force of ¼. If the gap between the two bodies were five times what it is now the gravitational force would be only 1/25th of its present value. The calculation is again elementary: ($5^2 = 25$). Inverting 25 gives 1/25.

Assuming the validity of the Inverse Law, one can reasonably infer that at some earlier time (say about ten or fifteen billion years ago) the universe must have been much smaller in size than Hubble's Law now projects it to be. It must at that point have been so shrunken that individual galaxies would have been compacted together with no intergalactic spaces between them. Indeed, if calculations based on Hubble and Newton are correct, there must have been a time when there were no galaxies. The universe would have then been severely diminished in size. On the assumption that the total volume of galactic material would have been the same as is now observed, it follows that the density of matter would have been driven up to nuclear values and beyond. There would thus have been a contest between the compressing forces of gravitation and an expansionist response involving an immense increase in heat due to the augmented density of matter. If we pursue the scenario further we arrive at an object that is virtually squeezed to zero but having an infinite density and with an increasing propensity to explode. This compacted object is sometimes referred to as "The Original Atom." It is this inchoate fireball which burst forth with unimaginable violence and whose pieces are now the galaxies, stars, planets and comets that populate the cosmos we know. The enormous eruption that occurred is familiarly known as the Big Bang.

What would the state of the universe have been immediately after the big bang? The current, controversial answer is called "Inflation Theory." It is not sheer speculation that generates this theory but rather an extrapolation from observational data concerning background radiation left over from the big bang. Its central idea is that moments after the colossal explosion of the primeval fireball, space may have been in a state described as a "false vacuum," a condition, according to particle physics, that differs in complex ways from a true vacuum. This false vacuum was characterized by immense outward pressure that created a huge bubble of gas that eventually cooled to become the present universe. The evidence for inflation theory is based on discoveries made in 1965 of very short wavelength radio waves, so-called "microwaves." Measurements showed that these emanate from extragalactic space, and that they have an energy spectrum just a few degrees above absolute zero (−270°C). Most cosmologists are now convinced that these microwaves are remnants of a heated, diffuse gas from which the galaxies and other clusters were formed as the gas cooled. The evidence in support of this conjecture is that the radiation is equally strong in all directions, thus ruling out any local point of origin within the Milky Way. The suggestion, as I have indicated, is that this is a remnant of the primeval heat generated by the big bang.

The narrative based on the Einsteinian theories of relativity and on Hubble's Constant provides a persuasive account of the early history of the universe that takes us back to the moment when the primeval fireball exploded. But the scientific story stops at that point. With respect to the question, "Where Did the Original Atom come from?" we are offered a different sort of response – one that philosophers will find familiar. The suggestion is made that the question is meaningless since it presupposes that time existed before the big bang. The idea is now advanced by some theorists that time was created with the big bang; hence there was no before.

In *The Edge of Infinity: Where the Universe Came From and How It Will End* its author, Paul Davies, says this explicitly. He writes:

What, then, happened before the big bang? The simple answer is "nothing," for there was no "before." If the big bang singularity is accepted as a complete past temporal boundary of all the physical universe, then time itself only came into existence at the big bang. It is meaningless to talk about a "before." In the same way it is meaningless to ask what caused the big bang, for causality implies time; there were no events that preceded the singularity (p. 167).

But this statement hardly settles the issue. Clearly something existed before the big bang occurred. According to the tale that modern cosmology provides, that something was a rudimentary entity of incredible density, composed of all the material that comprises the present universe. The original question can then be rephrased – where did all that material come from? Was there a creation moment that created such a totality?

To one's surprise, perhaps, a number of scientists provide a positive answer to this last query. I will quote two. Here is what Professor Davies says:

The big bang was the beginning of time. Whether there will be an end of time for the whole universe is still an open question.

We can now view the creation as a special case of a naked singularity. Anything can come out of a naked singularity – in the case of the big bang the universe came out. Its creation represents the instantaneous suspension of physical laws, the abrupt flash of lawlessness that allowed something to come out of nothing. It represents a true miracle – transcending physical principles – that could only occur again in the presence of another naked singularity (p. 168).

Frank Shu also speaks of a creation event. Like Davies he suggests that the universe could have arisen from nothing.

Taken together, the discoveries of Hubble and Einstein gave rise to a new worldview. The new cosmology gave empirical validation to the notion of a creation event; it assigned a numerical estimate for when the arrow of time first took flight; and it eventually led to the breathtaking idea that everything in the universe could have arisen from literally nothing (p. 766b).

The idea that something could come from nothing is indeed breathtaking. It is perhaps the mark that distinguishes philosophy from science and theology. From the time of the Greeks to the present, philosophers have agreed that it is impossible that something could come from nothing. The principle expressed in Latin *ex nihilo nihil fit* – that from nothing nothing comes – is perhaps the motivating apophthegm for the many arguments that philosophers have advanced to prove there is a First Cause. The arguments were felt to be necessary since it was ruled out as a possibility that something could come from nothing. Yet as the quotations cited above establish, some modern scientists say the opposite. In this respect, they join forces with numerous theologians who have expressed just such a view. Does this mean that for these scientists modern cosmology is a form of religion – one that supports the existence of a single God?

Davies confronts the question and provides two different answers to it. The first is that science and theology are not incompatible.

There is certainly no incompatibility between these theological ideas and the scientific version, because the singularity, by definition, transcends the laws of nature. It is the one place in the universe where there is room, even for the most hard-nosed materialist, to admit God. Yet surely a God that is pushed off the very edge of spacetime is a pale shadow of a deity that most people would wish to accept. In this fascinating subject area, where science mingles with religion and philosophy, the urge to push science to its limits is compulsive. Can our, albeit fragmentary, know-ledge of singularities reveal anything about the nature of the god who created the universe, to use theological language? (p. 169)

The second is that science cannot support the Deistic position that God is an artificer, a *deus ex machina*, who instantly created the universe:

... it must be admitted that, at the present state of our understanding, science does not support the religious picture of a creator who produced a ready-made cosmic organization. The old idea of a sort of "package universe," set up in cosmic splendour, does not accord well with the evidence. The organization ... of the universe ... has emerged slowly and apparently automatically from a fiery start (p. 170).

Up to this point we have described what contemporary physics presents as the best theory about the origin of the universe – which is that the so-called "big bang" was a case of something emerging from nothing. Whether this account provides an acceptable answer to the first part of our original question, "Where did the universe come from?" is a matter we shall postpone until the end of the chapter. But that question had two parts, the other half of which was: "What is the universe expanding into?" How do string theorists like Max Tegmark deal with this part of the query? In fact, they do not. Instead they give an interesting twist to the puzzle. Rather than speaking about the universe, they speak about space, and state that space is expanding endlessly. Here is Tegmark's description of the cosmic situation:

Inflation is an extension of the big bang theory and ties up many of the loose ends of that theory, such as why the universe is so big, so uniform and so flat. A rapid stretching of space long ago can explain all these and other attributes in one fell swoop (see "The Inflationary Universe," by Alan H. Guth and Paul J. Steinhard; *Scientific American*, May 1984; and "The Self-Reproducing Inflationary Universe," by Andrei Linde, Nov. 1994). Such stretching is predicted by a wide class of theories of elementary particles, and all available evidence bears it out. The phrase "chaotic eternal" refers to what happens on the very largest scales. Space as a whole is stretching and will continue doing so forever (p. 44).

It is obvious that Tegmark has not answered the question: What is space stretching into? Perhaps current theory cannot answer it. So, in summary, what is the response of modern science to our original query: "Where did the universe come from? And what is it expanding into?" If my characterization of the present state of astrophysical knowledge is accurate the answer is that the universe emerged from nothing at all. With respect to the second part of the question, theory remains silent. We are told that the universe (or at least space) will expand forever – but what it will expand into is not addressed.

Up to this point we have described what contemporary science presents as the best theory of the origin of the universe – that is, the Big Bang Hypothesis plus Inflation. But looking at the other end of this process, we should now ask "What does physics say about the ultimate fate of the universe?" Here we definitely enter the realm of speculation. There are two different scenarios that are commonly advanced which depend on whether the universe is conceived of as infinite or as finite. If the latter should turn out to be the case, cosmologists believe that gravitation will inevitably cause a contraction of its existing contents; the cosmic background radiation will be blueshifted, raising the temperature of matter and radiation to incredible levels, and what is called the Big Squeeze which led to the original fiery atom will be repeated. The suggestion is that this will be a repetitive cyclical process of contraction and expansion, taking place over vast stretches of time. The conjecture recalls the writings of the ancient Greek poet, Hesiod, who argued that the cosmos will recycle endlessly.

If the universe is infinite, however, the current thinking is that cosmological expansion will continue forever, and that eventually the galaxies, stars, and planets will die, leaving the universe a cold, dark, and lifeless place. Newton's Second Law of Thermodynamics will have prevailed, and all motion will have ceased. It is a bleak picture, but fortunately a distant one.

THE THEOLOGY STORY

At the beginning of the chapter and elsewhere I distinguished between theology and philosophy. Some persons might find this contrast questionable on the ground that theology is a branch of philosophy. It is true that some theologians are philosophers, and that some philosophers are theologians. St. Augustine (354–430 C.E.) is perhaps the most notable example of someone who falls into both categories. Apart from his voluminous writings on religious topics, he was also the author of a work, *On the Teacher*, a straightforward philosophical treatise on semantics, which was remarkably advanced for its time. It is also true that many theologians are not philosophers and that many philosophers are not theologians. Thrascius Caecilius Cyprianus (200–250 C.E., also known as St. Cyprian) is an example of a pure theologian. He was mostly concerned with justifying the role of the church in remitting deadly sins, including apostasy. Eutyches (c. 375–454 C.E.) is still another. An opponent of Nestorius, he was a monophysite who argued that Jesus, as the son of God, had a single nature and that it was divine – a view rejected in 451 C.E. as heretical by the Council of Chalcedon, which held that Jesus was both fully human and fully divine. Both of these persons were unalloyed theologians whose basic concern was church dogma. W. V. O. Quine, G. E. Moore, Gilbert Ryle, and J. L. Austin are examples of twentieth-century philosophers whose writings exhibit little or no interest in religion. From these illustrations it is clear that theology and philosophy should be discriminated, and indeed many historians support such an interpretation. What then is the difference? In *A History of Philosophy* by Frederick Copleston, S.J., we find a characterization which most contemporary scholars would accept. The difference, according to Copleston, lies in the fact that the theologian receives his principles as revealed and considers the objects with which he deals as revealed or as deducible from what is revealed, whereas the philosopher apprehends his principles by reason alone and considers the objects with which he deals, not as revealed but as apprehensible and apprehended by the natural light of reason. In other words, the fundamental difference between theology and philosophy does not lie in a difference of objects concretely considered. Some truths are proper to theology, since they cannot be known by reason and are known only by revelation, the mystery of the Trinity, for example, while other truths are proper to philosophy alone in the sense that they have not been revealed; but there are some truths which are common to both theology and philosophy, since they have been revealed, though at the same time they can be established by reason. It is the existence of these common truths which makes it impossible to say that theology and philosophy differ primarily because each science considers different truths: in some instances they consider the same truths, though they consider them in a different manner, the theologian considering them as revealed, the philosopher as conclusions of a process of human reasoning.

vol. 2, pt. 2, p. 31

I accept the distinction as Copleston draws it, but with a slight modification. I emphasize a difference of attitude. Theologians are willing for authorities or experts, on the basis of scriptural or conciliar decisions – this is what is generally meant by "revelation" – to decide for them what is true, whereas philosophers are not. With respect to conceptual problems, their view is that there are no authorities or experts. Their attitude toward a problem thus mandates the suspension of belief until evidence, whether observational or logical, can lead to a rationally defensible judgment. This is a different mental set from that of the theologian. In practice, the distinction is obvious and I will base the ensuing discussion about the universe on it.

I shall begin with theology. It is important to distinguish between religions that have explicit theories about the universe from those whose focus is local. The Japanese creation myth is an example of the latter. It begins with a god (Susanowo) and a goddess (Amaterasu) who marry and give birth to the four islands of Japan. The tale includes a naming ceremony based on the idea that Amaterasu is a personification of the sun. The word for Japan in Japanese is "Nihon" or "Nippon." It is composed of two *kanji* (or characters) "ni" and "hon." "Ni" means "sun," and is a particularly interesting idiograph. In many ancient languages, the sun is drawn as a disk with rays extending from its perimeter. In early Japanese calligraphy this was also the case, but as the language became simplified, the disk was replaced by a small rectangular box which is the printed form used today. (In a type of shorthand, *sosho* or "grass writing," the box reduces to a dot.) In the box there is one horizontal line. It represents the many rays of the sun. The character for "hon" means origin. Taken together these two *kanji* mean the origin of the sun. The creation narration is thus confined to what today would be called ingredients of the solar system.

Many anthropologists claim that the concept of the environment as a totality is unknown among primitive peoples. Instead, only individual phenomena, such as stars, rain, and animals, are considered worthy of veneration or placation. As one sociologist puts it, "Nature as an entity in itself, in contrast with man, human society and culture, or even God, is a philosophical or poetic conception that is found only in advanced civilizations." The creation accounts of the three most important "Western" religions – Judaism, Christianity, and Islam – are not so limited. They each speak about the origin of the cosmos, probably because all have the same source, the Old Testament. There are three arresting features in these narratives. First, each proclaims itself to be monotheistic (although Muslims deny that Christianity's triune God satisfies this condition). Second, none of them raises the skeptical question: "Where did God come from?" And third, each of them states (based on biblical passages I shall mention in a moment) that God created the universe from nothing. These three features constitute a background that is accepted by every major theologian in each of these religions from the beginning of the historical record we have until our own day. As far as I know, there are no significant exceptions.

The basis for the creation story they accept in common is to be found in two places in the Hebrew bible. The first occurs in Genesis, the first of the five books that comprise the Torah or Pentateuch. Chapters 1–11 deal with primordial history; they begin with the creation of the universe, and then turn to the origin of mankind. Many theologians have referred to the opening sentences of Genesis in support of the belief that God created the universe from nothing. These read as follows:

> In the beginning God created the heavens and the earth. Now the earth was a formless void, there was darkness over the deep, and God's spirit hovered over the water.

> trans. *The Jerusalem Bible*, 1966

The Hebrew words for "formless void," *tohu* and *bohu*, are sometimes translated as "trackless waste and emptiness." According to the *Jerusalem Bible*, these terms, like "darkness over the deep" and "water" are negative images that attempt to express the idea of "creation from nothing."

That the quoted sentences from Genesis actually speak about God's creation of something from nothing has been challenged. But there is another entry in Scripture that is more explicit. It is found in Second Maccabees. This document is not one of the twenty-four canonical books of the *Tanach* or Old Testament, but its inspiration has been recognized by the Roman Catholic Church and is accordingly categorized as "deutero-canonical." Like First Maccabees it treats of the Jewish struggle for religious and political freedom from the Seleucid kings who reigned in the second century B.C.E. It is generally thought to have been written around 100 B.C.E. The words in question are:

> I implore you, my child, observe heaven and earth, consider all that is in them, and acknowledge that God made them out of what did not exist, and that mankind comes into being in the same way.

> 2 Macc. 7:28

It will be noted that in speaking of *all* that is in heaven and earth the author seems to be referring to the totality of what exists, that is, to the cosmos; and there is no doubt that he is stating that God made that assemblage out of what did not exist, that is, out of nothing. Like many other religious tenets, the claim is not provable by reason. But having been "revealed" in an authoritative document it is accepted by devotees as true. As I mentioned earlier, I do not know of any major theologians who have challenged the thesis that God created the universe from nothing.

It would clearly be impossible in a single chapter to explore the substantial differences that exist in the main monotheistic religions about the mode of creation or the future of the universe, a topic which involves such complex ideas as eschatology, apocalyptics, and millenarianism. I shall therefore limit my discussion to the views of two medieval Christian theologians who debated the issue about the origin of the universe vigorously and with great subtlety. They are St. Thomas Aquinas, described by Copleston as one of "the greatest of the Fathers both from a literary and from a theological standpoint," and his colleague at the University of Paris, St. Bonaventure.

CHRISTIAN THEOLOGY ON THE ORIGIN OF THE UNIVERSE

Thomas and Bonaventure were Italians, close friends, and almost the same age. Bonaventure, whose birthname was Giovanni Fidanza, was born in Tuscany in 1221, and Aquinas, three years younger, was born near Naples. Both died in 1274, Aquinas on 7 March and Bonaventure a few months later on 15 July. Both were intellectual prodigies and both were enormously productive, Thomas especially. His most famous work, the *Summa Theologica*, was composed between 1265 and 1273 and is longer than the entire extant works of Aristotle. The *Summa* is only one of about sixty books that Thomas dictated – sometimes to four amanuenses at once – all in the last twenty years of his life, while at the same time energetically performing a host of administrative and professorial duties. This is an incredible performance by any standard, but it is especially impressive when one considers that he died at the age of forty-nine.

Two issues that exercised these highly intelligent men were typical of the debates, most at a lower order of sophistication, that took place in the thirteenth century about the universe. The first was, "What was meant by saying it was created from nothing?" The second, closely related, was: "Is creation from nothing possible if the universe is infinite?" This last question arose because Aristotle had asserted as a fact that the universe was infinite and therefore had always existed. Though a pagan, Aristotle was regarded as an authority without parallel, and therefore as someone whose pronouncements had to be taken seriously. Indeed, Thomas's most important overall achievement is to have created what historians call the *Medieval Synthesis*, a fusion of Aristotelianism and Christianity that has become the official philosophy of the Catholic Church. As ecclesiastics, neither Bonaventure nor Aquinas doubted that the cosmos had a beginning in time, since that is taught by theology; but they differed over the tantalizing question of whether if it were infinite, as Aristotle had affirmed, it could have been created from nothing. The difficulty arose, as they saw it, from a tension between the scriptural account of a creation moment and the apparent impossibility of such a moment if the universe were infinite. If the latter were the case there could have been no beginning event and the universe would have existed from eternity.

CREATION FROM NOTHING

In their debate both Bonaventure and Thomas agreed that if the universe were infinite it would be eternal. If they were thinking of the universe as consisting of an endless regress of causally connected events ending in the present this would be a plausible assumption. The texts do not allow us to decide the question, although there is some evidence in its favor. However, they also frequently used the terms "infinite" and "eternal" as synonyms; that is, they tended in practice to identify infinity with eternality, and this was a mistake. As we shall see later in discussing the views of the Greek philosopher, Parmenides, eternality and infinity should be distinguished. Parmenides developed a line of reasoning in which Being (his name for reality) exists eternally, but without being infinite. In his version of eternality, neither causality nor temporality plays a role. But Bonaventure and Thomas did not make such a distinction; and their arguments, pro and con, are frequently couched in terms of a contrast between a creation moment and the eternality (or, alternatively, the infinity) of the cosmos.

Bonaventure, for example, argued that the idea of creation from eternity involves a contradiction, since if the cosmos existed from eternity it is logically impossible that it could have had a first moment. Accordingly, there would have been no time in which it did not exist, and in that sense it would have been eternal. In opposition to this conception, he asserted that there was an initial creation event. But he gave this idea a special twist, meaning by it that the universe acquired Being only after Not-Being (*esse post non-esse*). This led to an issue between him and Thomas about the meaning of "creation from nothing." Thomas, as a defender of Aristotle, disagreed with Bonaventure's interpretation. He stated that the doctrine of creation should not be construed to mean that the universe was made *after* nothing, but that it was made *out* of nothing, the antonym of which is "out of something." Bonaventure's position, he pointed out, presupposed that there was a time "before" the creation and this inference, as Scripture assures its devotees, is manifestly untrue. The idea that the universe is not made out of something, rather than being created after nothing, has become part of the official creed of the Church. Following Thomas, dogma makes no reference to the concept of time – that is, to the notions of before or after nothing, *ante et post nihilum* – in its interpretation of the creation thesis.

INFINITY AND CREATION

Influenced by Aristotle, Thomas therefore saw no inconsistency between the claims that the world was infinite and that God had created it out of nothing. Since it is not clear what Thomas meant by infinity or eternality, one can only speculate as to the grounds for his judgment. Perhaps he thought that God in one fell swoop could make the causal equivalent of the negative integers out of nothing. This would allow for the universe to be infinite and yet not created after anything. In contrast Bonaventure found this idea incomprehensible and stated that it still entailed an initial creation moment. If this was indeed his view, it would suggest that he thought of God as a kind of artificer, only one who created *de novo* the materials he worked with rather than collecting and organizing them from an existing pool. According to such a conception, the universe would have had an initial creation moment, as Scripture states, and each event that has occurred down to the present would represent one concrete happening. Since the present is the last event in such a series, the causal sequence leading to it would be finite – that is, it would consist of a limited number of occurrences, like the discrete ticks of a clock. Whether this was his actual thought pattern is not known; I suggest it only as an illustration of the kind of argument he might have had in mind.

In any case, the notion of infinity turned out to be the turf on which an intense intellectual contest about the nature of creation played itself out. In this struggle, Bonaventure was consistently on the attack, devising clever arguments to prove that an infinite universe is inconsistent with creation; whereas Aquinas assumed the posture of a counter-puncher, blocking Bonaventure's assaults. Although Bonaventure generated a panoply of arguments against the thesis of an infinite universe, I will consider only two. Both are shorter reworkings of longer originals. In my rendition, I will present them as having the structure of thrust, parry, and thrust.

Argument one:

I: Bonaventure states:
Suppose the universe were infinite. Then there would have already been an infinite number of lunar revolutions around the earth and every twenty-four hours another would be added. But it is impossible to add to the infinite. Therefore, the world cannot have always existed.

II: Thomas responds:
It is a mistake to assert that no additions can be made to an infinite set. Let us assume that an infinity of events has already occurred. These end in the present. So a lunar revolution that occurs today can be added to the

past total. It is true that one is adding to the finite end of such a sequence; but Bonaventure's point is that it is impossible to add any new member to an infinite sequence and my counter-example shows he is wrong.

III: Bonaventure rebuts:
If one is referring to an infinite past, one would have to admit that an infinite number of lunar revolutions has already occurred. But there are a dozen lunar revolutions to every revolution of the sun. Therefore we have two infinite numbers, one of which is a dozen times larger than the other; and this is impossible.

Argument two:

This argument is especially complicated. Its beginning part is a variation of the cosmological proof that we shall consider in detail later in the chapter.

I: Bonaventure thrusts:
It is impossible to pass through an infinite series; so that if the universe had always existed, that is, had no beginning, there would have been no second, third, or any subsequent day. But we have arrived at the present day; so there must have been a first moment just as Scripture indicates.

II: Thomas parries:
The claim that it is impossible to pass through an infinite series is correct but it does not apply to the present case; for it is also true that every journey requires a beginning moment and a final one. But if the universe is infinite and therefore lacked a first moment, then no journey could begin; hence Bonaventure's objection does not arise.

III: Bonaventure thrusts:
There is either a revolution of the moon which is infinitely distant in the past from today's revolution or there is not. Let us consider each possibility. If there is not a revolution that is infinitely distant from today's then the distance between them is finite and so the series must have had a beginning. If there is a revolution that is infinitely distant from today's, then the revolution immediately following that infinitely distant one must either be infinitely distant or finitely distant. If it is finitely distant, then the supposedly infinitely distant revolution cannot actually be infinitely distant since the interval between the two is finite. If the

revolution immediately following the infinitely distant one is also infinitely distant then the revolutions following it must also be infinitely distant; and hence they must be infinitely distant from today's revolution. If they are, then today's revolution is no less distant from them than from the first. It follows that there is no succession of revolutions at all and instead they all are synchronous; which is plainly absurd.

History does not record Aquinas's answer, and I shall not try to answer for him. The sensible course instead is to follow Wittgenstein's advice. He writes at the end of the *Tractatus Logico-Philosophicus*: "Whereof one cannot speak, thereof one must be silent" (p. 7).

So silent we shall remain.

WHO WAS RIGHT – BONAVENTURE OR AQUINAS?

There are at least two factors that make it difficult to decide who was right in their debate about creation. First, the conception of infinity they were appealing to was vague. They were, of course, men of their time and used this term as it was employed in the thirteenth century, and as it is commonly employed by ordinary speakers today. The first precise definition of "infinity" was formulated by a German mathematician, Georg Cantor (1848–1918), at the end of the nineteenth century or some seven centuries after the seraphic doctors had died. Precise though it is, its primary application is in number theory, and not in theology. Yet, we cannot wholly ignore it either, since some of the arguments that Bonaventure and Aquinas used are, as we shall see, best understood via Cantor's conception, even though the Saints could not possibly have anticipated the sophisticated arithmetical concepts on which that notion rests.

But there is a second difficulty. Several different meanings of "infinite" were in ordinary use in the Middle Ages, as they still are today, and the two contestants wobbled between them more or less indiscriminately, thus augmenting the exegetical difficulties. The term has been used to mean the same as "great" ("an infinite number of stars"), "immeasureable" ("a truth of infinite importance"), "inexhaustible" ("a person of infinite energy"), "unending" ("an infinite series"), "unbounded" ("an infinite expanse"), and "unlimited" ("the infinite wisdom of God.") The term was used in this last sense by Sir Walter Raleigh who claimed that "there cannot be more infinities than one; for one of them would limit the other."

Let us return for a moment to the first argument, and a statement in it that Bonaventure makes. He says there that it is impossible to add to the infinite. He later supports this assertion by producing an example of two infinite numbers, one of which is supposedly a dozen times larger than the other, and claims that this is impossible. Note that he here explicitly uses the term "number," which strongly suggests he is thinking in mathematical terms about infinity. Note also that in his rebuttal Thomas states that it is possible to add to the finite end of an infinite series, a remark that would be true if one added some or all of the positive integers to the terminal member of the negative integers. There is thus some textual evidence that both are thinking of infinity in terms of certain arithmetical sequences. If this is a plausible conjecture – and one must emphasize that it is indeed only a conjecture, since the textual evidence is indecisive – their arguments can be reassessed in the light of Cantor's 1895 treatment of infinity or what he called "transfinite numbers." I again stress that what I am about to say about Cantor's conception could not have been known by either Saint. But if we look at their debate anachronistically through the eyes of Cantor their arguments suddenly assume a kind of clarity that they do not possess if restricted to the fuzzy concepts of their time.

CANTOR'S CONCEPTION OF INFINITY

There is an important respect in which Bonaventure's views are similar to those of Cantor, and different from those of St. Thomas. Thomas was an Aristotelian, and Cantor and Bonaventure were Platonists. Like Plato in the *Republic*, they supposed there is a realm of abstract objects (points, numbers, classes, and sets) that exist external to and independent of any investigator. Cantor's view was thus that the mathematician is like an astronomer who does not create the stars, comets, and galaxies he studies, but investigates such mind-independent entities in order to discover their properties and truths about them. Cantor was thus part of the Logistic or Platonic tradition which holds that numbers, unlike numerals, do not reflect light, possess bulk or mass, or have causal properties, and hence are not physical objects. If a bowl holds three apples, the apples, being physical objects, are not themselves the number three but belong to one of the many sets that are triples. A set is determined by its members. The number three is thus a second order abstraction containing all classes of triples as members. Accordingly, numbers are classes of classes.

This point brings us to an important contrast on which Cantor's account of infinity depends. This is the distinction between cardinal and ordinal numbers. Ordinals represent a sequence, such as the first, second, third, etc. If one is counting the succession of the days of the week, for example, and if Sunday is the first day in the series, then Wednesday is the fourth. Cardinals, in contrast, are such numbers as one, two, and three. Cardinality thus determines the number of members a class has. In the case of a week, for example, the number of its members is seven. In the light of this dichotomy, Cantor asked the question: "How do we determine when two numbers have the same cardinality?" His answer is simple and convincing, and can be illustrated by an example. Suppose you have a room in which there is a large number of chairs and there is a person sitting in each chair. Suppose also that there are no other persons in the room and that there are no empty chairs. Finally, assume you do not have time to count the number of persons. Nevertheless, you can be sure that the number of chairs and the number of persons is the same, that is, that both sets have the same cardinal number. For Cantor, therefore, sameness of cardinality is established by means of a one-to-one correlation between the members of differing sets. So if the membership of two sets satisfies this condition, the sets have the same cardinality.

Cantor then called attention to a familiar property of finite numbers. Suppose I have a bowl holding five apples and I give two to a guest. It follows that I am left with three. I have, in mathematical parlance, performed the operation of subtraction on the number of apples. If I had three apples to begin with, and my guest brought two, I would then have five apples. The sum is arrived at by addition. Cantor noted that the well-known operations of subtraction, division, multiplication, addition, and exponentiation necessarily change the cardinality of any integer other than zero. It follows that part of a finite number can never be put into a one-to-one correspondence with the number itself. But this result does not hold for transfinite numbers, and represents the main distinction between them. This is another way of saying that the arithmetics of transfinite and finite numbers differ. I submit that Cantor's discovery will assist us in understanding and perhaps resolving the controversy about infinity between Bonaventure and Aquinas.

To proceed in this endeavor, let us begin with what are called "the natural numbers." These are the familiar digits that begin with 0 and are followed by 1, 2, 3 ... n. Cantor named this set Aleph, which is the first letter of the Hebrew alphabet. Since he later discovered that Aleph was the smallest transfinite number, he gave it a subscript: zero. It is thus generally called "Aleph Null," and is represented by the symbol $\aleph_0$. This number has the peculiar property that it is possible to put its members into a one-to-one correspondence with a proper part of itself. (A proper part is a part short of the whole.) One can illustrate this property by removing the even numbers, and since $\aleph_0$ consists of both odd and even numbers, the even numbers are thus only a proper part of $\aleph_0$. One can easily show that a one-to-one relationship exists between Aleph Null and the set of even integers by multiplying any number in Aleph Null by two. This will result in a one-to-one correspondence with the even numbers, as follows:

$$1, 2, 3, 4 \ldots \text{etc.} \times 2 = 2, 4, 6, 8 \ldots \text{etc.}$$

This same correspondence or isomorphism can be obtained by multiplying the numbers in Aleph Null by four or eight, and so forth. In each of these cases the sequences that are proper parts of Aleph Null will have the same cardinality as Aleph Null itself. This consequence was noted by Leibniz, who rejected it as contradictory on the ground that no whole number can be equal to a part of itself. In effect, he was applying a principle that seemed to hold universally. But Cantor showed that it did not. As he pointed out, it was valid for finite numbers but not for infinite numbers. It was Cantor's genius to have recognized that this feature defined a different sort of number from the digits that belong to Aleph Null. He thus rejected an assumption that Leibniz had assumed to be unassailable: that no number can be equal to a subset of itself.

It will be useful to give a few examples of the radical difference between the arithmetics of the finite numbers and the infinite numbers. For instance, in standard arithmetic $3 + 3 = 6$, but in transfinite arithmetic $\aleph_0 + \aleph_0 = \aleph_0$. Or again, $3 \times 3 = 9$, but $\aleph_0 \times \aleph_0 = \aleph_0$, and $3^3 = 27$, but $\aleph_0^{\aleph_0} = \aleph^0$. Cantor also proved by an argument too lengthy to be reproduced here that there are larger transfinite numbers than $\aleph_0$. The argument concludes with the theorem that 2^n is always greater than n, even when n is infinite. This proposition entails that there is no largest infinite cardinal number. However great an infinite number n may be, 2^n will be still greater. $2^{\aleph_0}$ is thus greater than $\aleph_0$. Cantor called this number $\aleph_1$. He argued that it was next in rank in size to $\aleph_0$. An interesting and as yet unsolved problem in mathematics is whether $\aleph_1 = C$. C is a transfinite number that designates the real numbers, that is, the number of points in space or of instants of time. C thus represents the continuity of space and time, a continuity that is assumed in analytical geometry and kinematics. The question of whether these two numbers are identical is called "the problem of the continuum."

The relevance of these remarks to the controversy between Bonaventure and Aquinas is easily shown. From a Cantorian perspective both are wrong. Bonaventure holds that there cannot be two infinite numbers one of which is greater than the other; but as Cantor's analysis shows this statement is false since $\aleph_1$ is greater than $\aleph_0$. Bonaventure also asserts that it is impossible to add to the infinite. As he says: "But it is impossible to add to the infinite. Therefore the world cannot have always existed." The claim that it is impossible to add to the infinite is mistaken, since as we have indicated $2\aleph_0$ is greater than $\aleph_0$. In response to Bonaventure's assertion that it is impossible to add to the infinite, Thomas states that this can be done if one adds a single lunar revolution to the terminus of an infinite series. But if he means that adding an integer to $\aleph_0$ or to any transfinite number will increase its size he is also in error. It is part of transfinite arithmetic that $\aleph_0$ + n where n is any natural number will always equal $\aleph_0$, and this theorem also holds of all the larger infinite cardinals. Of course, I must again emphasize that it is not clear what either of these divines meant by infinity; and accordingly, that to assert categorically that both are wrong may well be unwarranted. We shall have to be satisfied with the decision that no firm judgment can be reached in this matter.

Still, there is no doubt that these Christian theologians believed that God had created the universe from nothing; and in this respect, their views, like those of their counterparts in the other monotheistic religions, are not dissimilar to the outlooks of many scientists, among them Frank Shu and Paul Davies. As mentioned earlier, the possibility that something could emerge from nothing has been consistently rejected by philosophers from the time of the ancient Greeks to the present. Nonetheless, there has been a vigorous debate in this discipline about whether the universe has always existed and whether it is infinite in scope. It is thus clear that unlike some scientists and virtually all theologians, philosophers have dealt with these puzzles independently of the question of whether something can be created out of nothing. So let us now turn to some of the answers they have given to the two parts of our original question: "Where did the universe come from? and what is it expanding into?"

PHILOSOPHY AND THE ORIGIN OF THE UNIVERSE

Let us begin with the ancient Greeks, who were obsessively speculative thinkers. Perhaps the most challenging problem they addressed was: "What is the cosmos really like?" They came at this issue in a variety of ways. Another common formulation was: "Is the world made of some fundamental stuff, and if so, what is it?" Both questions led to speculations about the eternality of the universe.

Two incompatible replies were given to these questions. One response, advanced by Heraclitus (540?–475 B.C.E.), was that the universe is in a constant state of flux so that from moment to moment its ingredients are changing. As he remarks, "You cannot step into the same river twice." The only thing that does not change is a cosmic balance maintained by the continuous alteration of everything. There is no underlying "stuff," such as water, as Thales believed, that remains invariant through all temporal processes. Though Heraclitus apparently did not draw explicit skeptical implications from this view, some of his followers did. One of them, Cratylus (after whom Plato named a dialogue), held that reality is unknowable. Since it does not stand still long enough to be described, our words and their meanings are constantly changing, as is each speaker. Thus human language has no fixed meanings; and accordingly the attainment of accurate information about the world is impossible. Like Heraclitus himself, his epigones held that the universe is ephemeral. For whatever totality exists at any moment, that totality will be substantively different in the moment that follows.

An opposite point of view was espoused by Parmenides. His theory starts from the common-sense observation that if something, say a leaf, changes, then to speak of it as a "leaf" is to imply that some essential feature remains constant while other features, such as its color and shape, mutate. In a Heraclitean world, a so-called "leaf" would consist of a number of unconnected states that appear successively in one's visual field. But for Parmenides such a sequence of discrete events is not change. Change requires, as a matter of logic, a degree of cohesion in the changing object; and that requires that something remains constant. The Parmenidean thesis thus entails the existence of some "stuff" that "underlies" the features that change but which is itself immune to change. This "stuff" he calls Being. Plato was later to invent the term "essence" for it.

Given this intuition about change, Parmenides produced a set of arguments to show that Being is eternal. Suppose one believes that Being must have come from something. If true, that belief would imply that there was a time at which Being did not exist. But then what could it have come from? It could not come from itself, so it must have come from something other than Being. But anything other than Being is

Non-Being, and by definition Non-Being does not exist. Non-Being (the Non-Existent) cannot produce anything, since it is nothing. Therefore, Being cannot come into existence at all, and this means that it has always existed. Another argument proves that Being is a single cohesive stuff. Suppose one assumes that Being is composed of parts. Then either these parts would be real or not real. If they are not real, they do not exist and cannot be part of anything, let alone Being. If they are real, then they are not different from Being. Being is therefore one indissoluble stuff.

By a similar argument Parmenides deduced that Being cannot move. To move to a place means to move to something that either exists or does not exist. But nothing can move to what does not exist, since it is not a place. But then every existing place must be occupied by Being. Therefore it cannot move, and hence it cannot pass away. Accordingly, these arguments, taken conjointly, demonstrate that Being cannot come into existence or cease to exist, which is equivalent to proving that it is eternal. Furthermore, in showing that Being occupies every existing place, Parmenides is identifying Being with the totality of what exists, that is, with the universe. Therefore the arguments also establish that the universe is eternal. This conclusion bears directly on the previous discussion between Bonaventure and Thomas since both thought of eternality in terms of an uninterrupted sequence that had no first member. But the Parmenidean arguments distinguish between infinity, regarded as an endless regress, and eternality. They demonstrate that eternality does not depend on any form of causality or temporality. Parmenides also provides answers to both parts of our query: "Where did the universe come from? and what is it expanding into?" His reply to the first half of the question is that the universe did not *come from* anything since it has always existed. His reponse to the second half is that the universe is not expanding into anything because, being immobile, it is not expanding at all. Note that his analysis presupposes the *ex nihilo nihil fit* principle. As he points out, Non-Being cannot produce Being. Thus, Parmenides, like most of his philosophical congeners, would disagree with those theologians and scientists who believe that something can come from nothing.

THE COSMOLOGICAL ARGUMENT

In Chapter 3, I stated that there have been three important arguments for the existence of God and that the cosmological argument was one of them. I also stated that in order to avoid duplication I would be deferring a discussion of it until this chapter. I had another reason for such a postponement. Although the argument is regarded by the Catholic Church as primarily designed to demonstrate the existence of a personal deity, it can be given an interpretation that does not directly touch on that issue. As so construed, it attempts to prove that the universe is finite in at least one direction and it does so by attempting to show that it must have had a beginning event or first cause. Theologians have understandably tended to identify the first cause with God.

But the theological interpretation does not capture the essence of the argument. Let us, therefore, investigate it as a piece of secular reasoning. As so viewed, its main aim is to deny that the universe is subject to an infinite regress. It is important in understanding the argument to see that it is essentially retrospective. It thus does not speak about the future of the universe. It is also important to see that its scope is limited. Unlike the theological views we have just discussed it leaves open the question of whether the universe was created from nothing or from something. Hence, it does not deal with the *ex nihilo* issue at all. It also has no bearing on Bonaventure's claim that finitude and eternity are incompatible. Questions about the nature of the first cause or its mode of creation are also bypassed. So it says nothing about whether the non-existence of the first cause is inconceivable.

I do not wish to minimize its importance for natural religion, but I am convinced that one cannot get a perspicuous grip on the argument unless it is stripped of its theological baggage. I think that Kant's understanding of the argument was flawed in just this respect. He saw it as attempting to prove that nothing could be a first cause unless its essence included its existence. For Kant, the argument was thus a variant of the ontological proof and failed on the ground that existence is not a property. I wish to avoid such partisan conflations and to pare the argument down to its logical essentials. To repeat: its main concern is whether the universe had a beginning. If it did, it follows that it is not infinite in at least one direction. It thus answers the first part of our question: "Where did the universe come from?" by saying it had an initiating moment or event while leaving the nature of that moment unexplained.

Like the ontological proof, it is an indirect argument or *reductio ad absurdum*. Such an argument, as I explained earlier, begins by assuming the negation of the conclusion it wishes to reach. It then proceeds to show that the assumption leads to a falsehood, and accordingly that the negation of the assumption must be true. In this particular case, the falsehood it leads to is that there is no present event. This is a false statement since for any T, where T = today, T is a present event. The argument can be broken down into the following steps:

1. The universe had no beginning event (Assumption).
2. Therefore there would be no second event. (2) follows from (1).
3. Therefore there would be no third event. (3) follows from (2).
4. Then there would be no successive events. (4) with certain additions follows from (3).
5. If there were no successive events, there would be no present event. (5) follows from (4).
6. But (5) is false, since today is a present event.
7. Therefore, the universe must have had a beginning event.

The finitude of the universe in one direction follows from this pattern of reasoning. It establishes that starting from today there cannot be an unending regress of events. The universe is thus not like the series of negative integers, which lacks a beginning, although it does have an end, namely -1. If there is a parallel in mathematics it would be to the natural numbers. They are to be distinguished from the integers. Their logical basis derives from Peano's Postulates, whereas the integers are based on Dedekind cuts. The natural numbers have a beginning, which is zero, but no final or largest number. That the series does not have a last number follows from two of Peano's postulates: that every number has a successor and that no two numbers have the same successor. The integers include the negative and positive numbers and hence have neither a beginning nor an end. But even the analogy with the natural numbers is strained. It does not follow from the cosmological argument that there will be an endless number of events that follow the present event. It is thus neutral with respect to that issue.

The power of the argument rests on three premises. The first is that there is no beginning event. This is the proposition that is to be disproved. The second follows from the first. It is that there is no second event. This seems obviously true since if there is no first event there cannot be a second. (Some wits have argued that this move is equivalent to the thesis that there cannot be a Second Coming unless there is a First Coming.) The third proposition is also true – that there is a present event, namely any T, where T = today. Unlike the second proposition its truth is established on empirical grounds. The argument conjoins these premises to reach the conclusion that there must be a first event in a sequence that terminates in the present.

Despite its plausibility the argument has some serious defects. We can begin to expose these by asking: "Why does it follow that if there were no first event there would be no second event?" The obvious answer is that the second event would not occur unless it were caused or produced by the first event. This dependence on causality seems to hold for all the events from the second to the last event. Each has been caused by its immediate predecessor. But this reply creates a puzzle about the status of the supposed first event. Either it had no cause or was self-caused or was caused by something else. Each of these options leads to mystification. For example, if the presumed first event was caused by something else it could not really be the beginning member of a series ending in the present. If this option is excluded, we are left with only two possibilities: either it was self-caused or was uncaused. On the common understanding of causation, to say that A causes B entails that A and B are not identical. So it makes no sense to speak of any B as self-caused. This leaves only the possibility that it was uncaused. But to assert that it was uncaused would violate the *ex nihilo nihil fit* maxim that all philosophers accept. It is this last objection that theologians attempt to meet by arguing that the first cause is God and that God is uncaused. Because of such difficulties with the secular interpretation some philosophers have advanced a different argument that does not presuppose that the members of the sequence are causally related. Instead, this argument invokes the dependent/non-dependent (technically known as the "contingent/non-contingent") distinction to explain why an infinite regress is impossible. But now let us see if this maneuver, traditionally referred to as the argument from the principle of Sufficient Reason, manages to avoid the difficulties the cosmological proof engenders.

THE ARGUMENT FROM THE PRINCIPLE OF SUFFICIENT REASON

The intuition that underlies the argument can be expressed in various ways. In the *Tractatus Logico-Philosophicus*, Wittgenstein writes:

> Not *how* the world is, is the mystical, but *that* it is (6.44).

Another version states:

> Why something rather than nothing: that is the question?

Historically the most famous attempt to give formal expression to this intuition is due to the German philosopher, Gottfried Wilhelm von Leibniz (1646–1716). He was also the first to call it the argument from the Principle of Sufficient Reason (*Ausreichenden Grund*). Leibniz asserted that there are an infinite number of possible historical sequences, but that out of this set only one is actual. This sequence consists of the total number of events that have occurred and will eventually occur in the history of the universe. It includes the assassination of Julius Caesar in 44 B.C.E., the signing of the Concordat of Worms in 1122 by Pope Calixtus II and the German emperor, Henry V, the ascension of Elizabeth to the throne of England in 1558, and so forth. Since from a logical point of view all series are equally possible, Leibniz claimed there must be some reason why this particular sequence came into existence. But only a sentient being can have a reason; so the actual sequence of events mandated an intelligent selector. He also claimed that the selector necessarily existed outside of all the sets, including the actual one. This was required because the selector had to survey all available options before choosing one of them. For Leibniz, God was the selector. The argument in its original form was thus devised to be a proof of God's existence.

It will be noted that in this Leibnizian version the dependency/non dependency (or its analogue, the contingency/non-contingency) distinction does not appear. Yet most formulations of the argument require such a contrast. Let us look at a later construction that does embed this opposition. It was advanced by Copleston in a debate that was originally broadcast in 1948 on the B.B.C. Copleston's opponent was Bertrand Russell. Here is how Copleston presented the argument.

> First of all, I should say, we know that there are at least some beings in the world which do not contain in themselves the reason for their existence. For example, I depend on my parents, and now on the air, and on food, and so on. Now, secondly, the world is simply the real or imagined totality or aggregate of individual objects, none of which contain in themselves alone the reason for their existence. There isn't any world distinct from the objects which form it, any more than the human race is something apart from its members. Therefore, I should say, since objects or events exist, and since no object of experience contains within itself the reason of its existence, this reason, the totality of objects, must have a reason external to itself. That reason must be an existent being. Well, this being is either itself the reason for its own existence, or it is not. If it is, well and good. If it is not, then we must proceed farther. But if we proceed to infinity in that sense, then there's no explanation of existence at all. So, I should say, in order to explain existence, we must come to a being which contains within itself the reason for its own existence, that is to say, which cannot non-exist (pp. 145–146).

Copleston provides an interesting analogy as to why the series must have a being who exists outside of it. He says:

> If you add up chocolates to infinity, you presumably get an infinite number of chocolates. So if you add up contingent beings to infinity, you still get contingent beings not a necessary being. An infinite series of

contingent beings will be, to my way of thinking, as unable to cause itself as one contingent being.

Copleston's version, like Leibniz's, is designed to establish the existence of God. God, for him, is a being "which contains within itself the reason for its own existence." He also describes God as a "being which cannot non-exist." This characterization is virtually identical with that of the onto-logical proof. Yet the argument leading to that conclusion is radically different. The intuition behind it is that if everything were contingent the totality of beings would be like a house suspended in air. Nothing would hold it up and that would be impossible. Therefore the house must have a foundation. Think of the foundation as a concrete slab. Think of the series of contingent beings as also requiring a base. As a theologian, Copleston identifies the foundation with God. But that identification is not needed if our focus is on the issue of whether the universe had a beginning. That is a different sort of question and not necessarily a reli-gious one. Therefore, let us secularize the argument to see what it proves.

We can get some sense of why a foundation is necessary by con-sidering Copleston's ingenious metaphor of the chocolates in the light of Hume's sarcastic comment about the Indian philosopher and the ele-phant in Part IV of the *Dialogues Concerning Natural Religion*. The ques-tion was: "What holds the world up?" The Indian philosopher said it was resting on the back of an elephant; the elephant on the back of a great tor-toise; and the great tortoise on the back of he knew not what. Hume says: "After all, what satisfaction is there in that infinite progression?" Copleston agrees with Hume. As he says: "But if we proceed to infinity in that sense, then there's no explanation of existence at all." So to explain existence, the sequence of contingent events must have a foundation. Copleston infers from this picture of things that the foundation must be non-contingent. But a secularized version of the argument does not require that conclusion. It merely requires that there be some sort of foundation. The nature of the foundation raises a variety of different considerations. Let us therefore construe the argument in this stripped down version as a form of classical foundationalism – a type of argument that many philosophers, past and present, have advanced independently of any religious association. As so secularized, we can then ask: "Does it serve to establish the finitude of the universe?"

The answer to a considerable extent depends on what is meant by "foundationalism." As we shall see this is a complicated matter, but it is necessary to deal with it if we are to understand the attraction that the argument from Sufficient Reason has exercised on so many philosophers. I will therefore begin with some historical remarks about foundationalism as mode of argumentation. From at least the time of Aristotle many philosophers have asserted that some of the knowledge human beings possess is more fundamental or basic than the rest. If we call such primordial knowledge "F" and the remainder "R," we can roughly express their intuition by saying that R depends on F but not conversely and that F depends on nothing. Let us sponge the epistemological gloss from this statement, that is, we shall leave F and R uninterpreted and in particular not take them to be pieces of knowledge or even to be contingent events. What remains is just a formal structure. It holds that there is some asymmetrical relationship of dependence between F and R, whatever these are taken to be, and that F is not dependent on anything else. So given some unanalyzed notion of "dependence" and some unanalyzed conception of what sorts of items F and R may be, we can say that this skeleton gives us the basic foundationalist intuition. The main thrust of the conception is that F somehow supports R and is itself not supported by anything. The idea that F is not supported by anything is generally taken to be another way of saying that it is foundational.

In the realm of philosophy there are many mansions that conform to this model – in religion, logic, epistemology, and ethics, to mention the most important cases. A typical example would be an axiomatic logical system, such as that developed by Whitehead and Russell in *Principia Mathematica* (*P.M.*). The set of axioms is the foundation of a logical mansion whose rooms are the various calculi that eventually allowed Russell and Whitehead to derive arithmetic from logic. The totality of theorems deduced from the set of axioms is R. The theorems have a different status from the axioms. Unlike the axioms which are assumed to be true, they can be proved to be true. If we think of the theorems as dependent on the axioms, the parallel with Copleston's analogy is very close. The theorems are thus like the pieces of chocolate and the axioms are the foundational support they require. That R depends on F (no matter what R and F are) is the theoretical model that every traditional foundationalist accepts.

Even in this skeletal form, the model needs some further explanation. For example, what does it mean to say that F depends on nothing whatever? Consider the axioms of *P.M.* for a moment. A critic might ask: Don't the axioms depend on something? For instance, don't they depend on somebody's writing them down or at least conceiving of them as axioms? But doesn't that entail that such a person be alive and conscious, and doesn't that require that his/her heart be pumping blood, and doesn't that in turn necessitate the satisfaction of an infinite number of other conditions? So how can one say that the set of axioms – taken to be F in this context – depends on nothing?

I am sure that Russell would have dismissed this objection. He would probably have said something like this:

> Look, I am distinguishing between theorems and axioms and the point I am making is that the latter are more basic than the former. Consider the principle of commutation, for example. This axiom in the notation of *Principia Mathematica* states that (pvq ≡ qvp). In arithmetic it would appear as the formula that $1 + 2 = 2 + 1$. It is obviously true but it cannot be proved within the system of *P.M.* as Kurt Gödel demonstrated in 1930. But the theorems that depend on it can be. Thus, the relationship runs one way. This is what it means to say that the axioms are more basic. It is thus irrelevant to talk about the notion of dependence in linguistic, physiological or medical terms. They just do not apply to the case in point. It would be like asking, "What color are the natural numbers?" The question makes no sense. The question at stake is whether any of the axioms can be derived from any of the theorems and this I deny.

This secular version of the argument, which treats it as a form of foundationalism, thus agrees with the theological interpretation in holding that a distinction must be drawn between F and R. But it disagrees that F is therefore a sentient being or one which contains within itself the reason for its own existence. The axioms of *Principia Mathematica* are to be distinguished from the superstructure they support, but they are not conscious beings. Moreover, since they were invented by Whitehead and Russell, there was a time when they did not exist; hence their non-existence is conceivable. These remarks show that the secularized form of the argument does not prove that God exists. But do they even establish the existence of a first cause, that is, the finitude of the universe in one direction? There are severe criticisms of the argument in this respect. We shall examine three:

1. There is a problem about the meaning of the phrase "the reason for their existence." In the first passage from Copleston I cited, he identifies this notion with the concept of dependence. He says: "I depend on my parents, and now on the air, and on food, and so on." I shall have more to say about this conflation below. But in the second passage I quoted (concerning chocolates), he states "An infinite series of contingent beings will be, to my way of thinking, as unable to cause itself as one contingent being." In this passage, the role played earlier by "the reason for their existence," is now taken over by "the cause of their existence." It thus appears that at times "reason for" means the same as "cause of."

But if that is so, his version of the argument from the principle of Sufficient Reason turns out to be a terminological variant of the cosmological proof. As we have just seen, the cosmological proof attempts to prove that the universe is finite in one direction, in the sense that the sequence of events ending in the present had an initial cause. But as we also noted in our analysis of the argument, if one is speaking about causality in reference to the initiating event, one runs into a set of difficulties that are insuperable. Either there is no first cause because the supposed first event must itself be caused by something else, or it is self-caused (which violates the ordinary meaning of "cause"), or it is uncaused (which leads to mystification). Hence, this secularized version of the argument from Sufficient Reason does not serve to establish that the universe is finite in one direction.

2. However, let us assume that the phrase "reason for its existence," does not mean "cause of its existence," but means "depends on

something else for its existence." As so used it is a non-technical synonym for "contingent." But if so, it generates other difficulties. Although the theorems of *Principia* depend on (i.e., can be deduced from) the axioms, they are analytic or necessary truths. It would therefore be be wildly misleading to describe them as contingent. Furthermore, the argument, as Copleston construes it, contends that all experienced beings are contingent, and because that is so, we cannot account for their existence, since the thesis of universal contingency would lead to an infinite regress. But is the assumption even sensible that every experienced being is contingent? If every object is said to depend on something else, then the correct inference to draw is that the notion of "dependence" has no application to the things that we in fact experience. For example, some persons are wholly dependent on welfare, some are partially dependent, and some are not dependent at all. The claim that everything experienced is dependent or contingent is thus a case of the monistic fallacy. It would be like holding that every object is red. If everything is said to be red we could not distinguish the things we now call "red" from those we call "green" or "blue." It would follow from such a usage that "red" does not pick out a particular color, and hence does no real work in the language we use for describing the world. According to this criticism, the argument depends on a concept that is empty of content; and hence it can be rejected as providing any information about the origin of the universe.

3. For Leibniz and later proponents of the argument, the actual causal sequence needs a reason for its existence, and that reason derives from a sentient being who selects it from an indefinite number of possible causal series. It follows that such a selector exists. For Copleston the selector is God. In his debate with Copleston, Russell points out that the argument is fallacious. He says:

> I can illustrate what seems to me your fallacy. Every man who exists has a mother, and it seems to me your argument is that therefore the human race must have a mother, but obviously the human race hasn't a mother – that's a different logical sphere (p. 152).

Russell's point is well taken. The argument from Sufficient Reason presupposes that a notion (causality) that applies to individual events also applies to the totality of which they are members. But if the totality, as Copleston admits, is simply the aggregate of its members, then it is a mistake to infer that the totality itself is another singular event requiring a reason for its existence.

Given the aforementioned criticisms, it is difficult to believe that the universe had a beginning; but it is equally hard to see how if it did not there could be a present event. One is thus confronted by a dilemma in which both of two contradictory positions seem true. In most such cases, philosophers tend to defend one of the alternatives. But Immanuel Kant (1724–1804) proposed a highly original solution which rejects both options. Let us see what it is and whether it manages to resolve the problem.

KANT AND THE ANTINOMIES OF PURE REASON

Kant calls the dilemma an "antinomy." In the *Critique of Pure Reason*, his *chef d'oeuvre*, he describes four such antinomies. Each consists of a thesis and an antithesis. The first is the dilemma just discussed. Its thesis is that the world has a beginning in time and is limited as regards space. Its antithesis is that the world has no beginning in time and no limits in space. It is this antinomy that we shall discuss in what follows although we shall set aside the complexities raised by its reference to space. The second antinomy is that every composite substance both is, and is not, composed of simple parts. The thesis of the third antinomy holds that there are two kinds of causality, one defined by the laws of nature, the other involving freedom. Its antithesis maintains that the only form of causality is defined by the laws of nature. The fourth antinomy proves that there is, and is not, an absolutely necessary Being.

Let us begin with Kant's formulation of the first antinomy, and then turn to his solution.

Here (with some editing by me) is his version of the thesis:

1. The world is the totality of whatever exists.
2. The world has no beginning in time (Hypothesis).

3. It follows that up to the present moment an eternity has elapsed.
4. The world consists of an infinite number of successive events that have actually occurred.
5. Its final event is the present moment.
6. Therefore, an infinite series of successive events has been completed.
7. It is a logical truth that an infinite series can never be completed by successive events.
8. The concept of a world that consists of an infinite series that has been completed is thus self-contradictory.
9. Hence, the world had a beginning in time (i.e., a first event).

The conclusion, 9, entails that the world is finite in at least one direction.

Now let us look at the antithesis which leads to an opposite judgment. (Like the thesis, it has been edited by me.)

1. The world is the totality of whatever exists.
2. The world has a beginning in time (Hypothesis).
3. The concept of a beginning entails there was a time when the world did not exist.
4. It follows that before the world began nothing existed.
5. It is impossible for something to come from nothing.
6. It is therefore impossible for the world to have had a beginning in time.
7. Consequently, the world has always existed.
8. It is therefore infinite in one direction.

The thesis is an indirect or *reductio ad absurdum* argument. In this respect it resembles the cosmological proof. The hypothesis that the world lacks a beginning leads by a series of valid steps to premise 6, the falsehood that an infinite series of successive events has been completed. It follows from 6, 7, and 8 that 2 is false. Its falsity thus entails that the universe had a beginning in time. However, it is important to note that the antithesis is not a reverse mirror image of the thesis. It is not an indirect argument at all, although it superficially resembles one in that its conclusion contradicts its hypothesis. It fails to satisfy the formal condition that its hypothesis leads to a falsehood, since no premise that follows the hypothesis is false. The antithesis also differs from the thesis in not depending on the proposition that an infinite number of successive events have occurred. Indeed, it does not mention infinity at all. Its key premises are 3, 4, and 5. Note that 5 is the *ex nihilo nihil fit* principle. Kant, like Parmenides, can thus be added to a long list of philosophers who take this proposition to be an indubitable truth. Both arguments use the term "world" as a synonym for "universe."

Although the thesis and the antithesis differ in important respects, they both contain a premise that seems obviously true. This is the assertion that the world is the totality of whatever exists. Yet Kant held this set of words to be meaningless. Since it is an essential premise in both the thesis and the antithesis, he contended that both arguments are fallacious, and that the supposed dilemma is spurious.

KANT'S SOLUTION

An adequate explanation of why this group of words is bereft of meaning would require a full immersion in Kant's complex philosophical system in the *Critique of Pure Reason*. Since whole tomes have been dedicated to such an explication, it is obviously impossible to provide such an account here. But there is one apophthegm that is central to the Kantian philosophy. It is his statement: "Concepts without percepts are empty; and percepts without concepts are blind." This maxim will provide the entry we need. It represents Kant's compromise between an extreme rationalism and an extreme empiricism. For Kant, pure rationalism is the doctrine that unassisted reason can provide a true description of reality. Pure empiricism, in his view, asserts just the opposite thesis. It is the doctrine that all knowledge derives from experience. For empiricists, such as Locke and Hume, reason can never tell us anything substantive about the world. On Locke's view, the human mind is a *tabula rasa*, a blank tablet. It is experience that imprints information on the tablet. It follows that *all* human knowledge arises from experience. Kant rejected both views. His theory was that both sense experience and the mind contribute substantively to the apprehension of the world. Exactly how this takes place is what makes the Kantian philosophy so difficult to explain.

Simplifying drastically, we can say that the mind imposes structure and organization on experience. Kant calls the forms by which experience is organized "categories." There are twelve of them, the most important of which are substance and cause. These categories are innate features of the human mind. If Locke were correct in saying that the human mind is entirely passive, the world that we experience would be "a blooming buzzing confusion." But it is not and that is because human reason, by means of the categories, unifies experienced events into coherent unities. So when we see a dog run across a lawn we do not experience a patchwork of disconnected impressions, such as unrelated colors, movements, shapes, sizes, and textures; but something recognizable as a particular kind of animal moving across a stretch of something recognizable as turf. It is the mind that enables us to organize such impressions into meaningful wholes. Without the activity of the mind, percepts would be blind (chaotic), and without perceptions, our concepts would apply to nothing – would be empty of observational content. Thus, Kant's "Copernican revolution," emphasized the contributions of reason and experience in the acquisition of knowledge.

In holding that concepts without percepts are empty, Kant is thus criticizing the rationalist tradition, stemming from Descartes and running through Spinoza and Leibniz, which held that *pure* reason – reason exercised independently of experience – can be informative about reality. These rationalists assumed that there is a symmetry between reason and reality; that somehow and in some inexplicable way the structure of the human mind mirrors the structure of reality. Because this is so, unassisted reason can issue in truths about the world. The paradigm they appealed to in this connection was mathematics. It is indeed a remarkable fact that a formula such as $s = \frac{1}{2}gt^2$ should accurately depict the behavior of all freely falling objects. These thinkers were thus enormously impressed by the power of pure reason, as expressed in mathematics, to be informative about the world. In contrast, the empiricists thought that pure reason was empty of factual content – that the world could only be understood *posterior* to our experience of it. But for Kant such a view failed to comprehend that the mind also makes an essential contribution to the understanding of reality. Thus, one knows *prior* to any experience that anything observable has to occur in space and time. Time and space are thus among the a priori features contributed by the mind.

In the light of this compromise view, we can now begin to appreciate Kant's idea that the set of words "the world is the totality of whatever occurs," is meaningless. His point is that these words are expressions of pure reason without a substantive grounding in experience. Lacking any tie to experience they are "empty" of factual content. This is so, he held, because the very concept of a *total* world transcends the bounds of actual or even possible experience. We do not and cannot experience such a totality. The concept can thus tell us nothing about reality. Since both thesis and antithesis crucially depend on this concept, the dilemma they supposedly create is spurious and can be rejected. For Kant it is an interesting feature of the human mind that it has the power to put words together that seem to formulate genuine questions. But if such collections of words have no tie to what is in principle experienceable, they are devoid of meaning. His view is thus a form of "verificationism." This is the thesis that if a set of words purports to refer to a situation which in principle is incapable of verification it is cognitively meaningless. Kant's solution to the question: "Where Did the Universe Come From?" is therefore that the question needs no answer, since the concept of the universe that it incorporates is without cognitive content.

BERTRAND RUSSELL

As we have seen throughout this chapter, many scientists, theologians, and philosophers have assumed that "Where did the universe come from? and what is it expanding into?" is a significant question. Kant is, of course, a notable exception. Suppose, following the tradition, we accept the logical equivalence between the concepts of "the universe" and "the totality of whatever exists." If we do, we can make another plausible supposition – that the phrase "the totality of whatever exists," means pretty much the same as "all that exists." If so, we can replace "totality" with "all," and accordingly the question, "Where did the universe come from?" can be reformulated as "Where did all that exists come from?" Kant's position can now be interpreted as holding that the question, "Where did all that exists come from?" is meaningless for the reasons he gives. This series of inferences thus leads one to focus on the logic of "all." Is there any reason to think that it is "all" that is the real source of such metaphysical vacuity?

In one of the most surprising and brilliant analyses in the history of philosophy, Bertrand Russell answered yes. He even gave a formal demonstration of why this is so. To explain his thinking will require a detour through the early terrain of mathematical logic. I will keep the journey brief. It begins not in logic but in geometry. For more than two thousand years Euclidean geometry was regarded as a true, *unique* description of physical space. But in the middle of the nineteenth century, new theories were advanced by Reimann and Lobachevsky that cast doubt on the privileged role of Euclidean geometry. A number of logicians were thus spurred to show that not only geometry but all of mathematics could be reduced to formal logic, whose foundations were the most impregnable of all the intellectual disciplines. This endeavor is called "the logistic thesis." In 1879 a German logician, Gottlob Frege (1848–1925) published a book, *Begriffschrift* (Concept-Script) that contained the first major effort to prove the thesis. The demonstration required the development of a new kind of logic, later to be called symbolic or mathematical logic. Frege is thus regarded as the inventor of modern logic.

It is one of the oddities of intellectual history that Frege's work was generally unknown and unappreciated until long after his death. But from the Second World War on, his reputation has soared and he is now regarded as one of the seminal figures in the history of analytic philosophy. In particular, his contributions to logic have turned out to be of the highest importance. Mathematical logic is now the only game in town; it has totally eclipsed scholastic logic, a theory of inference that had existed since the time of Aristotle. This development would have astounded Kant who at the end of the eighteenth century stated that logic was complete and beyond further development.

After the publication of *Begriffschrift*, Frege continued to work at the logistic thesis and discovered, as Russell was to do later in *Principia Mathematica*, that he had a monumental task on his hands. Indeed, most logicians believe that no successful proof has ever been achieved. Volume 1 of his *Grundgesetze der Arithmetik* (*Fundamental Laws of Arithmetic*) was published in 1893 and a second volume in 1903. Both were dedicated to new attempts to prove the logistic thesis. In reading the second volume of *Grundgesetze* Russell discovered that Frege's system was susceptible to an irreparable contradiction, now known as "Russell's Paradox." The technical part of the story, considerably simplified, runs as follows. In attempting to prove the logistic thesis, Frege had made use of the concept of a class and gave this notion a particular interpretation, namely that a class was the referent (*Bedeutung*) of a concept. Thus, the concept, *dog*, denotes the class of canines, and the concept, *ardvaark*, the class of ardvaarks, and so forth. Russell pointed out that the principle that each concept denotes a class leads to a contradiction, and hence that Frege's attempted proof of the logistic thesis fails.

The paradox arises from the fact that there are some classes that are members of themselves and some that are not. The class of all classes is itself a class, and therefore is a member of itself; but the class of dogs is not a dog and therefore is not a member of itself. It is thus possible to form a class, K, which is the class of all classes that are not members of themselves. And now a key question: Is K a member of itself? Either it is or it is not. Either answer leads to a contradiction. If K is a member of itself, then since K is the class of *all* classes that are not members of themselves, it follows that it is not a member of itself. If it is not a member of itself, then by parallel reasoning it is a member of itself. But it is a straightforward contradiction to assert that something can both be a member of itself and not a member of itself.

The basic difficulty can be explained in ordinary English. Consider the sentence:

H: "All rules have exceptions."

Let us suppose that H is true. If so, it has exceptions and is therefore false. Let us then suppose that H is false. Since it is a rule and says that all rules have exceptions what it says is true. Therefore, H is both true and false. But this is impossible. No significant locution can be both true and false. H is speaking about *all* rules, including itself. K is a class and speaks about *all* classes including itself. Russell argued that to apply "all" in an unrestricted way to anything, whether it is to God or the universe, will inevitably generate a contradiction. This is thus the source of the paradox about K. Let us return to H to illustrate why.

Think of rules as forming a hierarchy, a system of pronouncements in a graded order. There are many types of hierarchies, some of them non-linguistic. The Roman Catholic Church, for example, is a hierarchy consisting of various levels of authority. The Pope is at its apex, cardinals have a lower rank, bishops a still lower status, and so forth. In a hierarchy of rules, some will stand higher in the system than others. They stand "higher" in the sense that they refer to or are about rules that occupy a lower position in the system. This is what Russell means by the "theory of types." He thinks that this theory both explains and solves the paradox. So H would be a rule of Type 1, and a rule such as "Do not step on the grass," would be a rule of type zero. The rule "All rules have exceptions" would apply to rules of type zero but *not to itself.* H has to be excluded from the rules it speaks about. We can think of exceptions to rules of type zero. In an emergency – say a fire – it is perfectly legitimate to step on the grass. It is this rule, and all others of type zero, that H is referring to when it states that all rules have exceptions. But H (like K) cannot itself be included in the set of items it is referring to. If it is the result will be a contradiction. The conclusion that follows from this line of argumentation is that if one means by the universe "all that exists," the claim that the universe is all that exists will lead lead to a contradiction if "all" is treated as having unrestricted scope.

Russell's solution to the paradox is thus another way, via logical theory, of explaining and justifying Kant's position that taken as an expression of pure reason, and without any ties to experience, the concept of the totality of whatever exists is without conceptual content. This conclusion depends on a further assumption: That to assert both p and not p is not to make any claim at all; and accordingly that such a formula says nothing about the world. In opposition to this point of view, some logicians have held, for formal reasons, that contradictions are false and therefore meaningful. But a widely held contrary view, based on semantic considerations, is that they lack meaning. Here the argument is that if one asserts p and then asserts not p, one has first asserted something and then withdrawn it, and accordingly that nothing has ultimately been said. From such a perspective, contradictions are devoid of cognitive content. Without the verificationist gloss, Russell's line of argumentation thus supports Kant's position that "the totality of whatever exists" is meaningless.

SUMMARY

The central question of the chapter falls into two parts. The first asks: "Where did the universe come from?" and the second: "What is it expanding into?" I have more or less followed this division, exploring some of the answers that cosmologists, theologians, and philosophers have given. A branch of theology called "eschatology" is entirely devoted to discussing the future of the cosmos, including God's plan for mankind and what will happen in "the final days." Science has also made some predictions – for example that the universe will continue to expand forever – but philosophers have tended to concentrate on the first half of the question. Of course, that issue has been treated in depth both by science and theology as well. As a result of this somewhat disparate emphasis, I have tended to follow the mainstream and accordingly to focus mostly on the first half of the question. Here the answers are quite diverse.

Some scientists take the position that one should suspend judgment with respect to questions that go beyond the available evidence. This is a conservative point of view that claims there is evidence that allows researchers to trace the origin of the universe back to the big bang, but no further; and that is the point at which significant inquiry must stop. The difficulty with this position is that it leaves a profound question unanswered: "Where did the original fireball come from?" Disssatisfied with this cautious viewpoint, some astronomers and astrophysicists think that there is some evidence, admittedly faint and hardly decisive, that will allow for speculation to proceed. String theorists tend to belong to this coterie. They think inflation theory may provide some information about the origin of the cosmos, and even about the possible existence of parallel universes. These views tend to be highly technical and not easily comprehended by the ordinary person. I have therefore mentioned but not explored them. There is a third group of cosmologists who admit frankly to being puzzled. They regard the question as significant but do not think that any evidence is currently or even prospectively available that will produce a satisfactory answer. Paul Davies and Frank Shu represent such a position. They assert that one must simply acknowledge that there are singularities in nature in which the laws of physics are suspended. They speak of the creation of the original atom as a "miracle" and suggest that it is a case in which "something emerged from nothing."

The idea that the universe was created from nothing has been grist for the theological mill. In the three great monotheistic religions of the West – Judaism, Christianity, and Islam – there is a consensus among its theoreticians that God created the universe from nothing. The evidence they cite is scriptural. A deutero-canonical text, Second Maccabbees, contains the most explicit passage to this effect. It states that God made heaven and earth "out of what did not exist, and that mankind comes into being in the same way" (2 Macc. 7:28). As far as I know, every major theologian has accepted this account. But within this consensus some interesting problems have arisen. I have focused on one of these, a controversy between two of the greatest Catholic exegetes, St. Thomas Aquinas and St. Bonaventure. Both believed on biblical grounds that the universe was created from nothing. But their philosophical backgrounds were different. Thomas was an Aristotelian and Bonaventure a Platonist. Aristotle held that the universe is infinite and Plato held it to be finite. So a dispute developed between these two ecclesiastics over the question whether the universe could have been created from nothing if it were infinite. I have described this controversy at some length. My position is that since the concept of the infinite was not well understood until the work of Georg Cantor in the nineteenth century it was necessary to look at their debate from a modern, admittedly anachronistic, standpoint. On that basis, I decided, though with considerable exegetical trepidation, that they were probably both wrong. I was thus left with their original concurrence that the universe had been created from nothing. But from a contemporary perspective, even this turned out to be an intriguing result. It meant that some scientists and the vast majority of theologians were banded together against philosophers in thinking about the cosmos. Since time immemorial, philosophers have regarded the claim that something could come from nothing as irrational. The existence of a joined opposition to this principle is thus one of the interesting findings of the chapter.

On the assumption that to ask "Where did the universe come from?" is a significant query, philosophers have tried to provide rational answers to the question. Two of the most celebrated – the cosmological proof and the argument from the Principle of Sufficient Reason – have usually been advanced in support of a religious agenda. But the arguments can be stripped of any religious associations and considered as specimens of purely secular reasoning. As such they directly bear on the issue of whether the universe consists of an uninterrupted regression of causally connected events or whether it began with a first event, that is, whether the universe is infinite or finite. A careful examination of the merits of these two arguments leads, in my judgment, to an intellectual standoff. Both positions strike one as compelling.

A wholly different approach to the question was developed in the eighteenth century by Immanuel Kant. In his greatest work, *A Critique of Pure Reason*, Kant argued that the concept of the universe as the totality of whatever exists is meaningless. Since this concept plays a crucial role in the arguments pro and con, Kant contended that the arguments on both sides of the issue are fallacious. Additional, unexpected support for this conclusion was supplied more than a century later by Bertrand Russell. He demonstrated that the concept of an unrestricted totality (or of an unlimited use of "all") is self-contradictory. On the assumption that a contradiction says nothing about the world, Russell's analysis bolstered Kant's conclusion that the concept of an unlimited totality is vacuous. In their different ways, both philosophers "solve" the puzzle about the origin of the universe by denying the legitimacy of the question. Both approaches depend on technical moves whose validity it is impossible for the ordinary person to assess.

A study of the history of this problem thus leaves the impartial observer perplexed. It seems to make sense to think of the universe as existing, and also to think of it as the totality of what there is. It therefore seems to make sense, to ask "Where did it come from? and what is it expanding into?" On the assumption that the question makes sense, the arguments that it must have had a beginning, and that it could not have had one, seem equivalent in strength. The scientific evidence that it is expanding and the counter explanation that being all that there is, there is nothing for it to expand into, seem equally potent. That the question makes no sense, for the reasons advanced by Kant and Russell, also strikes one as forceful. What should one infer from this melange of intuitions and arguments? Given the lengthy history of the dispute, and the amount of conceptual ingenuity that has been expended on it, I reluctantly conclude that the issue is irresolvable.

GLOSSARY

Aleph Null The lowest of the transfinite numbers. It designates the natural numbers as defined by Peano's five postulates.

Analytic One half of the so-called "analytic/synthetic" distinction. In its narrowest interpretation the term refers to a sentence (proposition, statement) in subject-predicate form and in which the meaning of the predicate term is included in the meaning of the subject term. Example: "All husbands are married." More broadly, it is sometimes used as a synonym for any logical truth.

Antinomy A conceptual difficulty involving two principles each of which seems true and yet which are contradictory.

Apnea Cessation of respiration whether normal, as in hibernating animals, or abnormal, as in the case of someone who has recently died.

Apocalypse A writing in Jewish or early Christian circles (usually between 250 B.C.E. and 150 C.E.) professing to reveal the future by means of a symbolism understandable to the faithful but hidden from others. The Book of Daniel in the Old Testament and the Book of Revelation in the New Testament are examples of such works.

A posteriori A term applied both to arguments and to statements (propositions, sentences, assertions. An a posteriori argument is one whose premises do not offer conclusive proof of the truth of the conclusion but provide evidence for it. Sometimes called "inductive reasoning." It is thus possible for the premises to be true and the conclusion false. Example: All the swans I have observed are white; therefore all swans are white. An a posteriori statement is one whose truth can be ascertained only after some exploration of the world.

A priori A term applied both to arguments and to statements (propositions, sentences, assertions). An a priori argument is one whose conclusion logically follows from its premises. Example: All Greeks are human. All humans are mortal. Therefore, all Greeks are mortal. A statement or proposition is said to be a priori when its truth can be established independently of experience.

Avatar The descent and incarnation of a deity in earthly and usually in human form.

Big Bang The explosion of an incredibly dense and indescribably hot fireball that created the observable universe.

Boson An elementary particle named after the Indian physicist Satyendra Nath Bose (1894–1974). According to the standard model, matter consists of two kinds of particles, quarks and leptons. They interact by means of bosons (force particles) which range from W and Z (weak force) to gluons (strong force).

Compatibilism Also called "Soft Determinism." The view that causality is universal but does not necessitate either choice or action. Freedom of the will is thus *compatible* with predictability based on foreknowledge and scientific laws.

Contingent A term applied both to events and to statements (propositions, assertions, etc.) about events. An event is said to be contingent if its existence depends on something else. A statement is said to be contingent if its negation is not self-contradictory.

Determinism The view that every event has a cause and that antecedent causes produce predictable effects, provided that no intervening factors are present.

Docetism A version of monophysitism – the view that Jesus had one nature. The Docetists held that he was divine, and accordingly that what appeared on the cross at his crucifixion was not a human body but a phantasm. For this reason, Docetists were also termed the Phantastiastae. The view was declared heretical at the Council of Chalcedon in 451 c.e.

Doppler Effect A common physical phenomenon connection with motion. In the case of sound, an object moving toward a stationary observer will appear louder as it approaches the observer and fainter and higher as it moves away. In the case of light, an object moving toward a fixed point will exhibit a shift toward the blue end of the visible spectrum and an object moving away will exhibit a shift toward the red end of the visible spectrum. The Doppler Effect is one of the major pieces of evidence that the universe is expanding.

Dualism The theory that the universe consists of at least two fundamentally different ingredients, neither reducible to the other. Its opposite is monism, the doctrine that the universe is composed of one fundamental stuff, such as matter or mind.

Eliminativism The idea that a sophisticated science of the mind can dispense with reference to mental phenomena, such as ideas, thoughts, beliefs, and intentions. Such references are eliminated in favor of descriptions of neural activity. This is a radical form of materialism.

Empiricism The doctrine that all non-analytic knowledge derives from experience, that is, from data provided by the five senses. Historically its main proponents were John Locke (1632–1704) and David Hume (1711–1776). It is sometimes described as the philosophy of modern science.

Eschatology A branch of theology that deals with the final moments of history. What the "final days" are taken to be depends on the particular religion.

Ex nihilo nihil fit Latin sentence meaning "From nothing nothing comes." That nothing can come from nothing is taken to be an axiom in philosophy.

Some cosmologists and most theologians belonging to the Western monotheistic religions believe it to be a true description of the origin of the universe.

Fate The doctrine that all happenings are fixed in advance such that no humans or animals can change them.

Foundationalism The idea that any complex system of thought must rest on fundamental principles that themselves rest on no other principles and must be accepted without proof or evidence. An elegant expression of this notion is Wittgenstein's remark "If the true is what is grounded, then the ground is not *true*, nor yet false" (*On Certainty*, 205). The most important versions of foundationalism are found in religion, logic, epistemology, and ethics.

Higgs boson A yet unidentified elementary particle named after Peter Higgs, Professor Emeritus of Physics at the University of Edinburgh. It was posited to explain why particles have mass.

Hubble's Constant Named after the American astronomer, Edwin P. Hubble (1889–1953), it is an application of the Doppler Effect to galactic phenomena. It states that velocity = H × distance. This formula denotes the rate at which the expansion of the universe is occurring. The current figure places the rate of expansion as between 9.3 and 18.6 miles per second per one million light years.

Indeterminism A defense of freedom of the will on the ground that mental phenomena are exempt from causality.

Inverse Square Law First formulated by Isaac Newton (1642–1727) it describes the gravitational attraction between bodies. It implies that if the earth were twice its present distance from the sun the gravitational force between the two bodies would be one-fourth of its current value. The algorithm states: square the distance and invert the total. Thus, twice the distance $2^2 = 4$. Invert 4 thus arriving at a gravitational attraction of ¼.

Lepton Matter consists of two kinds of particles: quarks and leptons. Quarks congregate in groups, whereas leptons travel alone. Leptons consist of electrons, muons, taus and their corresponding neutrinos. Our world is mainly built up of leptons (electrons) and up and down quarks.

Logicism A form of Platonism in mathematics, usually contrasted with Intuitionism and Formalism. It holds that mathematical entities exist independently of any form of sentience.

Logistic Thesis First advanced by Gottlob Frege (1848–1925), it is the view that arithmetic is a proper part of logic. In *Principia Mathematica* (1910–1913) Alfred North Whitehead and Bertrand Russell attempted to prove a generalized version of the logistic thesis, namely that all of mathematics is reducible to logic.

Metempsychosis The passing of the soul into another body, either human or animal. Also called "transmigration of the soul."

Millennarianism The view mentioned in Revelation 20 that as history comes to an end there will be a period of one thousand years during which holiness will be triumphant and Christ will reign on earth.

Mitigated skepticism The view that absolute certainty is unattainable but that probable information about matters of fact is possible.

Monism The thesis that the universe is composed of one fundamental "stuff." In philosophy the two main versions of this view are materialism and idealism.

Monophysitism The doctrine that Jesus had one nature. There were two main forms of this view, one of which held that Jesus was human and the other that Jesus was divine. Both were declared to be heretical at the Council of Chalcedon in 451 C.E.

Natural Religion (Natural Theology) A product of the new scientific age, it confines its discussion of religion to what can be proved on the basis of reason. It thus excludes any attempt to establish the existence of God by means of revelation, faith, or dogma.

Nicene Creed One of the major formulations of the basic creed of Christianity. So-called because it was first expressed at the Council of Nicea in 325 C.E. It rejected Arianism, the doctrine that Jesus was of a lower order than God.

Pathetic Fallacy The ascription of human traits or feelings to inanimate nature, as in "the road consents to bend," "cruel sea," or "pitiless storm."

Phlogiston theory A theory in eighteenth-century chemistry disproved by Antoine Lavoisier (1743–1794). It was designed by earlier chemists to explain the nature of combustion. It held that phlogiston was an inflammable substance that was the cause of combustion. Lavoisier demonstrated that the substance in question was oxygen and that there was no such thing as phlogiston.

Phthartolatrae A Greek word meaning "worshippers of the corruptible." Also known as Aphthartodocetae. A monophysite sect that held that Jesus was a human being who suffered and died for mankind. What appeared on the cross was thus a human body. The view was declared to be heretical at the Council of Chalcedon in 451 C.E.

Predestination The theological doctrine that all events throughout eternity have been foreordained by divine decree or purpose. Also called "predetermination."

Quark Along with Leptons one of the two kinds of particles that make up matter. Quarks form a large class of particles with amusing names, "up," "down," "charm," "strange," "top," and "bottom." Our world is mainly built up of electrons and up and down quarks.

Rationalism The view that pure reason can arrive at substantive truths about the world. Its model is mathematics and its aim is to attain the kind of certitude about matters of fact that mathematics can achieve in its own domain.

Reincarnation The incorporation of a soul in a new human body.

Reductionism The transposition of one level of explanation to another that is simpler or more basic.

Resurrection In Christianity, the term has several meanings. In its most general significance, it denotes the rising again to life of all the human dead before the final judgment; more specifically, it refers to the rising of Jesus Christ from the dead. The commemoration of this event is celebrated at Easter.

Sabellianism The doctrine that the Father, the Son, and the Holy Spirit are three different manifestations of the one God. Also known as Modalistic Monarchianism.

Scholasticism The philosophy of the "schools", that is, the philosophy strongly intermixed with theology taught throughout the medieval period in Christian universities. It combined Aristotelianism with Christianity. Its foremost representative was St. Thomas Aquinas (1224–1274).

Skepticism The view that knowledge and/or certainty are impossible.

The Standard Model A recent physical theory that attempts to reduce to a handful the number of basic particles that comprise matter and to explain how they are related. It describes particles and forces previously unknown but later identified – a stunning confirmation of the theory's predictive power.

String Theory Instead of particles, string theory claims that matter is ultimately made of tiny loops of strings that vibrate at different frequencies in a universe composed of 10 or 11 spacetime dimensions, not just four. Different vibrations become different particles or forces, such as quarks or leptons.

Synthetic The other half of the so-called "analytic/synthetic" distinction. It refers to sentences (propositions, statements, assertions) whose negations are not necessary. Synthetic propositions hold for some states of affairs and do not hold for others. Thus, the statement "This door is white" may be true of a particular door but false when asserted of another door. The negation of any synthetic statement is thus always conceivable.

Tabula rasa The term means "a blank tablet." Locke held that the human mind was such a blank slate until imprinted on by sense data. This view is thus connected with the thesis that all human knowledge derives from experience.

Tautology A trivial truth, for example, "All men are men." According to some philosophers (notably Ludwig Wittgenstein) all logical truths are tautologies, that is, they can be reduced to statements of the form "A is A."

Teleology A metaphysical theory explaining natural events as being directed toward an end or as being motivated by a purpose.

Transmigration The movement of the soul at death from one body to another.

Trinitarianism The Christian doctrine which holds that God is a single substance composed of three persons, The Father, the Son, and the Holy Spirit.

Unitarianism The term denotes those who believe that God exists only in one person. This group includes some Christians and most Muslims who contend that the triune God of standard Christianity is inconsistent with any form of monotheism.

Vitalism The position that the processes of life are not explicable by the laws of physics and chemistry alone, but are due to a vital principle such as an élan vital (life force) or entelechy.

Verifiability Principle The thesis that the meaning of any synthetic or contingent statement is identical with a description of the conditions under which it can be determined to be either true or false.

BIBLIOGRAPHY

Allison, Henry. 1983. *Kant's Transcendental Idealism.* New Haven and London: Yale University Press.

Anselm, Saint. 1948. *Proslogion,* in *St. Anselm.* Trans. S. N. Deane. La Salle, IL: Open Court.

Aquinas, Thomas Saint. 2003. *A Summary of Philosophy.* Ed. and trans. Richard J. Regan. Indianapolis and Cambridge: Hackett.

Aristotle. 1941. *The Basic Works of Aristotle.* Ed. with an introduction by Richard McKeon. New York: Random House.

Augustine, Saint. 1964. *On Free Choice of the Will.* Trans. Anna S. Benjamin and L. H. Hackstaff. Indianapolis: The Library of Liberal Arts.

—— 1995. *De Magistro* (On the Teacher). Trans. Peter King. Indianapolis and Cambridge: Hackett.

Austin, J. L. 1970. "A Plea For Excuses," in *Philosophical Papers.* Ed. J. O. and G. J. Warnock. 2nd edn. Oxford and New York: Oxford University Press.

Berkeley, George. 1988. *Principles of Human Knowledge.* Ed. with an introduction and notes by R. Woolhouse, based on the 2nd edn. of 1734. London: Penguin.

Bonaventure, Saint. 2003. *Works of St. Bonaventure.* Vol. 2. Trans. Z. Hayes. New York: Franciscan Institute Publications. Vol. 1, 1996.

Bouchard, T. J. 1990. "Sources of Human Psychological Differences: The Minnesota Studies of Twins Reared Apart," *Science*, vol. 250.

Bradley, F. H. 1959. *Appearance and Reality: A Metaphysical Essay*. Oxford: Clarendon Press.

Burnyeat, M. F. 1999. "Wittgenstein and Augustine. De Magistro," in *The Augustinian Tradition*. Ed. G. B. Matthews. Berkeley and Los Angeles: University of California Press.

Campbell, C. A. 1966. "Is 'Freewill' a Pseudo-Problem?" in *Freewill and Determinism*. Ed. Bernard Berofsky. New York: Harper & Row.

Copleston, F. 1962. *A History of Philosophy*. 2 vols. New York: Doubleday.

Davies, Paul. 1981. *The Edge of Infinity: Where the Universe Came From and How It Will End*. New York: Simon & Schuster.

Descartes, René. 1960. *Discourse on Method and Meditations*. Trans. Laurence Lafleur. Indianapolis and New York: Bobbs-Merrill.

Einstein, Albert. 1979. *Autobiographical Notes*. Trans. and ed. P. A. Schilpp. La Salle, IL: Open Court.

Frege, Gottlob. 1879. *Begriffschrift* (Concept Script). Selections in *The Frege Reader* (1997). Ed. Michael Beaney. Malden, MA: Blackwell.

—— 1892. "On *Sinn und Bedeutung*," in *The Frege Reader* (1997). Ed. M. Beaney.

—— 1903. *Grundgesetze der Arithmetik*. Vol. II. Selections in *The Frege Reader* (1997). Ed. M. Beaney.

Hannay, Alastair. 1990. *Human Consciousness*. London: Routledge.

Hegel, G. W. F. 1998. *The Hegel Reader*. Ed. S. Houlgate. Oxford: Oxford University Press.

Hobbes, Thomas. 1983. *Works*. Oxford: Clarendon Press.

—— 1991. *Leviathan*. Ed. with an introduction by Richard Tuck. Cambridge: Cambridge University Press.

Homer. 1965. *The Iliad*. Trans. with an introduction by Richmond Lattimore. Chicago: University of Chicago Press.

Hospers, John. 1966. "What Means This Freedom?" in *Free Will and Determinism*. Ed. Bernard Berofsky. New York: Harper & Row.

Hubble, Edwin. 1989. "Edwin Hubble 1889–1953" by Alan Sandage. In *Journal of the Royal Astronomical Society of Canada*, vol. 83, no. 6.

Hume, David. 1946. *A Treatise of Human Nature*. Ed. L. A. Selby-Bigge. Oxford: Clarendon Press.

Hume, David. 1987. *An Inquiry Concerning Human Understanding*. Ed. with an introduction by C. W. Hendel. New York: Macmillan.

—— 1998. *Dialogues Concerning Natural Religion*. Ed. with an introduction by R. H. Popkin. Indianapolis and Cambridge: Hackett.

Kant, Immanuel. 1929. *Critique of Pure Reason*. Trans. N. Kemp Smith. New York: St. Martin's Press.

—— 1950. *Prolegomena to Any Future Metaphysics*. Trans. L. W. Beck. Indianapolis: Bobbs-Merrill.

—— 1960. *Religion within the Limits of Reason Alone*. Trans. T. M. Greene and H. H. Hudson. New York: Harper & Row.

Leibniz, G. W. 1908. *The Philosophical Works of Leibnitz*. Trans. with notes by George M. Duncan. New Haven: Tuttle, Morehouse & Taylor.

Locke, John. 1963. *The Works of John Locke* [1777]. 8th edn. 4 vols. Ed. Edmund Law. London: W. Strahan.

Malcolm, Norman. 1963. "Anselm's Ontological Arguments," in *Knowledge and Certainty*. Englewood Cliffs, NJ: Prentice-Hall.

—— 1984. *Ludwig Wittgenstein: A Memoir*. New York: Oxford University Press.

Martinich, A. P. 1992. *The Two Gods of Leviathan*. New York: Cambridge University Press.

—— (ed.) 1996. *The Philosophy of Language*. 3rd edn. New York and Oxford: Oxford University Press.

—— 1999. *Hobbes: A Biography*. New York: Cambridge University Press.

Marx, Karl. 1906. *Capital*. Ed. and with a trans. by F. Engels, based on the 4th German edn. of 1890. Ed. Ernst Untermann. New York: The Modern Library.

Matson, W. I. 2000. *A New History of Philosophy*. 2nd edn. New York: Harcourt.

Melden, A. I. 1961. *Free Action*. London: Routledge & Kegan Paul.

Moore, G. E. 1970. "A Defense of Common Sense," in *Philosophical Papers*. London: Allen & Unwin.

Moyal Sharrock, D. 2000. "Wittgenstein Distinguished," in *Philosophical Investigations*, vol. 23, no. 1.

—— 2003. "Logic in Action: Wittgenstein's Logical Pragmatism and the Impotence of Scepticism," in *Philosophical Investigations*, vol. 26, no. 2.

—— 2004. "The Ladder & The Scaffolding," in *Proceedings of the Austrian Wittgenstein Society*. Vienna: Obvahpt.

Newton, Isaac. 1996. *Mathematical Principles of Natural Philosophy.* Selections by J. Bruce Brackenbridge. Trans. Mary Ann Rossi. Berkeley: University of California Press.

Parmenides. 1984. *Parmenides of Elea: Fragments.* Trans. with an introduction by David Gallop. Toronto: University of Toronto Press.

Pinker, Steven. 1997. *How the Mind Works.* New York: Norton.

—— 2002. *The Blank Slate: The Modern Denial of Human Nature.* New York: Viking.

Plato. 1945. *The Republic.* Trans. with an introduction by F. M. Cornford. New York: Oxford University Press.

—— 1974. *Phaedo,* in *The Last Days of Socrates.* Trans. with an introduction by H. Tredennick. Harmondsworth: Penguin.

Popkin, R. H. 1979. *The History of Scepticism from Erasmus to Spinoza.* Berkeley: University of California Press.

—— (ed.) 1999. *The Columbia History of Western Philosophy.* New York: Columbia University Press.

Popper, Karl. 1962. *Conjectures and Refutations.* New York: Basic Books.

Quine, W. V. O. 1960. *Word and Object.* Cambridge, MA: Harvard University Press.

—— 1974. *The Roots of Reference.* Chicago: Open Court.

Rudd, Anthony. 2003. *Expressing the World.* Chicago: Open Court.

Russell, Bertrand. 1919. *Introduction to Mathematical Philosophy.* London: Allen & Unwin.

—— 1956. *Logic and Knowledge.* Ed. R. C. Marsh. London: Allen & Unwin.

Russell, Bertrand and Frederick Copleston. 1959. "A Debate," in *Why I Am Not A Christian* by Bertrand Russell. Ed. with an appendix by Paul Edwards. London: Allen & Unwin.

Ryle, Gilbert. 1949. *The Concept of Mind.* London: Hutchinson's University Library.

Schlick, Moritz. 1974. *General Theory of Knowledge (Allgemeine Erkenntnislehre).* Trans. A. E. Blumberg. New York: Springer-Verlag.

Searle, John R. 1983. *Intentionality: An Essay in the Philosophy of Mind.* Cambridge: Cambridge University Press.

—— 1992. *The Rediscovery of the Mind.* Cambridge, MA. MIT Press.

Searle, John R. 1995. *The Construction of Social Reality.* New York and London: The Free Press.

Shu, Frank. 1990. "The Cosmos," in *The New Encyclopedia Britannica.* 15th edn. Vol. 16.

Singer, S. J. 2001. *The Splendid Feast of Reason.* Berkeley and Los Angeles: University of California Press.

Stroll, Avrum. 1998. *Sketches of Landscapes: Philosophy by Example.* Cambridge, MA: MIT Press.

—— 2000. *Twentieth-Century Analytic Philosophy.* New York: Columbia University Press.

—— 2003. *Wittgenstein.* Oxford: Oneworld.

Tegmark, Max. 2003. "Parallel Universes," in *Scientific American,* vol. 288, no. 5.

Thorpe, W. H. 1962. *Biology and the Nature of Man.* London and New York: Oxford University Press.

University of California Associates. 1949. "The Freedom of the Will," in *Readings in Philosophical Analysis.* Eds. Herbert Feigl and Wilfred Sellars. New York: Appleton-Century-Crofts.

Vendler, Zeno. 1972. *Res Cogitans.* Ithaca: Cornell University Press.

—— 1984. *The Matter of Minds.* Oxford: Clarendon Press.

Wittgenstein, L. 1922. *Tractatus Logico-Philosophicus.* London: Routledge & Kegan Paul.

—— 1958. *Philosophical Investigations.* Oxford: Blackwell.

—— 1960. *The Blue and Brown Books.* Oxford: Blackwell.

—— 1969. *On Certainty.* Oxford: Blackwell.

—— 1992. *Last Writings on the Philosophy of Psychology.* Vol. 2. Ed. G. H. von Wright and Heikki Nyman. Trans. C. G. Luckhardt and M. Aue. Oxford: Blackwell.

Wolgast, Elizabeth. 1977. *Paradoxes of Knowledge.* Ithaca: Cornell University Press.

INDEX